WORLD WAR ONE *SURVIVORS*

WORLD WAR ONE
SURVIVORS

Ray Rimell

Aston Publications

Sole distributors for the USA

Motorbooks International
Publishers & Wholesalers Inc.

Published in 1990 by Aston Publications Limited,
Bourne End House, Harvest Hill, Bourne End, Bucks.,
SL8 5JJ

ISBN 0 946627 44 4

Designed by Chris Hand

Photoset and printed in England by
Redwood Press Limited,
Melksham, Wiltshire

Sole distributors to the U.K. book trade,
Springfield Books Ltd.,
Norman Road, Denby Dale,
Huddersfield, West Yorkshire,
HD8 8TH.

Sole distributors in the United States,
Motorbooks International,
P.O. Box 2,
729 Prospect Avenue,
Osceola,
Wisconsin 54020.

Contents

CAPRONI

Caproni Ca.3	'4166'	Italy	43
Caproni Ca.36	2378	United States of America	44

CAUDRON

Caudron G.3	'3066'	United Kingdom	45
Caudron G.4	C1720	France	47

CURTISS

Curtiss HS-2L	A1876	Canada	48
Curtiss JN-4D	'4983'	United States of America	50
Curtiss JN-4D	34135	United States of America	51
Curtiss JN-4C (Can)	39158	Canada	52
Curtiss JN-4H	'38262'	United States of America	53

DE HAVILLAND

DH4	'No. 1'	United States of America	54

DFW

DFW C.V	'C17077/17'	Poland	54

FBA

FBA Type H	5	Belgium	55

FOKKER

Fokker D.III	?	Austria	56
Fokker D.VII	6810/18	Canada	56
Fokker D.VII	4635/18 (OAW)	United States of America	59
Fokker D.VIII	?	Italy	62
Fokker E.III	210/16	United Kingdom	64

HALBERSTADT

Halberstadt CL.II	C15459/17	Poland	65
Halberstadt CL.IV	8103/18	United States of America	65
Halberstadt C.V	3471/18	Belgium	66

HANRIOT

Hanriot HD.1	'515'	Italy	67
Hanriot HD.1	75	United Kingdom	69
Hanriot HD.1	'5934'	United States of America	70

HANSA-BRANDENBURG

Hansa-Brandenburg D.I	26.68	Czechoslovakia	71

PFALZ

ROYAL AIRCRAFT FACTORY

RUMPLER

SHORT

SOPWITH

SPAD

Acknowledgements

No book that attempts to cover an international survey of aeroplane museum specimens as well as survivors in private collections can even approach a comprehensive and up-to-date record without relying on the assistance of fellow enthusiasts from all over the world. The author is grateful to many individuals for their valuable contributions to this book, not the least of whom the curators of leading national aeronautical collections who have responded so willingly to requests for historical information and procurement of suitable photographs. To the following, my thanks: Dipl.Ing. Peter Rebernik (Director, Technisches Museum Für Industrie Un Gewerbe In Wien, Austria); Daniel Brackx (PRO, Musée Royal de l'Armée et d'Histoire Militaire, Belgium); A. J. Shortt (Curator, National Aviation Museum, Canada); Jan Mráz (Director, Národní Technické Muzeum V Praze, Czechoslovakia); Général Alain Brossier; Andre Lombard (Director and Deputy Curator, Musée de l'Air et de l'Espace, France); Captain Anthony Speir (Curator for Aviation, South African National Museum of Military History); Axel Carleson (Director, Flygvapenmuseum, Sweden); H. Wydler (Curator, Verkehrshaus Luzern, Switzerland); Hans Holzer (Deutsches Museum, West Germany); Graham Mottram (Curator, Fleet Air Arm Museum, UK); Major J. R. Cross AAC (Librarian, Museum of Army Flying, UK); J. A. Bagley (Curator, Science Museum, UK); Tim Moore (Skysport Engineering); Guy Black (Vintage Aero Ltd., UK); Barry Dowsett and Charlotte Hammond (Cole Palen's Old Rhinebeck Aerodrome, USA); Robert C. Mikesh (Senior Curator of Aeronautics, National Air and Space Museum, USA); William Johnson (Curator, Naval Aviation Museum, USA); Ray Wagner (Archivist, San Diego Aero-Space Museum, USA); and Wesley B. Henry (Research Division, United States Air Force Museum, USA). Thanks also to the staff of the Imperial War Museum at Duxford; the Royal Air Force Museum and the Shuttleworth Collection.

Aside from museum personnel there are a great many individuals who have a specialist interest and knowledge in WWI survivors and without whom this book could not have been completed. Among these enthusiasts I am particularly indebted to Gregory Alegi and fellow members of *Gruppo Amici Velivoli Storico* – the Italian national aircraft preservation society – for assistance with surviving Italian WWI aeroplanes; to John Garwood of New Zealand for sharing his treasured and extensive survivors files with me; to Bob Ogden for checking my master list against his computer-stored log of *all* the world's classic aircraft; and to Leo Opdycke of the US journal *WWI Aero* for releasing his precious card index of WWI survivors which virtually formed the 'core' of this book's content.

Thanks are also extended to the many readers of my journal *Windsock International*, who responded so generously to my requests for photographs and data: K. Brunner (USA); B.R. Cant (Australia); A. Casirati (Italy); H. van Dyk Soerewyn (USA); C. Emlich (West Germany); J. Francesco (USA); B. Green (South Africa); E. W. Gregory (USA); J. Hornát; (Czechoslovakia); D. Layton (USA); K. McCartney; J. L. Rosman (Belgium); R. B. Stone (USA) and A. A. Weir (New Zealand).

For general assistance and encouragement throughout the project, the author would also like to express his gratitude to the following: M. Blaugher; J. M. Bruce, ISO, MA, FRAeS, FRHistS; P. Calassin; J. Cundell; P. M. Grosz, J. Guttman, M. Hiscock; M. Hundertmark; Angela Hogan; P. C. Kirby; C. A. Owers; Group Captain W. S. O. Randle, CBE, AFC, DFM, FRAeS, FBM; K. Thomas and H. Woodman. Not to be forgotten is my publisher, Anthony Pritchard, for his continual encouragement and also Stuart Howe for valuable input and additional photographs. Last, and by no means least, I thank Mrs Fiona Parker, who so competently tackled the task of typing the manuscript.

Ray Rimell

Introduction

In the turbulent wake of the Armistice most of the world's population simply wanted to put the 'Great War' behind them as quickly as possible. Demobilization was swift as the instruments of war were consigned to the scrapheap, and suddenly countless men and women, their respective futures by no means certain, were thrust back into civilian life.

The great European conflict that bled a generation to death had witnessed the first deployment of modern mechanized weaponry: the machine gun; the tank; the submarine and the aeroplane. The latter had rapidly developed from frail under-powered reconnaissance machines which supported armies at the outset of the war to high-performance fighters and giant long-range strategic bombers used to good effect at its close. By the end of hostilities, according to some sources, France boasted the biggest air arm in continental Europe, but the fledgling Royal Air Force, born out of the Royal Flying Corps and Royal Naval Air Service in April 1918, was the largest overall with almost 20,000 machines on strength. By contrast, the German *Luftstreitkrafte* had some 2390 aeroplanes on Western and Home Fronts by the war's end; the French 4511 and the United States Air Service some 1480, most of the latter being French designed.

Today, over 330 genuine examples of 1914–18 aeroplanes have survived the ravages of time as well as a second global war. Most of these prized relics are displayed in museums throughout the world, although a number are privately owned. Many have been lovingly rebuilt and restored to their original configuration, some of the most recent examples of these being the finest of all, where modern materials and techniques have proved invaluable to the gifted craftsmen responsible. Certain machines remain in storage, inaccessible to all but the most persistent and diligent enthusiast, to await their turn in the workshops, while a precious handful of veterans still take to the skies on occasion thrilling air display spectators of all ages.

When the author was invited to compile this 'catalogue of classics' he was under no illusions as to the enormity of the task that lay before him. It might be reasonable to assume that over so many years the number of WWI survivors remains constant or that their locations never change. Such is not the case. Several surprising discoveries of 'new' specimens have been made as recently as the late 1980s, some in the most unlikely of places, while machines are frequently removed for renovation, changing in some cases not only museums but also continents for such specialized work to be undertaken. Then, of course, there are frequent auctions as smaller museums are

forced to close because of insufficient funds, their exhibits changing hands at ever upward-spiralling prices. Any work attempting to establish a 'definitive' compendium must, therefore, take such circumstances into account.

Perhaps the thorniest problem that presented itself during the writing of the book concerned the eligibility of certain types falling within the scope of its contents. At an early stage it was deemed necessary to work within strict parameters and include only authentic examples of warplanes built between 4 August, 1914, and 11 November, 1918. Pre-war types such as the Blériot, which may have seen combat, and immediate post-war derivatives or licence-built versions of WWI types are not, therefore, to be found here.

Another difficulty arose when it came to establish just how authentic some of these surviving aeroplanes really are. Many examples displayed throughout the world's major aeronautical museums are the result of virtual rebuilds, combining completely new components, albeit conforming strictly to original standards, with genuine, available portions of airframe. When one considers the large amount of wood and fabric used in the construction of these aeroplanes, together with the knowledge that their original creators did not really design them for longevity, partial reconstruction at some stage will become more or less inevitable.

As a working maxim it was decided to include those rebuilt aeroplanes which at the very least could boast a fuselage that was largely original, while complete *reproductions*, however well engineered, would be inappropriate. Similarly the author has not included those types for which only a handful of components or odd sections remain, and he has refrained from too much speculation on rumoured survivors where details are sketchy and sources unreliable.

Although over 330 extant World War I aeroplanes is quite a respectable figure, the various types that have survived are not a truly representative selection of the world's first warplanes. As far as I know, there are no genuine examples of an Albatros D.III, Fokker Dr. I, Pfalz D.III, Nieuport 27, British DII4, Handley Page 0/400 or Gotha to be found today, yet examples of all these aeroplanes are known to have survived the immediate post-war years. In Great Britain at one stage it was even suggested that a large national aeronautical collection would be established and at least one example of almost every major British type, not to mention a fair number of captured machines, would be earmarked for preservation. Obviously these plans never materialized and sadly most of these aeroplanes were broken up or burnt.

What is the difference between a reproduction and a replica? A placard at the Royal Air Force Museum's restoration and storage facility at Cardington spells it out ... (Author)

In the years immediately following World War I a great many ex-service pilots took to the air once again. For some it was to earn their living providing joyrides to an ever-eager public, giving exhibition flights, offering their services to film producers or even laying the foundations for fledgling airlines. War surplus aeroplanes were in great abundance and those that escaped the bonfire lived on even though the rate of attrition was high. Quite a few of today's most precious exhibits owe their survival to being immortalized in such Hollywood epics as *Hell's Angels* and *The Dawn Patrol*; to the many skywriting teams and flying circuses and, in rare cases, to a few forward-thinking individuals who believed that those old warplanes were actually worth saving.

For various reasons, not the least of which was the impracticality of personally touring all the world's aeronautical collections – as exciting a prospect as that was! – it has not been possible to illustrate, nor describe in equal depth, every single WWI survivor. In certain cases information is scanty at best, contradictory at worst, while frequent repetitious accounts of similar types would soon become tedious for the reader. As a compromise, almost a hundred of the most interesting and well-documented major types are recorded in the main body of the text and a supplementary appendix lists all *known* survivors and their current locations together with other pertinent data.

Despite lengthy correspondence with numerous museums, organizations, fellow enthusiasts the world over – to whom the author owes an enormous debt of gratitude – and careful checking and re-checking, omissions are probably inevitable, while individual aeroplane movements occur with sufficient frequency to render any listing out of date even as it is published. Neither is it beyond the realms of possibility that, even after seven decades, somewhere a long-forgotten, dust-laden airframe still lurks in a loft or barn awaiting discovery. Not unnaturally, therefore, the author welcomes *reliable* additions and corrections on any aspect concerning genuine WWI aeroplane survivors for future editions. He may be reached either through Aston Publications or through *Windsock International*, c/o Albatros Productions Ltd., 10 Long View, Berkhamsted, Hertfordshire, HP4 1BY, UK.

Raymond Laurence Rimell

Berkhamsted, 1990.

World War One Survivors A–Z

The descriptions that follow are arranged alphabetically by *type* and cover most of the major types preserved around the world. For a complete listing of all *known* surviving World War I aeroplanes the reader is referred to *Appendix I*, where these may be found listed by country of ownership. In both instances, where serial numbers appear in quotes this indicates an unconfirmed or spurious identity. While the information contained in both sections is accurate at the time of publication, readers are reminded that changes of ownership are frequent and that certain exhibits are liable to be withdrawn or re-exhibited without notice as restoration programmes are in almost continual progress.

AEG G.IV

G574/18. National Aviation Museum, Rockcliffe, Airport, Canada

The AEG G.IV was powered by the same twin Mercedes D.IVa powerplants as contemporary Friedrichshafen and Gotha bombers, but possessed neither their range nor lifting power. It was actually a somewhat refined version of the AEG G.I, G.II and G.III types, which had been used both as bombers and 'battle-planes'. Due to its limited load-carrying abilities the G.IV was used mostly for short-range bombing behind the Allied lines and on occasion it was used, without bombs, for long-range reconnaissance duties. Comparatively large numbers were constructed and the type continued to operate up to the Armistice, some 50 still being in service in August 1918.

Accommodation was sufficient for four crew members, although the normal complement was three. Crew positions were interconnected and the airmen could change stations in flight, but due to the G.IV's extreme sensitivity of longitudinal control the front (gunner's) cockpit usually remained unoccupied.

Towards the end of the war, several G.IVs fell into Allied hands. One of them, G1125/16, was brought down intact by AA fire and became the subject of several detailed technical reports. Another captured machine, G574/18, is currently displayed in the recently opened National Aviation Museum's new building in Ottawa, Canada, the only surviving example of a twin-engined WWI German bomber anywhere in the world.

Built by Allgemeine Elektrizitäts Gesellschaft (General Electric Company) of Hennigsdorf in Berlin during 1918, the wartime service history of G574/18 is obscure. What is known is that the machine was shipped to Canada on 23 May, 1919, from Dieppe

The National Aviation Museum's unique WWI twin-engined bomber, the AEG G.IV, seen here after its most recent restoration. (NAM 13986)

Cockpit of Rockcliffe's G.IV bomber. Most of the controls and instruments are original. (NAM 10431)

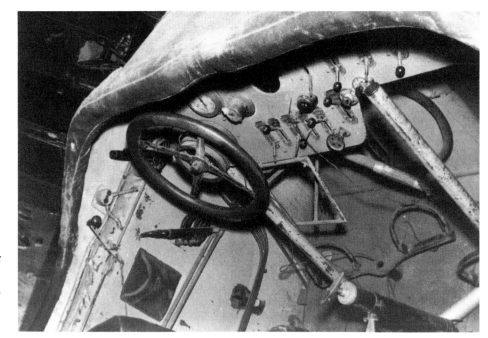

The AEG G.IV installed in the new museum complex at Rockcliffe in 1988. The CF100 wheels strike a jarring note, fitted pending full restoration of the original items. (Don Connolly, CAHS)

aboard the ss *Venusia* as war reparations and was stored at Camp Borden, Ontario, until 1939. During that year it was offered to the Aeronautical Museum of the National Research Council, who refused it, and the veteran was placed into storage with the Canadian War Museum instead. It was not until 1968–69 that G574/18 underwent partial restoration by No. 6 Repair Depot at RCAF Trenton, work subsequently completed by the NAC in 1970 for static display at Rockcliffe. A total re-covering of the airframe was necessary and a realistic 'night lozenge' printed fabric was re-created, copied from original material, which does much for the machine's current authentic appearance.

During restoration, most of the fuselage plywood covering had to be replaced and the engines that, presumably, accompanied the bomber to Canada were found to be of the incorrect type; 180 hp Mercedes rather than the 260 hp units which would have originally powered the machine, and which have been installed temporarily. No engine nacelles or original mountings were available and so the latter had to be fabricated to accept the 180 hp motors, the shafts of these being modified to accept the G.IV's original airscrews. Although one 260 hp Mercedes was obtained in 1981 by the museum it is currently in storage pending acquisition of another.

Much of the Canadian AEG's equipment is still intact: the bomb shackles, most of the cockpit interior, fittings, etc., but the radiators are wooden mock-ups and the original wheels were in such disrepair that temporary substitutes from a pair of Avro CF.100 'Canuck' jets have been used. At the time of writing the genuine wheels are being painstakingly restored. Eventually it is hoped that this unique aeroplane can be displayed in a more representative condition.

Airco De Havilland DH9

I.S 8. South African National Museum of Military History, Saxonwold, South Africa

The DH9 was designed to be a superior version of the highly successful DH4, but the numerous shortcomings of the Siddeley Puma powerplant had serious adverse effects on performance and the new machine was woefully underpowered. With both the Royal Air Force and Independent Force day-bomber units the DH9 saw widespread, but largely undistinguished, service until the end of the war.

Despite the intention that the 'Nine' should replace the 'Four', this never happened, and indeed, production of the DH4 had to be *revived* in 1918 to provide at least some day-bomber units with effective and

reliable equipment. It was planned to field over 30 DH9 Squadrons, a figure that was not achieved, although the type saw service in practically every theatre of war. Over 2000 were eventually built and in post-war years many examples were sold to emergent overseas air forces and one of these was I.S 8, part of the 1920 'Imperial Gift' of 110 aeroplanes for the fledgling South African Air Force, 48 of which were DH9s.

In 1938 DH9s still left with the SAAF came under the hammer, and were sold to private owners, including charter companies. Between June and August at least five were registered: ZS-AOD, AOE, AOG, AOI and AOJ. Three were scrapped before World War II – AOD, AOG and AOJ – and the other two were still the property of African Flying Services when the SAAF started impressing aircraft in 1939–40. ZS-AOE became 2001 and AOI became 2005 when they were taken on strength. Whether they flew again is unknown, but they were used as Instructional Airframes the latter becoming AI No. 8 (I.S 8) at No. 70 Air School, Kimberley. A Board of Survey sat on 5 December, 1942, to survey the aircraft. It was found to be 100 per cent damaged, and with no engine, the timber brittle and unsuitable for training. It was struck off charge on 19 April, 1943, when its value was placed at £5. A Puma engine was found for it and 2005 was subsequently issued to the South African National War Museum.

The machine was partially restored before delivery to the War Museum and in 1966 the SAAF carried out major restoration work, including re-covering all fabric surfaces and a complete repaint.

The cockpits remain in the final configuration after conversion to a dual-control trainer aircraft by the removal of the observer's Scarff ring mounting and the cutting down of the cockpit sides of the rear cockpit to pilot-type shape. The engine of this DH9 is clearly marked as being a Siddeley Puma of 200 hp, but no record exists of an engine with this output and it appears that all Puma engines sent to South Africa with the 'Imperial Gift' were of 230 hp output.

Two other DH9s survive. One of them, owned by the Australian War Museum, has the distinction of being the first single-engined aeroplane to fly from England to Australia, in 1920. Crewed by Lieutenants John C. McIntosh and Raymond J. P. Parer, the journey from England took over seven months in the face of an almost continuous succession of setbacks and disasters terminating in a crash-landing at Culcairn. The aeroplane finished its epic journey to Melbourne by rail. After acquisition by the AWM it was loaned to Lieutenant Parer's old school, but following adverse reports of its deteriorating condition was retrieved by the museum and remained in dismantled state until it could take its place in a long-term restoration programme. Painstaking efforts by the Restoration Group of the Australian Society for

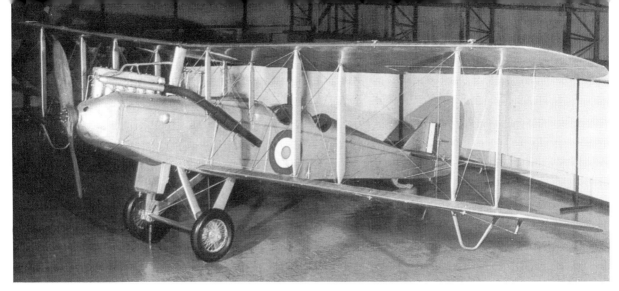

South Africa's Airco DH9 – note converted rear cockpit indicating the machine's post-war training role. (Bruce Green)

The Airco DH9 (ex-F1278) flown by Lieutenants J. C. McIntosh and R. J. P. Parer, the first to fly a single-engined aeroplane from England to Australia in 1920. The machine is seen here on its arrival at Sydney. (Colin A. Owers)

The Australian War Memorial's DH9 has been slowly restored in recent years despite a serious accident to the airframe in June 1987. (Colin A. Owers)

The AWM DH9 at RAAF Richmond in October 1988 nears completion after its recent restoration programme. (Stuart Howe)

The world's third DH9 survivor is F1258, preserved in its original finish by the Musée de l'Air. It is seen here as displayed during the late 1950s. (John Garwood)

F1258 is now beautifully displayed at Le Bourget in the recently opened La Grande Gallerie, one of the finest collections of WWI aeroplanes in the world. (Jon Guttman)

Aerohistorical Preservation to restore F1278 (ex-G-EAQM) to pristine condition suffered a serious blow in June 1987 when an out-of-control vehicle smashed into the building housing the aeroplane. At the time the DH9 was barely months away from completion, but the accident, which wrecked the DH9's rear fuselage and tail unit, set the task back many months.

The third DH9 is part of the *La Grande Gallerie* display at Le Bourget and is maintained by the Museé de l'Air in its original condition. Bearing the number F1258 it was built by furniture manufacturers Waring and Gillow Ltd. of London in 1918 and is powered by the standard 230 hp Puma. On the starboard fuselage side appears the legend 'A Battery, 2nd Siege Artillery Reserve Brigade'. Truly representative of its wartime configuration, the Musée DH9 is the world's most authentic example of the type.

Airco De Havilland DH9A

F1010. Bomber Command Museum, Hendon, UK

The DH9A, forever known by its crews as the 'Nine-Ack', was developed in the wake of the DH9 and proved greatly superior. When the redesigned airframe was fitted with the American 400 hp Liberty 12 powerplant, the product was the most outstanding strategic bomber to emerge from the war and the DH9A also saw extensive service use with the peacetime RAF.

The first squadron to receive the type was No. 110 at Henley, the cost of re-equipping the unit being met by His Serene Highness, The Nizam of Hyderabad, and an appropriate presentation inscription appeared on most of the squadron's aeroplanes. On 31 August, 1918, No. 110 embarked for the Western Front, arriving at Bettincourt, from where long-range day bombing sorties began on 14 September.

On 5 October, 1918 the DH9A squadron abandoned their original objective due to low cloud and attacked Kaiserlautern, where they were met by ground fire and attacks by German fighters. Four DH9As went missing, and one of these was F1010, which was forced down intact and subsequently put on display in the great Berlin Air Museum – the Deutsche Luftfahrt Sammlung.

The museum was seriously damaged by Allied bombing raids in November 1943 and it was at this time that many of the exhibits were transferred for safety to Czarnikau (today Czarnkow, Poland, about 19 miles south of Pila). At least 21 machines and a number of engines were stored there until March 1945. Next stop was Gadki, near Poznan, and from 1950 to 1954 the former exhibits were stored in Pilawa, near Warzawa, thence to Wroclaw. In 1963 came the foundation of the Polish Muzeum Lotnictwa i Astronautyki in Krakow and there most of the Berlin relics were stored not open to public display. In recent years several machines have been removed for restoration and in 1977 all that remained of F1010 – the fuselage and tail – were exchanged for a Spitfire XVI by the Royal Air Force Museum. The DH9A arrived at Cardington on June 28 and a long restoration/rebuild began which culminated in the magnificent specimen now displayed at the Bomber

The ex-Krakow Airco DH9A, having been painstakingly rebuilt by technicians at Cardington, arrives at Hendon in 1983 for assembly and eventual display in the Bomber Command Museum. (Stuart Howe)

The RAF Museum's Airco DH9A is undoubtedly one of the finest examples of a WWI aeroplane to be seen anywhere and has only really been surpassed by the museum's Bristol Fighter rebuild produced by the same talented team at Cardington. (Author)

Command Museum. Although little of F1010 is original, RAF Museum craftsmen have produced probably one of the finest re-creations of a WWI British aeroplane to be seen anywhere in the world today.

Albatros B.I

20.01. Heeresgeschichtliches Museum, Vienna, Austria

The Austrian Albatros B.I was the first aeroplane to enter production with the Ostdeutsche Albatros Werke, a subsidiary of the famous German manufacturer, established in Vienna during May 1914. The machine closely resembled the German Albatros B.II apart from having slightly swept-back wings and usually being powered by Austrian engines. In all, four series of the type were built, and as production began, the Vienna factory made progressive improvements to the basic design. These included additional

centre-section struts, an engine-mounted radiator replacing the original fuselage flank versions, and new wings designed by Professor Richard Knoller. Later production B.Is were armed, the observer being armed with a Schwarzlose machine gun on a tripod mounting. The Austro Hungarian *Feldflieger* units extensively operated the B.I well into 1916, when it was replaced by the Hansa Brandenburg C.I in front-line service.

Nothing is known of this machine's history, although its serial number suggests that it was the first experimental version built by the Austrian Albatros factory. The aeroplane, which still bears most of its original fabric and markings, differs in several respects from production machines. Although it does carry the extra central wing struts peculiar to the Austrian B.Is, they are located in different positions from 'standard', whilst its engine is a 150 hp Daimler rather than the Hiero or Mercedes motors that powered the majority of Austrian production machines.

The B.I displayed at Vienna boasts a fuselage plate inscribed 'Albatros Type ODD No. 1 Berlin-Johannistahl' which has puzzled many enthusiasts. Was the fuselage built in Germany and married to Austrian-originated wings or was the placard placed there at the behest of the parent company? Nobody seems to know for sure. . .

Albatros D.Va

D5390/17. Australian War Memorial, Canberra, Australia

During the 1960s this Albatros D.Va, one of only two genuine examples still extant, was restored by the Camden Museum of Aviation and placed on display in the Australian War Memorial. A rather unusual story surrounds the circumstances of the aeroplane's capture and is worth repeating. D5390/17 was presented to the Australian authorities having been brought down intact during a battle between an RE8 of No. 3 Sqn AFC and Albatros pilots from *Jasta* 29 on 17 December, 1917.

The RE8, A3816, crewed by Lieutenant J. L. Sandy and Sergeant H. F. Hughes, was engaged in artillery spotting when six German fighters began the attack. Despite the uneven odds the Australian crew put up stiff opposition and in the first few minutes managed to send down D5390/17, wounding its pilot, *Leutnant* Clauss. As the engagement continued another RE8 of No. 3 Squadron joined the fray and

for almost ten minutes the two-seater crews managed to hold the Germans at bay until the arrival of a third RE8 compelled the Albatros pilots to break off the engagement.

Although the RE8 crewed by Sandy and Hughes was seen to be flying in a normal pattern above the same area they had been observing before the attack, they never returned to the aerodrome. No news was forthcoming until the following evening, when a report was received that an RE8 containing two bodies had been found in a field 50 miles from the scene of the original combat. A subsequent medical examination revealed, incredible as it seemed, that neither man had been killed as a result of the crash, rather that a single bullet had fatally wounded the observer, passed through his body and instantly killed the pilot. At the time when the other RE8 crews had assumed they were resuming their patrol, Hughes and Sandy's machine was beginning the first of a series of 'ghostly' circles which would drift their RE8 to the south-west until it eventually ran out of petrol and crashed. . . Clauss' Albatros was salvaged by members of No. 3 Squadron despite heavy enemy fire and was sent to No. 1 Aircraft Depot at St Omer.

At the time of its capture, D5390/17 was described as having lozenge-type fabric under the upper wing, light blue under the lower wings and with light blue and red striped tailplane. The fuselage was partially painted in a 'dirty green'. For some reason the machine was not restored in its original colours and *all* flying control surfaces were covered in a carefully

Albatros D.Va D5390/17 seen here in December 1917 having been captured by Australian forces following one of the strangest air battles of the war. (Albatros/P. L. Gray Archive)

21

Today, the Australian War Museum preserves the Albatros of Leutnant *Clauss fully restored to its former glory, albeit with some finishing anomalies . . .* (Via John Garwood)

The NASM Albatros D.Va D7161/17 as originally exhibited in the USA shortly after the war, complete except for its tyres. (Albatros/P. L. Gray Archive)

Restoration of NASM's D.Va was painstakingly recorded and the result is extremely impressive. Meticulous research and attention to the smallest detail speaks for itself. (NASM)

created five-colour 'lozenge' fabric material.

Perhaps one of the finest restorations of any surviving WWI aeroplane is the only other known surviving Albatros D.Va, D7161/17, which is owned by the National Air and Space Museum in Washington DC. This particular example of the classic German fighter was completely restored over a three-year period and months of painstaking research was undertaken before work began in earnest. The museum's staff also had the foresight to carefully measure and photograph each component at every stage of the restoration process and later published the results, providing historians and enthusiasts with a valuable and comprehensive record of WWI German fighter design practices.

At least one other example of an Albatros D.Va is known to have survived the war and was displayed in later years at the Berliner Luftfahrtmuseum, together with many other German WWI types, before being transferred to the famous Deutsche Luftfahrt Sammlung in 1936, at that time the world's largest aeronautical collection, housing over 110 machines. This

The NASM's Albatros D.Va as recently desplayed inside a pseudo Western Front hangar. The green and yellow tail stripes define the machine as one which served with Jasta 46. (H. Van Dyk Soerewyn)

Albatros was no ordinary example, for it was D2059/17, at one time flown by Manfred von Richthofen, the 'Red Baron', who scored several of his victories with it.

During World War II the aeroplanes of the museum were thought to be at severe risk from Allied bombing and were moved to a safer location. Some of these aeroplanes are currently back in Berlin, the subject of an ambitious restoration programme, but the majority of the museum's original exhibits have 'disappeared'. For many years it was assumed that classic relics such as a Fokker Dr.I Triplane flown by von Richthofen, an AEG J.I, Spad A.2, several Albatros fighters (including D2059/17) and a Siemens Schuckert D.III were destroyed by bombing, but as recently as 1987 an individual responsible for assisting with wartime removal of the collection has claimed that *all* the aeroplanes were removed, undamaged, to a safe location. It is tempting to speculate that these precious aeroplanes still exist to this day hidden away to await their eventual discovery and restoration. For the moment, however, they remain 'missing in action' . . .

Albatros SK.1

04. Swedish Air Force Museum, Linkoping, Sweden

Based on the 1914 German Albatros B.II, the Swedish-built SK.1 was constructed under licence at Malmslatt, Sodertalge and Stockholm from 1915 onwards; 37 were built and five served with the air force from 1920 until 1929. The original Albatros design with its ply-covered fuselage was a sound one and the SK.1 served for many years as a 'pattern' for local manufacture. Initially these Albatroses were powered by a 100 hp Benz, replaced a few years later by a more powerful 120 hp engine, and in 1918 a 160 hp version became available to power later aeroplanes.

During the summer of 1917 at least one Swedish Albatros was fitted with floats. Records from the flight tests revealed a climb rate of 1½ hours to reach over 7000 feet and not surprisingly this marked the end of the career of the Albatros in naval service.

The Swedish-built SK.1, virtually a German Albatros B.II, constructed under licence, preserved at Linkoping by the Swedish Air Force Museum. Some 37 examples were built, this is number 4. (Swedish Air Force Museum)

More powerful engines permitted the extra burden of reconnaissance equipment and several ski-equipped machines took part in Swedish Army winter exercises. The SK.1 was produced at four factories: the Sodertalge Workshop's Aviation Division; the Swedish Aeroplane Company; Nordic Aviation Company and the Army Air Corps Workshop.

The original German-designed Albatros B.II operated in the reconnaissance role from the beginning of the war until late 1915, when they were replaced with the armed C-type two-seaters. The docility of the Albatros B.II's flying characteristics, however, made it ideal for training use and many examples were used in *Jastaschule* service up to the Armistice.

At least two other examples of Albatros two-seaters have survived. B.I, 20.01, preserved in Austria in the Heeresgeschichtliches Museum, and the remains of an Albatros C.I are stored in the Polish National Aeronautical Museum at Krakow. Formerly with the post-war airline Lloyd-Ostflug, only the fuselage and undercarriage of C197/15 have survived. The current whereabouts of the wheels, wings, tail and airscrew are not known.

Anatra DS

'11120'. National Technical Museum, Prague, Czechoslovakia

During the flight of the first Russian Anatra D in December 1915 it was found that the aeroplane was directionally unstable and required modifications including increased wing sweepback, relocation of crew seats, wing cellule moved rearwards and 7 kg of ballast attached to the base of the starboard leading outer bay strut. The fin leading edge was moved 30 mm to port, the upperwing span was reduced and the aileron chord and tail area increased.

Aeroplanes of the first series were delivered during May 1916 and 170 Anatras were produced during 1916–17. The type was widely used in the war and the following civil conflict, mainly in the trainer role. Information recently published in the Czechoslovakian journal *Letectvi-Kosmonautica* sheds more light on the history of the sole surviver: 'In March 1981, Austro-Hungarian forces entered the city of Odessa where the main Anatra factory was located. On arrival at the factory a large number of completed and partially completed aircraft were found. The Austro-Hungarian War Ministry ordered a batch of 200 machines to be built and on July 10, 1918, 42 Anasals were delivered and in August a further 51. The *KuK*

A unique WWI survivor is this Anatra preserved at Prague's Technical Museum. Built at Kiev in 1916 the machine bears the original form of Russian insignia. (Albatros/P. L. Gray Archive)

Luftfahrtruppen regarded the Anasal as unsafe and it was not used regularly. In spite of this the Anasals were given the series number 010, which was followed in the usual way by the serial number. Coincidently, the series number 010 was also given to the Ufag C.I

'A number of captured Anatra DS machines were stored in the Summer of 1918 in Plana near Pilsen. From there and also from Cheb and from the Al-Ma repair shops in Prague, 23 Anatras were taken over by the Czechoslovak authorities. Used initially in combat units, the Anatras were overhauled at the Olomouc aircraft maintenance unit in the Summer of 1920, a thorough reconstruction of the fuel system being carried out. After that the Anatras served as training aircraft at the Cheb flying school (the VLU). On October 20, 1921 some 20 Anatras were still available, one each with the 2nd and 3rd Regiments, six at the flying school, three under repair and nine in storage.

'On April 6, 1923 the remaining Anatras were withdrawn from the VLU at Cheb and despatched to the Olomouc maintenance unit. Of these, 010.117 was flying at the school and the following were in storage; 010.871, 010.091, 010.101, and 010.107. After withdrawal from service with the Czech Air Service some Anatras flew with aero clubs (these included 010.111 with the Moravian Aero Club).

The surviving Anatra DS now in the Technical Museum at Prague has the collection reference 10936. It bears the *fictitious* number 11120 on the fuselage side and came from the collection of the Liberation Memorial at Vikhov (along with Spad 7 and the LWF biplane.) Because of its Russian origin the erroneous story arose that the Anatra in question arrived with the Czech Legion from Russia after WW1, but this is not true. According to the caption of a photograph the Anatra in the Museum was probably originally 010.091.'

Ansaldo A.1 Balilla

16552. Museo Aeronautico Caproni, Trento, Italy

The Ansaldo A.1 was designed as a fighter and largely based upon the Ansaldo SVA. The all-wood fuselage, rectangular in section in front tapering to triangular at the rear, followed exactly along SVA lines and the two aircraft also shared the same 220 hp SPA.6 powerplant. The wings were different, however; the equal-span upper and lower mainplanes had four conventional wire-braced vertical struts instead of the SVA's so-called 'Warren truss' rigid bracing. The name, *Balilla*, referred to the legendary Genoese streetboy whose rock-throwing exploits against the city's Austrian occupiers in 1746 are to this day taught in Italian schools as examples of heroism and devotion to the fatherland.

166 *Balillas* were delivered during WWI, initially with the 70ᵃ *Squadriglia*. After the war, *Balillas* served around the world and at least six went to the USA. 16608 was flown by Eddie Rickenbacker in 1920 to set a Los Angeles–San Francisco speed record and after a brief Hollywood career it was fitted with a Hispano-Suiza and was still flying at St Louis in 1926. A young man who asked to fly it was turned down. His name was Charles Lindbergh.

A SPA 6.Aa-powered *Balilla*, flown by Bert Acosta, took third place in the 1920 Pulitzer Trophy and in 1921, equipped with a 400 hp Curtiss C-12 engine, it was placed fourth in the Pulitzer flown by Lloyd Bertaud. Several went to Latin America in 1919–22, Poland purchased 35 from Ansaldo and the Lublin firm Plage i Laskiewicz acquired a licence to build 100 machines, although only 57 were completed. The Soviet Union ordered 30 in 1922 and

Lettonia purchased 13 in the early 1920s.

The aircraft owned by the Caproni Museum was used in the closing stages of WWI by Natale Palli, one of the most famous Italian pilots of the war. His aircraft was preserved by the Aero club of Casale Monferrato (Alessandria province) and later passed to the Caproni collection most of which has been moved to Trento where a completely new museum building is being erected. The *Balilla* is currently under restoration at Rovereto near Trento. Its original markings include the large badge of Genoa.

Another *Balilla* survives in Italy. This is 16553, preserved in Bergamo's Museo del Risorgimento, and flown during the war by one of Italy's top pilots, Antonio Locatelli. The aeroplane was delivered to Locatelli at Borzoli, near Genoa, on 25 August, 1918, and Locatelli flew nine sorties in it between 28 August and 11 September. When Locatelli was later brought down and captured by Austro-Hungarian forces, 16553 was flown by F. Ferrarin but reunited with its original pilot after the war. The *Balilla*'s last flight was from Ghedi to Bergamo, after which the aeroplane was presented to the city for preservation. Like many Italian WWI survivors it still retains its original colours and markings and, like 16552, bears the famous Genoa badge.

The distinctive radiator of the Ansaldo A.1 Balilla *preserved by the Caproni Museum, which was closed to the public in 1988 for its move to Trento. This particular machine was flown by Natale Palli, one of Italy's leading wartime pilots. (Alberto Casirati)*

Caproni's Balilla *still bears its original covering and markings, which include the badge of Genoa forward of the fuselage roundel. (Alberto Casirati)*

Ansaldo SVA5

11721. Museo Storico AMI, Vigna di Valle (Rome), Italy

The SV was designed in 1916 by the *Direzione Tecnica dell'Aeronautica Militare* (Technical Directorate of Military Aviation). Designers Umberto Savoia and Rodolfo Verduzio sought a break with the pushers of French derivation then being built and a shortage of fabric and dope made them opt for an all-wooden fuselage, while the rigid 'Warren truss' wing bracing was to minimize rigging difficulties in the field. Metal parts were kept to a minimum and their design simplified. Production was turned over to the Ansaldo firm and the aircraft became known as the SVA.

Mario Stoppani made the first flight on 19 March, 1917 at Grosseto. Tests revealed that the SVA was much faster than Spads and Hanriots, but fighter pilots found it lacking in manoeuvrability. Production machines were thus assigned to the reconnaissance role, while Ansaldo developed many versions, production running to 1928, with over 2000 being built. Like the Avro 504K, many Ansaldos flew well into the 1930s.

Among the SVA's many feats are the Vienna leaflet raid (9 August, 1918) and the Rome-Tokyo flight of 1920. 11721 flew over Vienna in the hands of Lt Giordano Bruno Granzarolo, who acquired the aircraft after the war. In 1928 the five-year-old *Regia Aeronautica* was assembling a historic aircraft collection and Granzarolo asked for a flyable machine in exchange for his SVA. 11721 was exhibited in both the 1928 and 1934 shows, but does not appear to have joined the Caserta collection. Its subsequent whereabouts are unknown. In 1964 it was in the short-lived Turin museum and, when that closed, it was briefly in the Milan Science and Technology Museum before travelling to Vigna di Valle, where it was completely restored.

The aeroplane sports the enlarged long-distance radiator and an extra water tank on the top wing. It is currently in full 87ª *Squadriglia* markings, including the splendid 'Lion of St Mark' insignia. (The white tail and numeral 1 were applied for the Vienna raid.) The mission list on the nose is not in chronological order: 11721 did not carry it in Milan in 1934 and, furthermore, Granzarolo did not fly all the missions that are listed.

A second Ansaldo SVA5 (11777) is preserved in Italy by the Museo Caproni. This SVA also took part in the Vienna raid with Gino Allegri, nicknamed 'Fra Ginepro' by his comrades because of his long friar-like beard, as pilot.

Ansaldo SVA5 11721 seen here during the late 1960s while displayed, albeit briefly, in Milan's *Museo Nazionale della Scienza e della Technica*. (John Garwood)

11721 as currently housed by Musico Storico AMI at Vigna di Valle following its restoration after removal from Milan. (Alberto Casirati)

As with most other aeroplanes in the Caproni collection, no details of its early history are available. Since the end of World War II the SVA has been kept dismantled in the Caproni villa, venturing out only rarely. In 1968 it was loaned to Felice Gonalba as the basis for the replica commissioned by *Alitalia* for the Expo '70 in Osaka, and several years later it was again loaned to Gonalba as the basis for the SVA replica commissioned by Ansaldo for their newly established museum.

The Ansaldo is completely original and sports the long-distance radiator, while the wings still bear the original Ansaldo factory stencilling. Unfortunately, while in storage one side of the fuselage was exposed to sunlight, causing the Lion of St Mark to almost fade away completely.

Ansaldo SVA10

12736. Vittoriale degli Italiani, Gardone Riviera, Brescia, Italy

Gabriele D'Annunzio, born in Pescara on 12 March, 1863, had by 1889 established himself as a leading literary figure. His works were characterized by a decadent sensualism which ensured their commercial success even when their literary value thinned out. In 1897 D'Annunzio was elected to the Chamber of Deputies on an extreme right-wing ticket and in 1900 he shifted to the Socialists, but eventually landed with the Nationalists. In 1911 he was forced out of Italy by the huge debts he had amassed and returned from his French exile on the eve of war. The government agreed to underwrite his debts in exchange for a fiery pro-intervention propaganda. D'Annunzio took to the role with passion and eventually served operationally in all three services – the only Italian to do so. Aviation held a special place in his heart (he had written the aviation novel *Forse che si forse che no* in 1910) and his most famous exploit remains the Vienna raid of 9 August, 1918.

Not a pilot, D'Annunzio had envisaged using Caproni bombers, but their slow speed and limited range eventually made the High Command opt for the faster SVA scouts. This meant that the bomb-load was to be replaced by leaflets. This, incidentally, helped reduce the risk of Austrian retaliation. For D'Annunzio a special two-seater was built, which crashed on a test flight killing its pilot, Captain Luigi Bourlot. A second aircraft was hurriedly readied by Ansaldo, using an SVA10 fuselage. D'Annunzio sat in the front cockpit, directly atop the fuel tank. With his usual flair for catchy phrases, D'Annunzio dubbed it *la sedia incendiaria* (the fiery seat)! 12736 was flown to Vienna by Natale Palli.

In 1921 the SVA was reported to be in the care of the Cooperativa Nazionale Aeronautica, an abortive veterans' network for aerial work and propaganda. A few years later, 12736 was permanently preserved in the Vittoriale degli Italiani, the sumptuous house-museum D'Annunzio made for himself. In 1934 it was exhibited in Milan and in 1963 the aeroplane was hung from the ceiling to make room for a conference hall. It was lowered for the first time in February 1988, when members of the Turin and Alessandria

one which appears to have survived is this unique SVA10 two-seater. This final version of the SVA had the pilot in front and the observer in the rear with a Scarff-mounted machine gun.

In 1984 the French journal *La Fanatique de l'aviation* carried a photograph of an 'Ansaldo SVA' believed to be preserved in Peru, although details of its location are lacking. The wings and rear fuselage at least are clearly of SVA design, but the forward fuselage, undercarriage and wing strut arrangement are not original. Further details would be welcomed by the author.

Ansaldo SVA9

'13148'. Aeritalia Collection, Turin, Italy.

Herbert Fyfield, aeronautical engineer and World War II Corsair pilot, acquired this SVA in 1957 from a collector in Peekskill (New York), and for some ten years the aircraft lay unrestored. Work began in 1967 after the Air Attaché of the Italian Embassy enquired if the SVA could be exhibited at the Expo '70 in Osaka, Japan.

Restoration was undertaken by Aviation Techniques Inc. under Reno Brenner's direction. Adelaide and Carlo Ferrarin, wife and son of Arturo Ferrarin of the famous 1920 Rome–Tokyo raid, and Maria Fede Caproni supplied original handbooks and manuals; the Pirelli firm supplied suitable tyres; the Arrow Propeller Co. made a new propeller; Champion

An unlikely find in a New York barn during the late 1950s was this Italian Ansaldo SVA9 acquired by enthusiast Herbert Fyfield, who organized its full restoration. (John Garwood)

chapters of the *Gruppo Amici Velivoli Storici* carried out a much-needed cleaning operation. A general survey was also performed and certain details removed for restoration.

Markings are original and include the Lion of St Mark and a star-studded blue empennage. 12736 is noteworthy in that it is the *only* surviving SVA with the original short radiator.

Two other rare Ansaldos survive, one of which is SVA10 13164, held by the Museo Nacional de l'Aeronautica in Buenos Aires, Argentina, details of which are lacking. What is known is that an Italian Aeronautical Mission toured Latin America in 1919 and, as a result of the feats performed, several countries purchased Italian aircraft. Argentina, with its strong Italian contingent, bought several types. The only

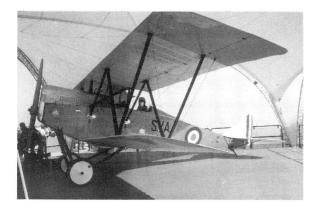

The fully restored Fyfield Ansaldo at Connecticut. It is now in Turin. (Via John Garwood)

Restored by Aeritalia, the ex-Fyfield SVA9 is seen here at Istrama on October 1 1989 making its first post-restoration display debut. (Diomiro Certaldi: GAVS)

manufactured new sparkplugs; Smiths overhauled the altimeter; Sperry took care of the compass. The magnetos were in poor shape, but Piero Vergnano, Fiat's aviation PR man, found another engine. Jesse Hackenburg and Joe Paag rebuilt the radiator coolant pipes, while George Krause made a new fuel tank.

Although this SVA was not exhibited in Osaka a replica was commissioned by *Alitalia* and presented to Japan. Since no original serial could be confirmed, Ferrarin's '13148' was applied. Although the FAA issued a Certificate of Airworthiness on 7 October, 1970, and the registration N92162, the SVA has never been reflown. In January 1989 it was sold to Aeritalia and following restoration in Turin is occasionally displayed 'away from home' in a purpose-built mobile exhibition hangar.

Aviatik C.I

C227/16. Musée Royal de l'Armée, Brussels, Belgium

The first Aviatik design to enjoy large-scale production, the C.I was introduced during 1915, powered by the 160 hp Mercedes D.III engine and armed with a single machine gun for defensive purposes. The aeroplane was unique among operational German C-class two-seaters in having its pilot occupy the *rear* seat with the observer in front with his gun clipped on to a sliding rail mounting either side of the cockpit. The gun was transferred from one side to the other as required and secured via a quick-release mechanism, an arrangement hardly advantageous in air combat. Subsequently Aviatik reversed the seating arrangements, but by that time more powerful types from the Albatros, LVG and Rumpler stables had already outclassed the type.

Aviatiks were used by *Flieger Abteilung* units for reconnaissance duties and occasionally operated in flights of up to six machines as escort to unarmed aeroplanes. The destruction of an Aviatik on 7 November, 1915, was instrumental in the award of the VC to Second Lieutenant G. S. M. Insall of No. 11 Squadron RFC, who, flying a Vickers FB5, forced down the German aeroplane and completed its destruction by dropping a bomb on it.

A rare example of the Aviatik C.I is currently under restoration by the Royal Army Museum. C227/16 was shot down by a Belgian anti-aircraft unit at De Panne in 1916. The remains were kept in store until 1978, when work began to renovate the airframe. At the time of writing the fuselage, its engine installed, has been completed and attention is latterly being paid to the wings.

Another Aviatik exists, a C.III, owned by the Polish Lotnictwa i Astronautyki Museum at Krakow. This machine was part of the original pre-WWII Berlin collection and is now awaiting restoration, although only the fuselage, engine, airscrew, rudder and undercarriage appear to have survived.

Aviatik (Berg) D.I

101.40. Champlin Fighter Museum, Mesa, Arizona, USA

During 1917 Julius von Berg, employed by Aviatik, designed a deep-fuselaged fighter with thin wings, the latter developed to accept the thermal currents encountered over the Austrian Alps without affecting the already precarious stability at high altitudes. The D.I's comparatively simple construction led to a number of firms undertaking licence manufacture

One of only two extant Austro-Hungarian Aviatik D.I fighters is 101.40, currently residing in Arizona's Champlin Fighter Museum. It has been fully restored in an authentic camouflage scheme. (H. Van Dyk Soerewyn)

and these included Lohner, Thone and Fiala, MAG and WFK. By 1918 some 700 machines had been built in various configurations as different engines were installed and other improvements continually made. The machine-gun mounting on the upper wing was soon replaced by twin synchronized weapons set over the instrument panel and within easy reach of the pilot.

Early problems with structural weaknesses were largely overcome and the D.I soon showed that its high rate of climb and manoeuvrability made it an effective fighter, although most Austro-Hungarian pilots preferred the much stronger Phönix designs. The various versions of the Berg never eliminated its one major defect of continual overheating problems with the Austro Daimler powerplant.

Of the total production from all manufacturers only two Bergs have survived. One of these is 101.37; built by Thone and Fiala in September 1918 it has been on display for many years at Vienna's Technical Museum with much of its structure cut away to reveal its construction. The only other remaining Berg was re-discovered as recently as the 1970s by Art Williams of Williams Flugzeug in Germany, who acquired the aeroplane at first unaware of the machine's true origins. On closer inspection the new owner became more and more intrigued as he tried to identify the type:

'Before me was a ply-skinned, slab-sided monster. The 100 Gnome had been attached on the front end, followed by a hammered metal top cowl, then a front seat, a bit of space and then the rear seat. Dual controls, less rudder in the front, were fitted. By measuring the position of the Gnome carburettor and the front seat I concluded that a backfire could provide the forward occupant a sensation he'd never forget!

'The whole machine was painted brown.... On both sides was a big white "A" and on the dirty white wings a big black "A". On the rudder was a small ruptured duck, supposedly an eagle, and decipher-

able below it: "Osterreichischer Luftverkeh–Wien" (Austrian Airtransport–Vienna). But nothing seemed to fit. I mean ... something didn't match up. A nice, clean fuselage then all this cowling, fairings, front seats that were impossible, etc. Something was very wrong....'

When Mr Williams began to disassemble the machine it was revealed that it had been cleverly disguised by its original owner to avoid the confiscation of military aeroplanes by the Allies following the Armistice. Since the deception included a front seat, the D.I seems to have been used for several years to carry a passenger and apparently it was *Frau* von Berg who kept her husband's precious machine hidden in a barn for many years.

101.40, thought to be an 'Austrian A–9' by 1924, was fitted with an 80 hp Le Rhône and purchased in 1965 by Otto Pavloro of Mauthausen, Austria, before being rediscovered by Williams Flugzeug in 1970, who subsequently sold it to the Champlin Fighter Museum in 1978 who completed the restoration. 101.40 is believed to be one of 60 Bergs built at the Oberursel factory in Wiener Neustadt and is fitted with a genuine 200 hp Austro Daimler engine acquired by trade from the US Air Force Museum. It currently wears an authentic three-colour mottled camouflage scheme researched by aviation historian Dr Martin O'Connor, who found the original colours on the only genuine existing fabric samples held in Italy's Leonardo da Vinci Museum.

In 1988 came unconfirmed reports that an original Aviatik (Berg) C.I, a two-seat version of the D.I fighter, had been found in a loft in Vienna. Further details are presently awaited...

Avro 504K

H5199. Shuttleworth Collection, Old Warden, Bedfordshire, UK

Probably the greatest training aeroplane of all time, the Avro 504 can trace its origins back to the 500 racing biplane of 1913. In the early months of WWI the Avro was used in an offensive role and the RNAS mounted at least one dramatic, albeit unsuccessful, attack against Zeppelin sheds by 504B pilots. From 1915 the type was mainly used in training units, although several examples were converted to make-shift single-seat night fighters for home defence duties.

The 504K appeared in 1918 and differed from the many versions that preceded it by having an open-fronted 'horseshoe' cowling and engine bearers designed to accommodate a number of different rotary powerplants such as the 110 hp Le Rhône, 130 hp Clerget and 100 hp Monosoupape. Over 8000 504s of various types were built during the war and by November 1918 the RAF could boast some 3000 on strength. Most of these were with the flying schools and were eventually superseded in post-war years by the Lynx-powererd 504N.

Although there are at least nine 504Ks preserved throughout the world the example belonging to the Shuttleworth Collection is one of very few maintained

The Science Museum's D7560 restored by Avro in 1954. This machine was originally powered by a 110 hp Le Rhône, but subsequently re-engined with a 130 hp Clerget. (Author)

in an airworthy condition. Built in 1918 (Factory No. 61400) as a K (H5199) it was converted to 504N configuration in RAF service and subsequently civilianized as G-ADEV. It was apparently sold by an aeroplane dealer sometime in 1936 and a year later won the Devon Air Race at 103 mph. Impressed into military service during 1940 as BK892 for glider-towing experiments, the aeroplane survived World War II and in 1955 was converted back to 504K status by Avro Company apprentices for the Shuttleworth

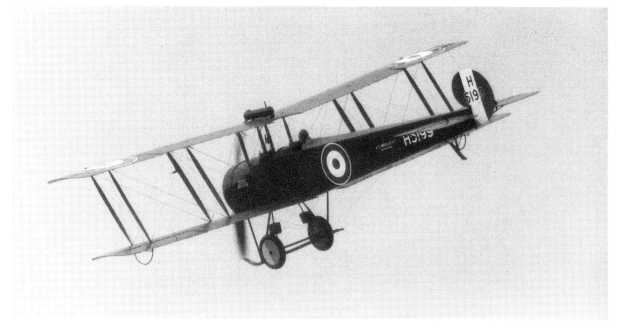

One of the world's best-known examples of the Avro 504K is the airworthy Shuttleworth specimen which was built in 1918, subsequently converted to 504N configuration and eventually restored to its original form by Avro apprentices in 1955. It has been renovated several times since by Shuttleworth engineers and currently bears its original identity. (Author)

Collection, who took delivery of the machine in 1958, following its star role in the classic film *Reach For The Sky*. A recent, thorough overhaul and complete re-covering has resulted in a more authentic RAF finish. Following an air display on 25 June, 1989 H5199 stalled during turning trials and crashed into a field 400 yards short of the runway. Although damaged, the aeroplane was repaired in time for the 1990 flying season.

Three other examples of the 504K exist in the UK. The Science Museum's D7560 was accepted by the RFC at Topcombe Corner on 22 March, 1918 and originally fitted with a 110 hp Le Rhône. Whilst at Topcombe the Avro was re-engined with a 130 hp Clerget and given the temporary serial 'C. Avro 7560'. After the Armistice the aeroplane was delivered to No. 3 Air Salvage Depot at Waddon, Croydon, on 8 April, 1919, and presented to the museum by the Air Disposal Board on 22 January, 1920. It was restored by Avros in 1954.

The Royal Air Force Museum boasts two Avro 504Ks, one of which is now under a long-term restoration at the Greater Manchester Museum of Science and Industry. This is 'H2311' (ex-G-ABAA), which for many years was kept in an airworthy condition following a rebuild in 1950. The serial number is not original but chosen to duplicate the 504K in which King George V learned to fly in 1919. At Hendon the museum's second Avro is displayed in RFC markings as 'E449', a hybrid machine rebuilt using wings from

The RAeS collection in the process of restoration at the BEA hangar, London Airport, September 1960, this formed the nucleus of the WWI collection at Hendon's RAF Museum. From left to right: Farman and Caudron nacelles; Blèriot XXVII; Fokker D.VII and F1 Camel – at rear the remains of Avro 504K G-EBJE. (John Garwood)

Avro 548 E449 (G-EBKN) mated to the fuselage of a genuine 504K, the former G-EBJE. The latter machine was originally owned by Captain R. G. Nash, who found it on a small farm where it had been stored for some 20 years.

The fuselage of Avro 504K (formerly G-EBJE) and wings from Avro 548 E449 (formerly G-EBKN) at London Airport prior to their combination. The resulting hybrid now stands in the RAF Museum at Hendon. (John Garwood)

Avro 504K

D8971. National Aviation Museum, Rockcliffe Airport, Ontario, Canada

One of 300 Avro 504Ks manufactured in 1918 by the Grahame-White Aviation Co. Ltd., at Hendon, D8971 (now registered 'G-CYCK') is the oldest aeroplane currently flying in Canada. The machine's early history is unknown, but it was probably not among the 62 504Ks that arrived in Canada during 1920 as part of the British Imperial Gift and used by the CAF and later the RCAF, the last of them being struck off charge in July 1928.

In 1961 Major James S. Appleby of California purchased D8971 from a Mrs G. H. Gallup of Connecticut and proceeded with restoration. He had completed almost 70 per cent of the work on the fuselage when, in 1966, he sold the machine to the RCAF, who flew it to Trenton inside a Hercules on 24 May. Once there the Avro was restored to flying condition by No. 6 RD RCAF Trenton, under Crew Chief H. Tate, and finished in the markings of G-CYCK. The veteran, powered by a 110 hp Le Rhône (No. 6202) and resplendent in its pristine new colour scheme first flew on 5 October, 1966, and was subsequently used for pilot training and demonstrations throughout 1967 for Canada's Centennial.

Hendon's rebuilt 504K 'E449'. (Author)

On 13 March the following year, 'G-CYCK' was transferred to the National Aeronautical Collection and is still operated by NAC/NAM for flying displays across Canada.

A second 504K is owned by the NAM and this is H2453, a machine built by A.V.Roe Ltd. of Manchester in 1918. Powered by a Clerget 9B (No. 9087) this Avro has also been restored by No. 6 RD Trenton and currently bears the fictitious registration G-CYFG.

The RAF Museum's second 504K was rebuilt to airworthy configuration in 1950. It was latterly in the Museum's reserve collection at Henlow. (Albatros/P. L. Gray Archive)

Avro 504K 'G-CYCK' is the oldest aeroplane currently flying in Canada. Originally built by Grahame-White in 1918 it was eventually restored by RCAF Trenton in the 1960s. (NAM 10315)

The first recorded owner of this machine was Frank F. Valcourt of Pantucket, Rhode Island, and in 1928 the machine had a US civil registration (5918) and was powered by a Le Rhône. Sometime during the early 1930s '5918' could be seen on display at the Roosevelt Field Museum, but changed hands again in 1951 when Cole Palen of Old Rhinebeck, New York, was flying the Avro for displays in both the USA and Canada. At that time it was registered as N8736R.

The RCAF purchased the machine on 19 May, 1966, and it was delivered to Trenton for restoration, several components from D8971 being used. It was assembled at Rockcliffe, fitted with a Clerget from the National Aeronautical Collection and displayed towards the end of 1967.

The Australian War Museum collection at Canberra includes an example of the 504K. This was presented to the museum by the RAAF in 1929 and bears its original service number A3–4. It is currently being restored to its original configuration. Another Avro is displayed in Finland at the Keski-Suomen Ilmailumuseo. This machine, the sole 504K operated by the Finnish Air Force, was bought from the Aircraft Disposal Co., and arrived in Finland on 22 September, 1926, being based at Santahamini, Utta and Kanhava before being retired in 1930 after logging almost 260 flying hours. Formerly E448 (G–EBNU), the Avro is powered by a Clerget 9b 130 hp rotary and was fully restored by personnel of the Rissala Air Force Base near Knopio between 1969 and 1971.

Avro 504J/K

B3182. Weeks Air Museum, Florida, USA

This American-based 504 was constructed by A.V. Roe in 1916, originally an early J model in the B3101–B3250 serial range. At some stage it was converted, along with many other Js, to 504K configuration with the universal engine mounting designed by Roe's and at a later date the lower starboard wing was damaged and replaced by another (dated November 1918) with fir spars. After the Armistice the aeroplane was brought to North America, probably by one of the many war surplus firms, and was subsequently purchased by a rancher in the early 1920s and flown in the

Rockcliffe's second Avro once belonged to Cole Palen and flew frequently from Old Rhinebeck prior to its 1966 purchase by the RCAF. (NAM 10306)

The Australian War Memorial's A3–4 as originally displayed in overall aluminium with olive drab undercarriage. (Via John Garwood)

Finland's 504K was originally E448 (G-EBNH) and is currently displayed at Tikkakoski (Keski-Suomen Ilmailumuseo).

Mexican Central Highlands; reportedly the first ever woman to solo in Mexico used the machine.

During 1925 the Avro was re-covered and loaned to a trade school six years later. It then lay disassembled in a shed until 1968, when it was brought to the United States and sold to a Mr J. L. Terteling, who initiated a full restoration to airworthy condition. Mr Dean Wilson was in charge of the project, which took three years to realize. When the machine arrived from Mexico it was virtually complete apart from the main undercarriage skid, compass and a number of turnbuckles. Many of the original aluminium parts, including rigging and control wires, were irreparably corroded and were replaced with genuine airworthy WWI parts or, as a final resort, duplicated with modern material using the original items for patterns.

All four longerons had to be replaced because of previous, rather crude, splicing work on all of them and the generally poor state of the oil-saturated wood. As received the Avro had copious amounts of castor oil and grime, almost a quarter of an inch in places, caking the entire fuselage interior. This was the result of the aeroplane being flown for some time without a firewall or lower forward engine pan! Every cloud has a silver lining it seems and it was true in the Avro's case, for the unwelcome quantity of oil had at least preserved most of the interior metal fittings.

The original landing gear was found to be badly damaged and had to be rebuilt. A swap was made with a museum for the main skid as well as a number of blueprints outlining three different undercarriage designs. The wide-axle version selected by the resto-

In May 1965, on Qantas airlines' 54th anniversary, the AWM 504K was acquired on long-term loan and converted to civil configuration which involved major surgery to install a 170 hp Sunbeam Dyack in-line engine. In 1988 the machine was returned to the Australian War Memorial to be restored to its original configuration. A replica takes its place at Qantas in Mascot, New South Wales. (Colin A. Owers)

This restored 504J/K in 'nightfighter' configuration is currently housed with Kermit Weeks's growing air museum in Miami, Florida. (Via John Garwood)

ration team used stacked rubber washers in place of the more usual bungee arrangement, but most of the original undercarriage fittings were salvaged and used. Indeed, throughout restoration, original items were incorporated wherever practicable and at least 70 per cent of the original wood was used. Both rudder and elevators are 100 per cent original and 95 per cent of the genuine 1916 hardware was restored to the airframe.

The completed Avro was finished in pseudo Home Defence markings and authentic-looking camouflage dope matched to original specifications. Dean Wilson first flew the restored Avro on 3 August, 1972, at Idaho and found it a stable machine, pleasant to fly. For a time hangared at the Glider Air Park in Boise, Idaho, the machine is currently part of the Kermit Weeks collection in Miami, Florida.

Breguet 14.A2

2016. Musée de l'air et de l'Espace, Le Bourget Airport, France

Undoubtedly the finest French day-bomber and reconnaissance aeroplane of the war, the Breguet 14 was extensively used in the latter part of World War I, serving in American, Belgian and French units. There were two basic versions; the A2, used for reconnaissance, and the B2 bomber. The latter boasted a lower wing of increased span fitted with automatic full-span flaps sprung by elastic cord and adjusted to drop at 70 mph. Michelin bomb-racks (32 16-lb bombs or their equivalent) could be carried and the

One of the true workhorses of the war was the Breguet 14 day bomber and reconnaissance machine and a fine example has been preserved by the Musée de l'Air. Here it is seen as originally displayed prior to recent restoration. (John Garwood)

Another intimate aspect of Breguet 14.A2 2016 which emphasizes its photo-reconnaissance role – note camera 'trap-doors' in fuselage underside. (John Garwood)

June 1988, La Grande Gallerie, Le Bourget, and the Musée de l'Air's Breguet, restored in somewhat untypical camouflage, nestles beneath the museum's DH9 and Pfalz D.XII. (Jon Guttman)

Bristol F2B Fighter

G-AANM. Vintage Aero, Northiam, East Sussex, UK

Generally regarded as the best fighter to see service with any nation in 'The Great War', the Bristol F2B enjoyed a long service with the Royal Air Force. After a somewhat disastrous operational début the 'Biff' soon established itself as a formidable combat aeroplane with a wide range of capabilities that included offensive patrols, photographic sorties, reconnaissance and ground attack. Undoubtedly the crack exponent of the F2B was the Canadian Lieutenant Andrew McKeever of No. 11 Squadron, who, with his observers, brought down 30 enemy machines between 29 June, 1917, and the Armistice – most of them scored while flying Bristols. By the time the war ended over 3000 'Biffs' had been delivered and a further 1369 had been built when production ceased in December 1926. The last operational 'Brisfits' – as they were known in post-war years – were those of No. 6 Squadron, which had served in Iraq and India until being replaced by Fairey Gordons in 1932.

There are two completely genuine surviving Bristol Fighters and at least three others which combine components of other machines and partially reconstructed airframes. One, in private hands, is owned by Guy Black's Aero Vintage of East Sussex. His G-AANM is being restored to fly as a 1917 Rolls-Royce-powered F2B, the engine, numbered '3 Falcon 13' (the third to be completed), is probably the earliest Falcon in existence.

Mr Black obtained a complete set of airframe components from the Shuttleworth Collection in 1983, including the original wings from their own, flying, F2B (D8096), which were being replaced with completely new panels at the time. The fuselage was one of six found at Weston-on-the-Green in the early 1960s by the Collection. Prior to their discovery the fuselages were being used as roof trusses in a barn,

B2 also featured illuminating panels each side of the fuselage beneath the observer's cockpit.

Despite heavy losses, the Breguet squadrons pushed home their attacks with determination, dropping a total of over 1800 tons of explosive on German targets. In an attempt to reduce casualties, pilots' seats were later armoured and downward-firing guns often fitted before heavily armed Caudron R.2s acted as escorts from July 1918.

An example of the classic two-seat 14.A2 is part of the incredible display of exhibits in the recently opened *La Grande Gallerie* at Le Bourget. The Breguet is in excellent condition. Fitted with a 300 hp Renault 12F motor it was overhauled and repainted before being moved to its current location and now boasts fairly authentic period camouflage. Fittings in the observer's cockpit reveal its one-time use for aerial photography and the legends 'Photo TSF' restored to the fuselage sides were copied from original markings. Few details of this Breguet's wartime service career appear to have survived and the author would welcome any additional data on this important aeronautical relic.

In storage is a fairly complete example of a Breguet 14.A2 (3C30), this one in Finland and held, pending a full restoration, by the Vesivehmaan Varastohalli.

Bristol F2B Fighter (G-AANM) in 1988 well on the way to full airworthy restoration. (Guy Black)

Bristol F2B Fighters of No. 39 Home Defence Squadron at North Weald in February 1918. The rearmost machine may be E2581 preserved by the Imperial War Museum – note fuselage markings. (Mrs A. J. Arkell)

having been bought from a surplus sale of ex-service machines after the war at a local airfield by a Mr Boddington.

The only major omissions from Aero Vintage's acquisition was the radiator and engine, the former being eventually manufactured by Lynx Engineering, the latter in an exchange for a Rolls-Royce Kestrel IIMS and 160 hp Gnome with the Royal Army Museum in Brussels.

The serial number stamped to the fuselage is 67626, but to date the machine's owner has failed to establish a reliable link between RFC/RNAS fuselage and serial numbers. However, amongst the components recovered from Weston-on-the-Green was a pair of cowlings with the number 7889 on both sides. It has been assumed that this is an RAF number, probably D7889 (which was an F2B), and pending further research the Bristol will be restored bearing this serial. By April 1988, fuselage restoration, undertaken by Skysport Engineering, was complete with 90 per cent of the original metalwork having been incor-

porated and about 40 per cent of the wood. The tail unit, which is completely original, is also finished, its components being merely cleaned, painted and re-covered. A second F2B (BAPC19) was recently restored by Skysport for the Historic Aircraft Collection of Jersey. This machine is a rebuild using many parts from several original Bristol fighters and is fitted with a Hispano-Suiza and finished in Belgian markings. On 22 June, 1989 it was transported to the Royal Army Museum in Brussels in exchange for Spitfire IX MK912.

Bristol F2B Fighter

E2581. Imperial War Museum, Duxford, Cambridgeshire, UK

This is possibly the most authentic WWI Bristol Fighter in existence and for many years was suspended in the Imperial War Museum at Lambeth before being taken down and re-covered during the early part of 1984.

E2581 was one of 500 F2Bs built by the British and Colonial Aeroplane Company (later Bristol Aeroplane Company) in September 1918. The origin of its unusual black/white diamond fuselage marking and numeral 13 has baffled many enthusiasts for years, but there is really no great mystery. E2581 was first issued to No. 39 Home Defence Squadron RAF at North Weald in Essex and at least one contemporary photograph showing a line-up of 39 HDS Bristols reveals a machine in similar markings, possibly the IWM aeroplane itself. From December 1918, E2581 was flown by a number of Communications and

The IWM's F2B at Lambeth during the late 1950s. The machine has been restored in recent years. (John Garwood)

Headquarters flights operating from aerodromes around London until its final flight in April 1920. In March the following year the RAF transferred the Bristol to the Imperial War Museum and from 1923 to 1931 it was on loan to the Science Museum and displayed at South Kensington. In 1936 E2581 returned to Lambeth.

The Shuttleworth Trust maintains a Bristol Fighter in airworthy condition at its famous Old Warden aerodrome near Biggleswade in Bedfordshire. D8096 was built during 1918, but did not see wartime service although it was on the strength of No. 208 Squadron in Turkey during 1923. It was acquired in 1936 by Captain C. P. B. Ogilvie, who kept the aeroplane stored at Primrose Garages, Watford, intending to restore it to flying condition, and although the civil registration G-AEPH was allotted, it was not used. It was restored by the Bristol Aeroplane Company and first flown in Shuttleworth ownership during February 1952 wearing an authentic pre-war overall aluminium finish. The 'Brisfit' entered the Old Warden workshops in 1980–82 for extensive engine and airframe restoration, to emerge in full WWI camouflage hardly appropriate for this particular machine.

The 'fifth' British-based F2B is displayed at The Royal Air Force Museum at Hendon, a superbly

The Shuttleworth Trust's D8096 is, as yet, the world's only original airworthy Bristol Fighter and is seen here at Woburn Abbey during the 1950s not long after its restoration by the Bristol Aeroplane Company.

Shuttleworth's E8096 wore its post-war No. 208 colour scheme for many years until a recent and thorough overhaul, when it emerged from the Old Warden workshops in a splendid, but entirely inappropriate, WWI finish. (Author)

crafted reconstruction based on F2B fuselage components from Weston-on-the-Green. A starboard lower wing panel from the Shuttleworth Collection and another five found in Ireland gave the craftsmen at the museum's Restoration and Storage Centre at Cardington a good start. The project took several years to complete and an amazing reproduction of a Rolls-Royce Falcon was created for installation into an airframe which has its starboard side uncovered to reveal the internal structure. Although not 100 per cent original, the RAF Museum's Brisfit is probably among the most impressive of their exhibits.

Bristol M1C

C5001. The Butler Memorial, Minlaton, South Australia

Had the Bristol Monoplane not been the victim of official prejudice in early 1917, it would have undoubtedly found a greater role in the history of air warfare, for it was a machine that boasted superior qualities to most contemporary machines and was sorely needed by the then hard-pressed RFC squadrons in France. The Bristol Monoplane was never allowed the opportunity to make a name for itself due to a deep-seated official suspicion of monoplane designs that went back to 1912.

During the war Bristol Monoplanes saw limited service in the Middle East theatre, but they were very popular with instructors at the various home-based training schools. Post-war years saw several examples being used for racing and one of these machines is now the sole survivor.

In the summer following the Armistice an Australian Captain, Harry Butler, AFC, bought Bristol M1C C5001 from the Aircraft Disposal Board. He took it back to Australia with him and at Minlaton, together with a partner, H. A. Kamper, and an Avro 504K, made several exhibition flights. The first of these was on 23 July, 1919, at Unley Oval in aid of the Repatriation fund, Butler flying the monoplane. The machine was given the Australian civil registration G-AUCH, and with Butler at the controls it won the first Australian Aerial Derby on 8 September, 1920. The Bristol, in its bright colour scheme, was universally known as 'The Red Devil', and Butler's frequent displays thrilled crowds and did much to make South Australia airminded. Butler's career came to an untimely end on 11 January, 1922, when flying the Avro. An engine failure resulted in a bad smash and although his passenger escaped unhurt Butler himself was badly injured. On 30 July the following year he died from cerebral complications as a result of the crash 18 months previously.

G-AUCH was stored in an Adelaide garage until 1930, when it was found and purchased by one H. Miller, who later replaced the original Le Rhône

Captain Harry J. Butler (in flying suit) stands before Bristol M1C C5501 during the latter months of WWI. He subsequently purchased the aeroplane after the Armistice and shipped it to Australia. (Colin A. Owers)

Butler's 'Red Devil' was purchased by a Mr Miller in 1930 who replaced the Le Rhône with an in-line DH Gypsy II engine. Renamed 'Puck', the aeroplane took part in many air displays and races until 1938. (Colin A. Owers)

rotary with a borrowed DH Gipsy II and removed the fairings from the fuselage sides. Re-registered VH-UQI, the modified Bristol won the Adelaide Aerial Derby in 1931 and 1932 and, known as 'Puck', was extensively flown in the Commercial Aviation Co.'s aerial circus. Its last flight was from Adelaide to Perth in 1938, after which it was stored in the roof of an airport hangar at Guildford. In 1956 the Bristol was rediscovered by C. B. Tilbrook of Minlaton and subsequently restored to exhibition standards by Aviation Services, Parafield (SA) Ltd. to form the centrepiece of the Harry Butler Memorial.

Although the machine in its present configuration bears little resemblance to Butler's 'Red Devil' and is hardly representative of Captain Frank Barnwell's original design it is the world's only example of a genuine British WWI monoplane fighter.

Caproni Ca.3

'4166'. Museo Storico AMI, Vigna di Valle (Rome), Italy

The Italian aviation pioneer Gianni Caproni began work on what would eventually emerge as the Ca.3 bomber biplane in 1913. In October 1914 Emilio Pensuti flew the prototype, powered by three Gnomes; a central 100 hp engine and two 80 hp laterals. Slow negotiations with the government and the small size of Caproni's firm meant that only three bombers had been built when Italy entered the war in May 1915, nine more being delivered by October. The aircraft's success prompted the Army to order more and, although production tempo never caught up with the orders, the Caproni bomber series was launched. Different versions utilized several engines in the 150–200 hp range and sported three- or five-piece wings. Many missions were flown, including bombings of Pola, Tarvisio and Cattaro; a group operated on the French front, while many American pilots were trained in Foggia. Among them was Fiorello La Guardia.

The Ca.3 now at Vigna di Valle is serialled 23174. It was purchased after the war for 30,000 lire by Lt.

Casimiro Buttini, a famous bomber pilot who won the Gold Medal for Military Gallantry while flying a Caproni over Tarnova in 1917. For nearly 40 years Buttini kept his aircraft on his farm at Casanova di Carmagnola and in 1959, shortly after his death, Buttini's wife sold it to the Air Force. By 1964 it was on display at the short-lived Turin museum, crudely restored. When the Turin collection closed it moved to Vigna di Valle, where it was restored. The rear turret was built from scratch; the engines were found to be SPA.6A instead of the original Isotta Fraschini V-4s. The lateral radiators are missing.

The aircraft was repainted as '4166', which operated on the Albanian front in July 1918 with the 11ᵃ *Squadriglia*. The logic of altering the identity and markings of Buttini's genuine aircraft is difficult to comprehend.

The Italian Air Force Museum at Vigna di Valle currently houses the magnificently restored Caproni Ca.3 bomber in the spurious markings of the 11ᵃ Squadriglia. (Stuart Howe)

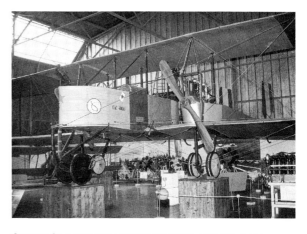

Caproni Ca.3 23174 is virtually complete although some missing components, including the rear 'turret', were built from original plans for its most recent restoration. (Stuart Howe)

Caproni Ca.36

'2378'. US Air Force Museum, Wright Patterson AFB, Ohio, USA

2378 flew many important war missions, including the 4 October, 1917, Pola raid. Its crew consisted of pilots Luigi Gori and Maurizio Pagliano, with the poet-soldier Gabriele D'Annunzio as observer. There is some doubt, however, as to whether this is the original 2378, which according to some sources was destroyed in action in late 1917. Certainly the five-piece wing belongs to a late-production machine, whereas 2378 was a relatively early product. Retro-fitting was fairly common, however, so the late model wing is hardly conclusive evidence.

Initial preservation history is unclear, although 2378 is reported as having been acquired by Gianni Caproni for his museum after the 1928 Turin show. 2378 was certainly displayed at the 1934 Milan historical exhibition and was then returned to the Caproni museum. At the end of World War II the Capronis did what they could to save their collection, although some aircraft were destroyed by the workers during the 1944–45 winter, including the Ca.5 tri-plane bomber. Others suffered the same fate in April 1945, when the Capronis were allocated insufficient time and transport to move the collection out of Taliedo. The dismantled 2378 was eventually walled up in a convent and only emerged in September 1987!

The US Air Force Museum has obtained the bom-

Nose detail of the Vigna di Valle Ca.3. (Alberto Casirati)

The Caproni Museum's Ca36 bomber on arrival at the USAF Museum. (Chuck King)

44

The completed Caproni was rolled out in March 1990 and is currently on display at Dayton. (USAF Museum)

ber on loan for 15 years. A small team travelled to Italy to pack the large aircraft into 14 crates, which were airlifted in a C-141 transport from Aviano airport – coincidentally named after Gori and Pagliano. By spring 1988 the crates lay unopened at Wright Patterson. Restoration began immediately after the Air Force took delivery of a new building in mid-year. The markings carried were inaccurate and were probably painted on for the 1934 show.

Recent research indicates that the Caproni may not be the original 2378 after all but a *post*-war Ca.36 25811. The curator at Wright Patterson discovered the number 25811 on several components, this serial belonging to the final production batch delivered during 1924–6. Until firm, irrefutable evidence is received this historic Italian bomber still remains classified by the author as a 'WW1 survivor.'

Caudron G.3

'3066'. Royal Air Force Museum, Hendon, UK

The Caudron G.3 was the ultimate development of the preceding C, D and E types, continuing the somewhat quaint combination of a basically pusher configuration with a tractor power unit. This WWI classic first appeared in French service during 1914 and as the war progressed a small number were purchased by the Royal Flying Corps, the first pair being delivered directly to No. 1 Squadron on 27 March, 1915.

In the field the RFC employed the Caudron G.3 for reconnaissance duties, but it never saw widespread service. Generally, RFC HQ had a low opinion of the aeroplane's operational qualities, although they pressed a small number into service with training

The ex-Royal Aeronautical Society's Caudron G.3 in its original Belgian civilian registration seen at Hendon in 1951. It is now back at Hendon in the markings of a typical machine from the RNAS. (John Garwood)

units. Production in France was substantial, the Caudron company itself turning out over 1420 of the type, and several modest production batches were made in England by the British Caudron Company. Some of these aeroplanes are thought to have been powered by the 70 hp Renault motor, others were fitted with the 80 hp or 100 hp Anzani radial, yet most RFC G.3s had the 80 hp Gnome.

Several examples of the G.3 may be seen today, 324 at Le Bourget and '3066' at Hendon's RAF Museum, in North London. The latter machine, once part of the Royal Aeronautical Society collection, was flying as late as 1935, in Belgium, where it bore the civil registration 00-LEA and was flown by M. J. E. Le Duc, who used the aeroplane for aerial advertising. In 1936 Ken Walter, then Chief Flying Instructor of Brooklands Aviation Ltd., purchased the machine and flew it back across the Channel to Brooklands. It never wore its intended British civil registration, but retained its original Belgian identity as it subsequently passed to the Nash Collection, thence to the

This Caudron G.3 is owned by the Musée de l'Air and seen here in 1974. (Stuart Howe)

2351 once belonged to the Musée de l'Air but is now displayed in Brussels following an exchange agreement in 1975. Note German Gotha G.V bomber engine, nacelle and propeller at extreme left. (Brussels Air Museum)

RAeS and ultimately the RAF Museum after being fully restored as '3066', representative of the RNAS Flying School at Vendôme in 1917.

Other examples of surviving Caudron G.3s include IE 18 preserved in Finland at the Hallinportti Ilmai-lumuseo (who also have the nacelle and parts of a second in storage); the aforementioned G.3 324 in the Museé de l'Air *La Grande Gallerie* and their second G.3 (2351) now displayed at the Royal Army Museum in Belgium following an exchange arrangement in 1975. A sixth Caudron G.3 was, until

recently, displayed at the Aeroflex Museum in New Jersey, USA.

Caudron G.4

C1720. Musée de l'Air et de l'Espace, Le Bourget Airport, Paris, France

The Caudron G.4, which was introduced during March 1915, was more or less a scaled-up version of the G.3 fitted with two engines. Originally these powerplants were 80 hp Le Rhônes with the 100 hp Anzani radial being used for late production aeroplanes. For the G.4, the vertical tail surfaces were increased to four and a machine gun with flexible mounting provided for the observer's cockpit. Some machines were further armed with an additional machine gun mounted on the upper wing intended to fire rearwards.

Although the Caudron G.4's bomb load was a modest one (about 100 kg) the machine boasted a useful performance and a surprisingly good rate of climb. It entered service with the French *aviation militaire* in November 1915 and proved to be a reliable workhorse and was not replaced until late 1916. AER in Italy built just over 50 G.4s, while the RNAS received 43 French-built G.4s and another dozen were completed by the British Caudron Co. During 1915–16 these machines were used for day and night raids on enemy airship and seaplane bases in Belgium by Nos. 4 and 5 Wings. Caudrons in French service included both A2 and B2 versions and in 1918 the American Expeditionary Force purchased at least ten G.4A2s for training purposes.

The Musée de l'Air's Caudron G.4 as displayed for many years at Chalais Meudon. This unusual angle emphasizes the one-piece lower wing. (John Garwood)

The Caudron G.4 displayed at Le Bourget is fitted with a pair of 80 hp Le Rhônes and has recently been fully restored by museum craftsmen. It is armed with a single Lewis machine gun and bears the red devil insignia of Caudron *Escadrille* C202 and the serial C1720 on its nacelle.

Recently restored the Musée G.4 is now marked in the colours of Escadrille *C.202 and is one of the star exhibits at Le Bourget.* (Jon Guttman)

The world's only other surviving Caudron G.4 is owned by the National Air and Space Museum at Washington DC: It is fitted with 110 hp Le Rhônes. (Via John Garwood)

Another G.4 survives and is owned by the National Air and Space Museum at Washington DC. It was acquired from the US War Department in 1919 and carries the serial C4263. It is fitted with two 110 hp Le Rhônes.

Curtiss HS-2L

A1876. National Aviation Museum, Rockcliffe Airport, Ontario, Canada

In mid-1917 the Curtiss Aeroplane and Motor Co. Inc. converted their three-seat H-14 twin-engined pusher flying boat into a single-engined type and assigned it the new designation of HS (model H, Single-engine). With America then involved in WWI, the US Navy ordered a modified version of the HS into full-scale production and since Curtiss themselves were unable to keep pace with demand, five other manufacturers were awarded licence contracts. There were several models in the HS series, including the HS-1L, powered by the 360 hp 12-cylinder Liberty engine, and the HS-2L, which followed, an improved version with greatly enlarged wing area. The vertical tail was also enlarged and a balance area added to the rudder.

An excellent example of an HS-2L is displayed at Rockcliffe as part of the NAM Collection. Although finished in post-war configuration this Curtiss was constructed before the Armistice, its hull being

manufactured by the Niagara Motor Boat Co. of North Tonawanda, New York, and completed by 9 August, 1918. As A1876 in USN service the flying boat was stationed at Halifax (Dartmouth) Naval Station by September and in February of the following year presented to the Canadian Government as a gift. The machine made the world's first 'bush' flights over the St Maurice River Valley area of Quebec until 2 September, 1922, when it crashed on take-off from Foss Lake in Ontario. The remains of the aeroplane were eventually recovered by NAM during 1968–69 with a view to full restoration. The wings, tail surfaces, struts and other vital components of another HS-2L (NC652–ex-USN A1373) were purchased from the Los Angeles County Museum in California during February 1971, while radiators and fittings

Finished in post-war colours Canada's National Aviation Museum's Curtiss HS-2L was completed during August 1918. The machine's restoration took place over several years and contains a number of parts from two other examples. (NAM 18222)

The most numerous WWI type still extant is the immortal Curtiss Jenny – over 50 complete examples are known to survive and a large number of these are still airworthy. One of many spendid Jennies to be found in the USA today is N5162, owned by Harrah's Automobile Museum in Reno, Nevada. (Harrah's Automobile Museum)

The Glenn Curtiss Museum, in New York displays two examples of the Jenny, and while one of them is fully restored, the uncovered fuselage of its companion is the more impressive exhibit. (Stuart Howe)

Curtiss JN-4D 8428 currently displayed at the Henry Ford Museum and Greenfield Village in Dearborn, Michigan. (John Garwood)

There are several classic Curtiss survivors at Pensacola's US Naval Aviation Museum – this is their JN-4D marked as '995'. (Stuart Howe)

from a third machine (G-CAOS) were recovered near Chipman Lake, Ontario, five years later. The restoration long planned by the National Aviation Museum could now begin in earnest and the result was wheeled out in May 1986 after nine years in the workshop.

Curtiss JN-4D

'4983'. Paul E. Garber Facility, Silver Hill, Maryland, USA

The Jenny, America's most famous training aeroplane, was developed by combining the best features of the J and N models. A 1915 version, the JN-3, was used operationally during Pershing's 1916 Punitive Expedition into Mexico, but its poor performance made it unsuitable. The same year saw the aeroplane being modified to improve its performance and it was designated JN-4. With America's entry into 'The Great War' on 6 April, 1917, the Army Signal Corps demanded large numbers of the new machine for training use and by the time production had ceased after the Armistice over 6000 had been delivered.

It is no overstatement to claim that the Jenny had more influence than any other type on the subsequent development of US aviation. After the war hundreds were sold on the civilian market and became the mainstay of 1920s Barnstormers, many of whom were still flying the aeroplane well into the following decade. Jennies also saw use in aviation films, even as late as the 1970s, and a relatively large number still survive in the USA.

A comprehensive record of all the known, extant Jennies would easily fill another book and with so many of them in various states of repair and frequently changing hands a definitive up-to-date listing is virtually impossible. Several occupy honoured positions in national museums, while others, in private hands, have been constantly – often drastically – altered. Different engines have been used, extra seats added, wings interchanged, even single-bay wings fitted. Remnants of Jennies have been found in hundreds of places across the United States – engines hidden away in old barns or hedgerows and wheels and wings in garages; struts, airscrews, and instruments even now are still turning up to the delight of vintage aeroplane enthusiasts. As a result many of the surviving Jennies have been assembled using com-

The Curtiss JN-4D of the USAF Museum at Dayton, Ohio, has been displayed to the public for many years. It is seen here in 1958. (Via John Garwood)

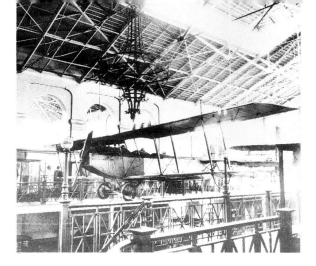

The NASM Jenny was acquired from the US War Department in 1919 – seen here as displayed in the museum during the late 1950s. (John Garwood)

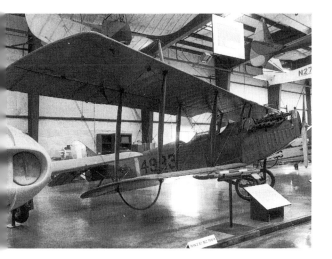

4983 has worn a white fuselage band and cartoon horse motif for many years. The origins of these markings are unclear. The Jenny is currently displayed at Silver Hills. (Stuart Howe)

A more recent photograph of the Dayton Jenny. 2805 was donated to the museum in 1956 by enthusiast Robert Pfiel of Taylor, Texas. (H. Van Dyk Soerewyn)

ponents from many sources, making it impossible to even guess their origins. (Readers are referred to Appendix I for the latest listings.)

One of the most authentic examples of a Jenny is currently held by NASM at Silver Hill. This is a JN-4D fitted with the standard OX-5 engine. It carries the Air Service serial number 4983 and the legend '46th', together with a white fuselage band and cartoon horse. The upper wings bear the later US star roundel, while the lower panels feature the earlier red, blue and white roundels. Formerly at Hempstead Field, New York, the aeroplane was acquired directly from the US War Department in 1919.

Curtiss JN-4D

34135. Central Flying Services, Arkansas, USA

This Jenny served with the US Signal Corps in 1918 and was subsequently owned for a time by the Huff Brothers of Redwood City, California, during the early 1930s and registered N1213. The next owner was Robert Ficklin of Madera, California, who purchased the Jenny in 1935 and in whose hands it remained for 22 years.

During the autumn of 1957, Al Kiefer, a purchasing supervisor of the Northrop Aircraft Company and member of the American Aviation Historical Society decided to finally fulfil a life-long ambition to restore

and operate a genuine Curtiss Jenny. Realizing the task was rather too much for him, Mr Kiefer easily persuaded fellow AAHS member R. T. Hood to join him in the project. Between them they located an OX-6 engine, radiator, almost a complete set of JN-4 fittings, 600 turnbuckles and a set of factory drawings. The only thing lacking was an airframe.

Working on rumours that a Jenny had been seen on a farm in 1950 the enthusiasts eventually tracked down Robert Ficklin's farm in Madera and found their prize – a battered JN-4D fuselage, together with boxes of spare parts, including seats, struts, a pair of fins and a radiator in its original olive drab dope. The owner of the Jenny accepted 500 dollars for the whole lot and Messrs Hood and Keifer loaded the remains onto their 14-foot trailer and towed it back to Torrance, California, for full restoration.

For the next six years the new owners spent all their spare time working on the aeroplane. Wooden parts were restored or replaced as necessary and all metal parts were sand-blasted, cadmium-plated, zinc-chromated and finally painted to match the original colours. The USAF Museum at Wright Patterson AFB yielded microfilm of some 1400 Curtiss factory drawings to aid the restoration, but even this mountain of data was insufficient. In an attempt to discover how the wingtip spars were tapered, Kiefer and Hood sorted through a number of aeronautical junkyards looking for Jenny components. They were fortunate to find exactly what they were after and when several spar sections were unearthed and examined it revealed that they were double-tapered – another mystery solved. A fellow member of the AAHS found a rotting Jenny airframe and forwarded dozens of record photographs, which provided valuable reference on wing rib shape and construction.

The completed Jenny received its registration in 1960 and made its first post-restoration flight on 6 July, 1963, at Meadowlark airport. It was immacu-

lately finished as 34135 in 1917 US Army markings of a training machine based at Kelly Field. The Jenny won several awards at air displays, but was almost written off in an accident at the Ontario Air Museum in November 1963. Damage to the machine, which was brought down by engine failure, was extensive, but pilot Al Keifer and his TV cameraman passenger were mercifully uninjured. Undaunted, Keifer and Hood rebuilt their JN-4 and it took to the air once more a year later. In 1967 the Jenny changed hands, its new owners, the Wings and Wheels Museum, displaying the machine at Orlando International Airport in Florida. At the 1981 Christie's Wings and Wheels auction the Jenny was sold to its current owners for $88,000.

Curtiss JN-4 (Can) Canuck

39158. National Aviation Museum, Rockcliffe Airport, Ontario, Canada

The JN-4C was almost entirely a Canadian development and production version of the Curtiss Jenny. Dubbed the 'Canuck', for obvious reasons, these aeroplanes featured more rounded ailerons and a redesigned rudder, while many were fitted with control wheels for bomber-pilot training. Nearly 2200 JN-4Cs were built by Canadian Aero Ltd., in addition to the 680 JN-4D machines built under licence for the USA. Only a handful of 'Canucks' have survived and 39158 is probably the most authentic example.

This superb restoration was originally built by Canadian Aeroplanes Ltd. of Toronto, Ontario, during early 1918. In US service the machine was allocated the serial 39158 and is thought to have been stationed at Love Field in Dallas, Texas, during May of that year.

Following expert restoration, the Canadian Canuck 'C227' is marked in the colours of the 85th CRS, RFC. (NAM 6723)

In 1925–26 the Canuck was purchased by Edward Faulkner of Honeoye Falls, New York, from George Reese of Naples and had received a US civil registration by April of 1927. In November 1932 it was stored in a barn at Honeoye Falls and its registration was officially cancelled five years later. Little is known of the machine's subsequent history until 15 February, 1962, when it was purchased by the National Aviation Museum. Fitted with a Curtiss OX-5 engine (No. M3491) it was restored by museum craftsmen and finished with the fictitious serial 'C227', in the colours of No. 85 CRS, RFC, and displayed at NAC Rockcliffe and NAM Uplands. Since 1967 this magnificent example of a Canadian JN-4 has been exhibited at the National Museum of Science and Technology.

Curtiss JN-4H

'38278'. Old Rhinebeck Aerodrome, New York, USA

On 30 January, 1957, Cole Palen received, by rail, 19 components of a wrecked aeroplane from a C. W. Adams Jr of Winter Haven, Florida. The aeroplane had been advertised as a Standard J-1, but on closer inspection turned out to be an engine-less Curtiss JN-4H, the Jenny variant powered by the 150 hp Hispano-Suiza Model A. Palen was unable to trace the aeroplane's history, but over the years some of the original missing parts, wings, radiator, etc., began to turn up and a suitable Hispano-Suiza was acquired

One of America's most well-known Jenny survivors is the JN-4H preserved in flying order by Cole Palen at Old Rhinebeck Aerodrome in New York State. (H. Van Dyk Soerewyn)

from the Franklin Institute in Philadelphia.

Restoration of the Jenny began in 1967, the aeroplane being built up from original sections and parts of several other Curtiss JN-4s, so it is something of a 'hybrid'. Finished in drab US camouflage olive it bears the fuselage number '38278' and has been flying at Old Rhinebeck since 1969.

De Havilland DH4

'No. 1'. National Air and Space Museum, Washington DC, USA

The De Havilland DH4 was destined to become the only American-built aeroplane to enter combat service in the war and enjoyed many years of peacetime employment after the Armistice. The aeroplane was based on the original classic design by the British engineer Geoffrey de Havilland and the fortunate result of some extraordinary steps taken by the US government and industry as the country entered the war in Europe. Funding, organization and industrial mobilization led to over 4800 DH4s being constructed in the United States, mostly by the Dayton-Wright Airplane Company.

In combat the 'American DH4' performed its dual role as bomber and reconnaissance platform to good effect. Despite some operational problems the type saw fairly widespread service in several American front-line units and 'The Liberty Plane', as it became known, proved a reliable workhorse despite the somewhat unjustified soubriquet, 'Flying Coffin', bestowed upon it by some crews. In post-war years the DH4 soldiered on in military and civil roles – many surplus machines were used in films, patrolled for forest fires and flew mail.

There are a number of post-war DH4Bs preserved in the USA, but it is believed that the recently restored NASM machine is the only survivor of those built during the last year of the war. Indeed, it is actually the first of all the DH4s built by Dayton-Wright, unique in several ways, and had been built with incredible speed by a dedicated team at Dayton's using converted British drawings and a specimen Airco DH4, less engine, as a pattern.

The first 'American DH4' had a long service life and logged over 1080 hours of test and routine flying. It was only the second machine to be powered with the Liberty 12 engine; it made more than 4000 flights; conducted 2500 experiments; flew more than 111,000 miles and pioneers Orville Wright and Glenn Martin made flights in it. Considering the service attrition of most aeroplanes of the time, the machine's longevity in service may be considered remarkable considering the number of flying hours it logged. After the Armistice, when DH4 production ceased, Colonel S. D. Waldoon of the USAS wrote to the Secretary of the

Smithsonian Institution offering the 'Original No. 1 De Havilland' for permanent exhibition. Before its arrival in early 1919 the DH4 was 'refurbished' by Dayton-Wright to service standard, its original finish replaced by overall olive drab and a full arsenal of military equipment fitted. Almost as an afterthought the serial number SC29159 was applied, which would have been assigned to the next machine in line had the 4000-aeroplane contract been continued. If nothing else it confirmed that Dayton-Wright completed 3100 machines by the Armistice.

Over the following years the DH4 was repainted, with markings added and deleted, and then placed into store. It re-emerged at one stage for exhibition at the Langley Air Force Base and hastily re-painted and refurbished by inexperienced craftsmen and then returned to storage at the Garber Facility. Despite the depredations of time and inept 'restorers', the DH4 was at least complete, an ideal candidate for a full restoration, and in April 1980 the talented team responsible for the magnificent NASM Albatros DVa project, Karl Heinzel and Richard Horigan Jr, were given the task.

The restoration was completed in November 1981 after 4163 manhours of dedicated work, and a total expenditure of just over $44,000. The result is magnificent and this historically important machine is undoubtedly one of NASM's most prized exhibits.

DFW C.V

C17077/17. Polish Museum Lotnictwa i Astronautyki, Krakow, Poland

One of the most successful all-purpose two-seaters used by Germany during the war, the DFW C.V, was produced in large numbers, by several contractors, for reconnaissance, artillery co-operation and infantry contact patrol duties. Introduced towards the end of 1916 it continued to equip *Flieger Abteilung* units for at least a year, a long time for an aeroplane to remain in production. Some DFW C.Vs continued in service late into 1918 and on the Italian front they were used right up to the Armistice.

The DFW C.V proved instantly popular with German aircrews, who were impressed with its tractable flying characteristics, all-round excellent performance, ease of handling and particularly with the rear cockpit's generous size, which provided ample room for wireless, photographic equipment and ammunition. The C.V was supplied to front-line units in greater numbers than any other German two-seater, reaching a maximum of 1057 aeroplanes in service by the end of August 1917. With such large numbers involved, a testimony to the recognized excellence of the type, it is perhaps surprising that only one survived in its country of origin, especially since several

An example of the German DFW C.V two-seater, circa 1917. One of these machines survives, stored for many years at Krakow in Poland before recent removal for restoration. (Albatros/P. L. Gray Archive)

were offered for sale after the Armistice. At least four examples were registered for civilian use, but their ultimate fate remains unknown.

Post-war, DFW C.V C17077/17 was displayed in Berlin's Deutsche Luftfahrt Sammlung with a dark grey-painted fuselage and narrow white crosses. It bore no armament and the distinctive 'wrap around' engine cowlings were missing. The aeroplane, along with many others in the collection, was removed in 1941 to escape Allied bombing and sent, subsequently, to Krakow. Only the fuselage, engine, airscrew, undercarriage and tail surfaces remain, and the present whereabouts of the wings are unknown. It is likely to be restored in the near future.

Franco British Aviation (FBA) Type H

5. Musée Royal de l'Armée et d'Histoire Militaire, Brussels, Belgium

During January 1915, Franco British Aviation built batches of flying boats (much on the lines of the Leveque boats) powered by a 100 hp Gnome engine as the Type B. In April 1916 the Type C appeared, which was similar but powered by a 130 hp Clerget engine. These flying boats operated from most of the French coastal bases, and were also supplied to Italy and Russia. The FBA flying boats were largely the result of close co-operation between M. Louis Schreck, from the automobile industry, and Lieuten-

ant de Vaisseau Conneau, better known by his pseudonym André Beaumont, who commanded *Escadrille de Dunkirk*, which flew FBAs exclusively.

First of the new series was the Type H, the first Hispano-powered flying boat, which accommodated a crew of three. Initially a 150 hp Hispano-Suiza engine was fitted, but later 170 hp Hispano-Suiza or 160 hp Lorraine engines were used.

The type H in modified form was also built under licence in Italy, powered by a 150 hp Isotta Fraschini engine and fitted with a fin. The dimensions were identical, but its performance was slightly inferior to the original version. The Italians built 38 in 1916, 367 in 1917 and 577 in 1918 – possibly more, a total of at least 982.

Records indicate that the FBA Type H was the most extensively built flying boat of the entire war,

The (FBA) Type H Flying Boat displayed at Brussels during the late 1950s. The aeroplane was donated to the Royal Army Museum in 1920. (John Garwood)

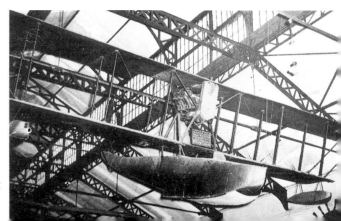

but very few appear to have survived. One of the best-known examples is that displayed in Belgium's Royal Army Museum. It still wears an original wartime finish with clear-doped wings and tail bearing Belgian roundels and a plain gloss varnished stained-wood hull. No other markings or serial numbers are visible, but the machine was believed to have been based at Calais for North Sea patrols. Donated to the museum in 1920, the Belgian FBA is powered by a 160 hp Lorraine-Dietrich engine.

Fokker D.III

Serial unknown. Technisches Museum, Vienna, Austria

Outwardly the Fokker D.III single-seat biplane fighter of 1916 differed little from the D.II that preceded it into service. It could be identified by the deep chord cowling necessitated by installation of the 160 hp Oberursel U.III twin-row rotary, and to allow for the extra weight of that engine, the undercarriage was suitably modified.

The D.III's operational career was a short one as its performance was eclipsed by superior Albatros and Halberstadt D-types, which equipped the first German fighter units. Even so such luminaries as von Richthofen, Boelcke and Udet flew the type. Some aeroplanes were used for training and others were sold to the Dutch, these being fitted with balanced ailerons. Total production of all D.II and D.III types neared the 300 mark and some were supplied to the Austro-Hungarian forces, with whom Anthony Fokker conducted considerable business.

In the Vienna Technical Museum, a complete, albeit uncovered, Fokker D.III fuselage is displayed. The exhibit is in mint condition (ex-factory?) complete with all controls and equipment: ammunition chutes and boxes; engine controls; instruments; fuel system, etc. The aeroplane's original identity is, at present, unknown.

Fokker D.VII

6810/18. Brome County Historical Society, Knowlton, Quebec, Canada

Considered by most aero historians as the finest German fighter aeroplane of the war, the Fokker D.VII proved a formidable weapon in the hands of a competent pilot. Early versions were powered with the 160 hp Mercedes D.III and in 1918 performance was improved even further with the introduction of the highly regarded 185 hp BMW engine. The D.VII was comparatively easy to fly yet extremely respon-

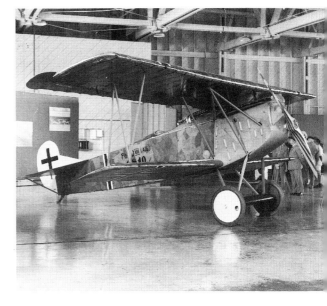

Probably the world's most authentic Fokker D.VII is 6810/18 displayed at Knowlton in Canada. The photograph shows the aeroplane at the 1963 Ottawa RCAF show just after restoration. (Via Leo Opdycke/WWI Aero)

sive, especially at its service ceiling of almost 23,000 feet, where many Allied aeroplanes were struggling.

Throughout the summer of 1918 the Fokker D.VII began to appear in ever-increasing numbers and by November over 750 were with front-line *Jagdstaffeln*. The D.VII was well respected by its Allied opponents and many of Germany's top pilots gained a considerable number of victories flying the type, amongst them Udet, Loewenhart and Göring.

One of the most authentic specimens of the seven known surviving D.VIIs may be found in Quebec, lovingly maintained by the Brome County Historical Society. Their Fokker was one of 22 D.VIIs sent out to Canada as war trophies, 6810/18 being despatched from Feltham in the UK on 12 March, 1919. Several German aeroplanes were initially stored at Camp Borden, Ontario, and records suggest that various machines were sent to McGill, Mount Allison, Acadia, Manitoba, Alberta and Saskatchewan Universities and to Brome County. At least seven of the 22 D.VIIs were loaned to a company formed by wartime aces Major William Avery Bishop, VC, and Lieutenant Colonel William George Barker, VC, which toured the country giving air displays. Brome County's D.VII appears to be the sole survivor and was shipped from Camp Borden to Knowlton on 27 May, 1920, at a cost of $112.50.

During the 1960s RCAF Trenton undertook to refurbish the Fokker whilst endeavouring to retain as much of the original five-colour 'lozenge' fabric covering as possible. Deterioration was evident in many places and careful patchwork had to be done using

Much of the Knowlton Fokker's covering is original and has been the target of several historians seeking to establish the correct colours of the five-colour printed camouflage fabric. (Deutsches Museum)

reconstructed material made available by NASM, Washington DC.

Recent study of 6810/18 by enthusiasts has revealed some interesting features of this historic aeroplane. It was noted that the D.VII, like so many other WWI museum exhibits, is a composite of several different machines. The number 6810 appears on the fuselage and all cowling panels except the nose piece, which bears 'OAW 6504'. Other components identified thus far include the tailplane (6506); elevator (8313); starboard aileron (8502) and port aileron (8502). Whether these substitutions were made to the aeroplane during its wartime service or in early Canadian ownership is not known.

There is another D.VII in Canada. This is '10347/18', which was used in several dogfight scenes for Howard Hughes's 1930 *Hell's Angels* epic piloted by its owner, a Mr Dewey Ward, who loaned the

machine for filming. The D.VII put in so many hours flying time during production that the original Mercedes had to be replaced by a 200 hp Hall Scott L.6 powerplant. From 1934 to 1953 the aeroplane lay in storage before acquisition by Mr James Mathiesen and Mr J. Nissen of San Jose, California, who subsequently sold it to the National Aviation Museum in February 1971. Since then the fuselage has been restored with a new undercarriage, radiator and engine cowling being fabricated, an airscrew donated by an English enthusiast/collector and an original Mercedes D.III (originally powering D.VII 6849/18) donated by the University of Manitoba in July 1975. The Fokker is currently well on the way to complete restoration and eventual display in the NAM's new exhibition hangar.

In Europe at least four genuine D.VIIs have survived. One of these is part of the Royal Air Force Museum collection and is currently at Cardington in dismantled state awaiting a long overdue restoration to its original configuration. Built by Albatros in January 1918, this D.VII (OAW) 8417/18 was issued to *Jagdstaffel* 71 at Ostend and when the Germans retreated in October the abandoned machine fell into Allied hands. R. G. Nash acquired it in May 1938 at Versailles and returned to the UK with his prize, which was kept at Brooklands until acquisition by the Royal Aeronautical Society after WWII. Since then at least two 'restorations' have taken place, the engine panels have been replaced by non-authentic versions along the way and the aeroplane currently sports a spurious all-red scheme with white nose panels.

D.VII '4404/18' has been displayed in West Germany's Deutsches Museum in Munich for many years, although since WWII, when it was damaged during an air raid, the D.VII has lost its armament, been fitted with sub-standard forward fuselage upper panels and re-covered and painted in an overall

Many WWI survivors were used by Hollywood during the 1920s and 1930s for film use and one of the most famous of these war movies was Howard Hughes's Hell's Angels *released in 1930. Here, Frank Clarke in the Fokker D.VII camera ship 'shoots' Ray Wilson's SE5a during a sortie over California. One* Hell's Angels *D.VII survivor is '10347/18', now being restored at Rockcliffe. (J. Barton via Harry Woodman)*

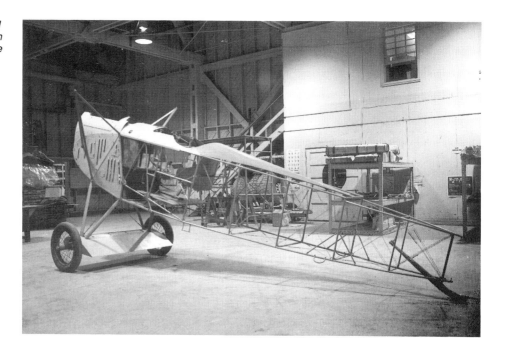

The other Canadian D.VII photographed in 1988. An ex-Hell's Angels 'star', the Fokker is currently being restored. (NAM 11417)

'lozenge' pattern of somewhat dubious authenticity. It is not known whether the serial number on the fuselage is authentic; some sources state that the aeroplane was formerly D-20 of the Dutch *Luchtvaart Dienst* (MLD) in post-Armistice years.

In the new *La Grande Gallerie* at Le Bourget hangs the Musée de l'Air Albatros-built D.VII 6796/18, which was one of many war prizes seized in November 1918 and displayed by the museum ever since. Recently renovated it currently bears an overall 'lozenge' fabric finish and is displayed alongside Georges Guynemer's famous Spad 7.

The most recent D.VII arrival in Europe can now be seen in the Netherlands at the Militaire Luchtvaart Museum in Soesterberg. The aeroplane was purchased by Fokker from the Wings and Wheels collection under auction at Orlando in Florida and following shipment was taken to Schipol for rebuilding. Recent research indicates that the Fokker's original serial may have been 436/18 (werke No. 2523), making it one of the earliest D.VIIs built, having been accepted on 28 May, 1918.

Following the end of WWI, the D.VII went to the USA, being allocated to McCook Field and subsequently used as a camera platform for filming use in *Hell's Angels*. For a time it was owned by Paul Mantz and in 1955 completely rebuilt, but because of its non-standard Hispano-Suiza powerplant (fitted in 1922) the nose contours were hardly of typical D.VII appearance. Superbly restored it is now displayed in post-war Dutch markings.

Albatros-built D.VII 4635/18 captured by the 95th Pursuit Squadron in somewhat unusual circumstances. It is seen here at Orly in early 1919. (Bill Jorgensen via John Garwood)

Fokker D.VII

4635/18 (OAW). National Air and Space Museum, Washington DC, USA

Another Albatros-built D.VII is the NASM exhibit, which was acquired from the War Department in 1919. The Fokker was captured near Verdun in September 1918 by Captain A. H. McLanahan and Lieutenants Curtis and Sewell of the US Air Service. In 1954 Captain McLanahan was able to give NASM the full story:

'On the actual day of the capture, the US 95th Pursuit Squadron was heavily engaged in the Verdun sector. Owing to the rapid advance of the Allied forces, the distance from the front line to their home aerodrome was expanding rapidly. When their Spad XIII pursuits were running low on fuel, the three pilots were forced to land in a field close to the front lines to refuel from two-gallon cans. Whilst they were busy pouring petrol into their tanks, heavy naval guns opened fire on a nearby railway line, and the concussion was so severe that it split the seams of the fuel tanks in all three Spads; thus they were grounded.

'The pilots retired to a small shack in the corner of the field to pass away the time. Presently they heard the sound of a hostile aircraft circling overhead, and on leaving the shack they observed the hostile aircraft

As currently displayed at NASM 'U.10' carries reproduction printed camouflage fabric applied in the correct manner. (H. Van Dyk Soerewyn)

The ex-Nash Collection Fokker D.VII was acquired in 1938 and taken over by the Royal Aeronautical Society after the Second World War. As seen here in the 1960s it carries dubious colours based on the original Jasta 71 red and white scheme. (Albatros/P. L. Gray Archive)

to be a Fokker D.VII. This particular field had only recently been evacuated by the German Air Force, and this gave Captain McLanahan an idea. As a ruse he waved to the German pilot, inviting him to land. Much to his amazement, the German proceeded to do so.

'They started to run towards the Fokker D.VII, but as the pilot climbed down from the cockpit he recognized their American uniforms and realized that he had been tricked. Hastily he attempted to set fire to his aircraft, but several warning shots from the Americans' pistols deterred him and he surrendered instead. Consequently the D.VII was taken intact. On interrogation the pilot proved to be Lt. Heinz Freiherr von Beaulieu-Marconnay of *Jasta* 65.

'All four aircraft were taken back to the airfield of the US 1st Pursuit Group, where the D.VII had the 'kicking mule' insignia of the 95th Aero Squadron painted on the starboard side of the fuselage, below the cockpit. Enemy insignia on the fuselage sides consisted of the large white symbols 'U-10'; the pow-

erplant is a 180 hp Mercedes.'

During the early 1960s the D.VII was restored by the Smithsonian's Preservation and Restoration Division in Maryland. The original fabric was, by that time, completely beyond repair and a realistic method of reproducing the 'lozenge' pattern fabric was sought. Eventually Greeff Fabrics of Port Chester in New York ran off some 125 yards of re-created fabric, carefully matched to the original fabric, using a silk screen process. Initially the original machine's distinctive 'U-10' on fuselage sides and upperwing centre-section were not restored, but in recent years they have been applied to the aeroplane in their correct positions.

The D.VII was restored in the 1970s for the RAF Museum and finished in less than authentic configuration and colour scheme. (Albatros/P. L. Gray Archive)

The RAF Museum D.VII is currently at Cardington in dismantled state awaiting its turn in the restoration programme. It is hoped that in time it will emerge from the workshop in authentic finish. (Author)

Germany's D.VII resides at Munich's Deutsches Museum in pseudo camouflage pattern and without armament. (Albatros/P. L. Gray Archive)

Fokker D.VIII

Serial unknown. Museo Caproni, Rovereto, Italy

After the war, Italy obtained some 300 German and Austro-Hungarian aircraft. These were tested and scrapped soon afterwards. General Costanzi reportedly put together a collection of Austro-Hungarian material, but does not appear to have included *complete* aircraft.

The D.VIIIs were unique among the vast war booty assortment in that they actually equipped an experimental unit based at Montecelio (now Guidonia) until about 1923. Some of these machines later found their way onto the civil register (two were I-ELIA and I-FRAK) and into collections (the Academy at Caserta had one in 1935 with Italian serial 24940; another (I-AANS) was preserved by Lt Cecconi's family near Rome, but was apparently burned in 1943-45).

The Caproni collection includes the fuselage and engine of the only original D.VIII extant today. A constructor's number 2916 has been often quoted, as

A fascinating glimpse of the Musée de l'Air collection during the 1930s reveals the Caudron G.3, Airco DH9 and Fokker D.VII 6796/18. (Via John Garwood)

has a serial, 194. These appear, however, to be just wild guesses and no real identity has been established. The D.VIII is destined for the USAF Museum at Wright Patterson for restoration.

The Paris D.VII in the 1950s still covered in its original fabric. (John Garwood)

A 1973 photograph of the Musée Albatros-built D.VII as displayed at Chalais-Meudon. It is currently displayed in La Grande Gallerie *at Le Bourget.* (Christian Emrich)

A post-war Fokker D.VIII parasol monoplane in Germany. (right) Only one of these fighters has survived, an unidentified fuselage currently stored by Italy's Caproni Museum. Restoration is planned. (Albatros/P. L. Gray Archive)

Fokker E.III

210/16. Science Museum, South Kensington, London, UK

The undoubted success of the Fokker E series of monoplane fighters in 1915 was largely as a result of their being armed with the first 'reliable' interrupter mechanism which allowed a machine gun to be fired through the airscrew arc without hitting the blades. The main production version was the E.III, powered by 100 hp Oberursel UI and of which about 150 were built. From autumn 1915 the 'Fokker-Scourge' took a heavy toll of the Allies' inferior reconnaissance types until the spring of 1916, when improved British fighters – mostly pusher designs – gave the Royal Flying Corps aerial supremacy by the summer.

The uncovered airframe of Fokker E.III 210/16, which has been suspended in the Science Museum's aeronautical galleries for many years, provides the enthusiast a rare opportunity to study the design and construction aspects of a genuine WWI fighter. The machine has an interesting history. It was captured intact on 8 April, 1916, when a lance corporal of the 5th *Feldflieger Abteilung* up from Valenciennes became disorientated and following an engine failure was compelled to make a forced landing at Renescure – behind the Allied lines. . .

Not surprisingly the arrival of a brand new, airworthy *Eindecker* was welcomed with open arms by RFC technicians, who made it the subject of detailed analysis, and several British pilots flew it against their own machines in mock combat to evaluate the monoplane's capabilities.

The Fokker was transported to England in May and was closely examined by The Test Flight of the Central Flying School at Upavon. Following

Fokker E.III 210/16 following its capture at Renescure on 8 April, 1916. After intensive evaluation the aeroplane was exhibited around the UK before being passed to the Science Museum. (Albatros/P. L. Gray Archive)

thorough and rigorous testing the monoplane was offered to the Victoria and Albert Museum, who passed the offer on to the Science Museum. In September 1916 the aeroplane was assigned to a nationwide National Economy Exhibition, which exhibited the Fokker in London, Manchester, Norwich, Chester, Sheffield, Keighley, Gloucester and Leeds.

Eventually the aeroplane was returned to the Science Museum *sans* engine, airscrew and instruments and in this form it was displayed until 1923 when 'souveniring' of its fabric forced it into storage for safe keeping, where it remained until 1935, when, reunited with its original engine, the E.III was put on display once again until World War II, when it was stored once again until the end of hostilities. As currently displayed the Fokker appears as it did in 1916, although it lacks instruments and the original airscrew.

The Science Museum has displayed their E.III without covering since WWI. Future plans may include partial re-covering of the airframe. (John Garwood)

Halberstadt CL.II

C15459/17. Polish Museum Lotnictwa i Astronautyki, Krakow, Poland.

The Halberstadt CL.II was designed to the 1917 CL (Light C type) specification to equip *Schutzstaffeln* (Protection Flights) and was built in large numbers. Introduced in the summer of 1917 the type was later supported by Hannover CL-class aeroplanes and operated mainly as an escort fighter to protect reconnaissance and photographic machines. By this time the German High Command, realizing the importance of close air support for their infantry, changed the Protection Flights to Battle Flights (*Schlachtstaffeln*), whose duties varied from close support to ground attack. With its communal single cockpit, which considerably improved co-operation between pilot and observer, the Halberstadt CL.II was ideally suited to the new roles. The CL.II, and other machines like it, provided highly co-ordinated infantry support and achieved a considerable measure of success.

In addition to its machine gun armament the Halberstadt CL.II had external racks fitted to the fuselage in which a number of anti-personnel grenades could be carried. The first of many successful operations involving the Halberstadt was the attack on the Somme bridges at Bray and St Christ on 6 September, 1917, where over 20 machines disorganized almost an entire division of British troops.

The remains of Halberstadt CL.II C15459/17 are stored at Krakow. This particular machine was built in 1917, and according to the notice it displayed whilst with the DLS collection prior to WWII, the CL.II was at one time used as the personal transport of the German Army Air Service's commander, General von Hoeppner. The wings are missing, but the Halberstadt's fuselage is in reasonably good condition, complete with upperwing centre-section, engine, undercarriage, rudder and fin.

Halberstadt CL.IV

8103/18. National Aeronautical and Space Museum, Washington DC, USA

Although it was intended to replace the Halberstadt CL.II, the CL.IV offered little improvement in overall performance other than in manoeuvrability; this was a useful asset, however, for its designed role as a close-support ground-attack machine. The CL.IV retained the same 160 hp Mercedes D.III motor of its predecessor but had provision for two fixed forward-firing machine guns, although one was normally fitted. Anti-personnel grenades were carried in external fuselage racks and rows of signal flare cartridges

One of at least three known Halberstadt CL.IV survivors is owned by the National Aeronautical and Space Museum at Washington DC. (Stuart Howe)

frequently strapped across the rear fuselage decking.

At least three examples of the CL.IV have survived to this day and their story is a remarkable one. When the war ended the former commander of *Jagdstaffeln* 18 and 57, Paul Ernst Strähle, victor of 14 combats, bought several Halberstadts and took them back to Germany. In December 1920 the former air ace operated a scheduled service between Stuttgart and Constance and subsequently Stuttgart and Nuremburg. Some of the machines remained in flying condition as late as 1939, when at least three of them and a CLS.I were carefully placed in storage at Schorndorf, about 20 miles east of Stuttgart. When Paul Strähle joined the *Luftwaffe* at the start of the Second World War he distributed his precious collection around the town.

In more recent post-war years, as the interest in vintage aeroplanes intensified, a number of individuals tried to persuade Herr Strähle to part with his Halberstadts without success until 1982, when the patience of American Airlines pilot Ken Hyde was rewarded, a price was agreed and the collection was shipped to Virginia, where Mr Hyde and Congressman Stan Parris formed *Halberstadt Enterprises* to handle the relics. It was the original owner's intention to retain enough components to complete one restoration, but realizing the task was beyond him, he released everything to Ken Hyde. Sadly Paul Strähle died in May 1983, one of the last of the 'Old Eagles'.

Once the Halberstadts had arrived at Ken Hyde's private airfield at Warrenton an inventory was begun. Some three months were spent cataloguing the collection before they were offered for sale to aeronautical museums, the American journal *WWI Aero* acting as broker. In mid-1984, the deadline for the disposal had passed and a buyer had not materialized – at least not one with the required price. Eventually a deal was

The most complete example of a Halberstadt CL.IV is the civilianized D.71 flown by Paul Strähle for many years after the war. (Via John Garwood)

made with the USAF Museum, who acquired the entire collection, less some parts sold individually to enthusiasts along the way. The National Air and Space Museum subsequently negotiated successfully for one of the Halberstadts (Roland-built 8103/18) for eventual restoration. Early in 1989 it was announced that all four Halberstadts were to be restored in West Berlin's Verkehr and Technik Museum. On completion the NASM and USAF Museum CL.IVs will be returned to the USA.

NASM's CL.IV was flown operationally in WWI and later became D-144 in *Luftverkehr P. Strähle* service. The machine was still flying in 1939, but was severely damaged when its hangar collapsed, breaking the rear fuselage aft of the cockpit. Otherwise the Halberstadt is complete and is mostly doped in aluminium over its wartime camouflage. Traces of its later civilian registration markings may still be seen.

Enthusiasts impatient to see a completed Halberstadt should travel to the Deutsches Auto-Museum at the Schloss Langenburg, 30 miles east of Heilbronn in West Germany. Here can be seen one of Paul Strähle's civilianized CL.IVs which has been restored in the airline's original, very striking, pale blue and aluminium finish and registered D-71. For many years this splendid machine was displayed at Stuttgart's Daimler-Benz Museum before transfer to its present location in 1981.

Halberstadt C.V

3471/18. Musée Royal de l'Armée, Brussels, Belgium

Designed principally for high-altitude, long-range reconnaissance and photographic operations the Halberstadt C.V initially appeared in the early part of 1918, becoming operational in mid-summer. The

The unique Halberstadt CL.V of the Belgium Royal Army Museum was suspended for many years in the main gallery where visitors could more readily appreciate the original printed fabric covering. (John Garwood)

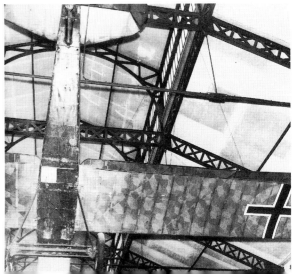

The Halberstadt CL.V, as yet unrestored, is currently displayed at ground level and carries no armament. (Brussels Air Museum)

high-aspect-ratio wings were of considerable span for a two-seat machine and contributed greatly to increased efficiency at altitude. The high-compression 220 hp Benz Bz.IV powerplant also improved the performance. Together with its contemporary, the Rumpler C.VII, Halberstadt C.Vs performed useful work during the war's closing months, providing much-needed photographic intelligence, a task burdened by difficulties imposed by frequent German retreats and increased Allied fighter opposition.

Few details of 3471/18's wartime career are available, although it is known that the Royal Army Museum received it during the early 1920s still wearing its original camouflage pattern. The fuselage is painted in mottled patches of violet and khaki-green with the wings and tail covered in both four and five-colour 'lozenge' printed fabric. No attempt as yet has been made to restore the machine, making it a valuable target for students of WWI colours and markings prepared to analyse its original covering. The Halberstadt is unarmed and is without a gun ring, leading one to suspect that it may have seen use as a trainer or communications aeroplane.

Hanriot HD.1

'515'. Museo Storico AMI, Vigna di Valle (Rome), Italy

In its compact, attractive appearance and nimble characteristics the French-designed Hanriot HD.1 may be ranked with the British Sopwith Pup and Bristol Scout as one of the prettiest of the WWI fighters, its flying qualities more than matching its aesthetic appeal. The Hanriot fighter failed to find favour in the country of its origin, the French authorities preferring Nieuport designs, but was readily accepted by the Belgians and Italians. At least 1700 HD.1s were ordered for use by Italian squadrons, most of these being licence built by *Società Nieuport Macchi* of Varese. Production of Hanriots by the company continued after the Armistice, a further 70 machines being built. In Italian service the Hanriot was used in greater numbers than any other fighter type of the war and when the Italian offensive of October 1918 began, of the 211 fighters operational on the Austrian front, 130 of them were HS.1s. Not surprisingly many of Italy's leading fighter pilots scored most of their victories flying Hanriots, among them *Tenente* Silvio Scaroni (26 victories), who brought down a Gotha bomber on 26 December, 1917.

Hanriots also saw widespread service with the *Aviation militaire belge*, and although Belgian use of the type was on a more modest scale than Italy's, at least 125 HD.1s were built by Hanriot for Belgium. Among its most celebrated exponents was Willy Coppens, whose speciality was the destruction of balloons.

Post-war, Hanriot HD.1s continued to serve in Italy and Belgium while at least 16 were bought by Switzerland in 1921, the type still operational with Swiss *Jagdflieger-Kompagnien* until 1928. Six Hanriots survive today in Belgium, the UK, USA, Switzerland, Venezuela and Italy, whose specimen has an interesting history.

Flavio Torello Baracchini ran up 20 victories while flying with 76ª *Squadriglia* and in April 1919 the government presented him with a Hanriot HD.1. The aircraft's subsequent history is unknown, but at some point this HD.1 belonged to the city of Florence, who presented it to the Air Force in the early 1960s. It was exhibited in the Turin museum, officially inaugurated in 1964 and closed in 1970 without ever having opened to the public. Like the other aircraft in the Turin collection, it was transferred to Vigna di Valle and completely restored by 1977, when the new museum opened.

Its current scheme represents an HD.1 flown by Baracchini. The fuselage carries a large 76 identifying the squadron and the four aces, which also appear on the tailplane. Tail number '515' is from a contemporary photograph, but the Italian serial Hd.19309 was found on the original fabric during the restoration.

Hanriot HD.1 '515' recently restored in the markings of Italian Ace Flavio Baracchini, who was presented with the aeroplane after the war. It is currently at Vigna di Valle. (Stuart Howe)

Unfortunately the fuselage is painted grey instead of being aluminium-doped.

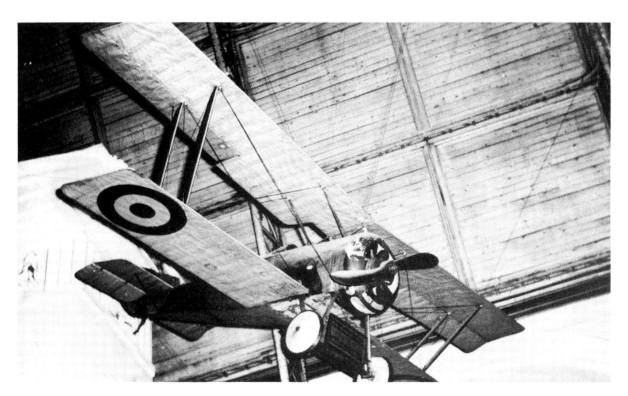

The Royal Army Museum's Hanriot HD.1 No. 78 has been displayed in the museum since the 1920s and restored in 1973 to its original scheme. (John Garwood)

Macchi-built Hanriot HD.1 653 as currently preserved by the Swiss Air Force Museum in Dubendorf. (Via J. M. Bruce)

Hanriot HD.1

75. Royal Air Force Museum, Hendon, London, UK

This Hanriot was constructed by *Société anonyme des Appareils d'Aviation Hanriot* at Billancourt in 1918 and on completion was sent to Beaumaris air-park for its camouflage to be applied. The machine was subsequently delivered to the 1ᵉ *Escadrille de Chasse* of the Belgian Flying Corps based at Les Moores in Belgium, where it was flown by Jan Olieslager, André de Meulemeester and other leading Belgian airmen.

After the Armistice the Hanriot was reassigned to the 7ᵉ *Escadrille* at Nivelles and in 1922 took first place in an aerobatic competition held in Nice, France. The aeroplane had a comparatively long service career as it was being used for training as late as 1928 and only declared surplus to requirements six years later. The first civilian owners were André, Jules and Paul Drossaert, whose initials formed part of the Hanriot's new Belgian registration OO-AJP. In 1937 the veteran changed hands, being sold to former Spad pilot Jacques le Dure, who based the Hanriot at Evere before accepting an offer of £15 by collector

Richard Shuttleworth!

Hanriot HD.1 75 was flown across the Channel by Shuttleworth himself to land at Lympne, the first stage of its flight to the now world-famous Old Warden aerodrome near Biggleswade. The Hanriot

Richard Shuttleworth's Hanriot HD.1 No. 75 in 1938 following restoration at Old Warden. With the civilian registration G-AFOX, the Hanriot participated in several air shows before storage. During WWII it was severely damaged and subsequently purchased in 1962 by American Marvin Hand. (John Garwood)

in Italy, who had preserved their original WWI blueprints on microfilm. Five years later, on 27 April, 1968, and finished in the wartime colours of the 1ᵉ *Escadrille*, the Hanriot took to the air with retired UAL Captain Walter Addems at the controls.

In 1973 the Hanriot was displayed at the Paris Air Show, where it attracted a great deal of comment. Soon after it was generously donated by Marvin Hand to the RAF Museum for eventual display at Hendon. For some reason the paper horse motif of the 7ᵉ *Escadrille* was applied to the wheel discs – since removed – but the green-and-white-striped cowling remains. Mr Hand believes it should be painted yellow as the aeroplane was known to have been in André de Meulemeester's flight. Enthusiasts studying the Hanriot, now displayed in somewhat incongruous company, may wish it had been returned to Old Warden – after all, when delivered to Hendon the fighter was still in an airworthy condition. . .

Hanriot HD.1

'5934'. Planes of Fame Museum, Chino, California, USA

One of the most celebrated French airmen of WWI was undoubtedly Charles Nungesser, the country's third ranking air ace, surviving the war with a total of 45 confirmed victories. The HD.1 currently residing at Chino was reportedly flown by Nungesser, but its history prior to 1924 is obscure. That year the airman arrived in the USA, along with two other pilots, to embark on a barnstorming career that lasted for three years. The Frenchmen brought with them the HD.1, a Potez and a Nieuport 10/83 and in 1925 the Hanriot was used during filming of *The Sky Raider*. Nungesser, who played an on-screen part, flew the HD.1 to 'shoot down' Paul Kotze's Thomas Morse S-4C, which was loosely disguised as a German fighter. After filming Nungesser took the Hanriot on a tour around the USA putting on flying displays until March 1927, when he made his ill-fated preparations to fly the Atlantic Ocean – east to west – in company with Major Francis Coli. The HD.1 was entrusted to the safe keeping of Mr A. J. Montee at Clover Field in Santa Monica, California.

The attempted Atlantic flight tragically failed, both Nungesser and Coli were lost at sea and no sign of them nor their aeroplane was ever found. When Mr Montee heard of Nungesser's death he auctioned off the Hanriot to pay for its hangarage. It was bought by Mr James Granger, who flew it in several war films, notably *Wings* and *Hell's Angels*, and kept it at Clover Field until 1933, where it was placed in storage until 1951 when Mr Edward Martoney purchased the fighter for his Claremont air museum, restoring the

Marvin Hand donated the rebuilt HD.1 to the RAF Museum in 1973, where it is now displayed. (Author)

was re-registered G-APDX and was flown regularly by Shuttleworth. During a 1939 demonstration at Brooklands one of the Hanriot's wheels was clumsily re-fitting during a tyre change and soon after taking off for Old Warden the wheel fell away and in the subsequent forced landing the machine's wings, rudder, undercarriage and airscrew all sustained damage. The wings were to have been repaired at the Chelsea Aeronautical College Workshops, but these were destroyed during a wartime blitz.

Richard Shuttleworth was tragically killed in a flying accident in 1940, but his mother established the Shuttleworth Trust in his memory, and it is now one of the world's leading collections of vintage cars and aeroplanes. The remains of Richard's Hanriot were sold in 1963 to Marvin Hand of San Francisco, although the Trust hung on to its engine, a 120 hp Le Rhône 9JB, for use in their Avro 504K. The long process of restoration began and Mr Hand slowly acquired missing parts over the next few years. *Mme* Hanriot, daughter of René Hanriot, made a significant contribution to the project by obtaining a complete set of factory drawings from *Aeroplani Macchi*

Nungesser's barn-storming film star HD.1 as currently exhibited at Chino's Planes of Fame Museum, California. (H. Van Dyk Soerewyn)

Charles Nungesser's Hanriot HD.1 '5934' seen at the Maloney Air Museum during the 1950s (John Garwood)

Hanriot to an almost airworthy condition. The fuselage sides for some years bore Nungesser's famous wartime insignia (inappropriate for the HD.1 however) – a black heart, skull and crossbones, a coffin and two candles – and the serial number 5934 on the tail, which was placed there in 1924 and may not be the original identity. The machine's construc-

tion number is 1398 and it is fitted with a 130 hp Clerget 9Ba.

Hansa-Brandenburg D.I

26.68. National Technical Museum, Prague, Czechoslovakia

Designed by Ernst Heinkel the Hansa Brandenburg D.I KD (*Kampfdoppeldecker*) was a sturdy single-seat fighter with an unusual arrangement of interplane struts which gave rise to its nickname of 'Star-strutter', although to most Austro-Hungarian pilots it had the more chilling soubriquet of *Sarg* (coffin). Early production models built by the Phönix factory in the 28 series were powered by the 180 hp Austro Daimler engine. The type was also built by Ufag (series 6S) and the type enjoyed widespread use on the Italian Front during 1916–17, being flown by many of the Dual Monarchy's leading airmen, including Linke Crawford and Julius Arigi.

Whether the sole survivor of this interesting fighter outlived the war intact is unknown, but the fuselage

The fuselage of Hansa-Brandenburg D.I 26.68 is preserved in Prague's Technical Museum. The whereabouts of the machine's wings, tail unit and undercarriage are not known. (Albatros/P. L. Gray Archive)

The 185 hp Austro Daimler of the D.I 'Starstrutter' is seen to advantage in this close-up. (Albatros/P. L. Gray Archive)

and engine at least are part of the transport collection in Prague's Technical Museum. The fuselage bears its original plain varnished finish with the distinctive Austro-Hungarian service number in black. The engine panels have been removed to reveal the Austro-Daimler motor and most of the cockpit fittings appear to be original and intact. Whether the machine will ever be completely restored is not known, but it is hoped that one day such work can be undertaken.

Junkers J.4 (J.I)

586/18. National Aviation Museum, Rockcliffe Airport, Canada

The Junkers armoured biplane was introduced in 1917 and it should be noted that the factory designation of the type was J.4, which has often led to confusion with the military designation J.I. In contrast to earlier plain metal sheet covering of earlier Junkers designs, the J.I's flying and control surfaces were sheeted with thin corrugated alloy over a dural frame. The rear fuselage was also of dural, fabric-covered, but from the rear cockpit position forward the J.I. was armour-plated with 5 mm chrome nickel steel sheet protecting both engine and crew compartments. Although the aeroplane was heavy on the controls and somewhat difficult to land and take off from rough fields, J.I crews welcomed the big biplane's armour protection and its great suitability for their contact patrol duties. Some 227 Junkers J.I biplanes were built altogether and one complete specimen has survived and is currently in storage at Canada's National Aviation Museum.

Manufactured at the Junkers/Fokker factory at Dessau during July 1918, J.I 586/18 became a war prize after the Armistice and was taken to Dieppe, from where it was shipped to Canada aboard the SS *Venusia* on 28 May, 1919.

The J.I was originally displayed at the Canadian National Exhibition at Toronto, Ontario, in August and by October had been stored at Camp Borden. Moved to Ottawa in the 1930s the machine became part of the Canadian War Museum collection and was recently stored pending possible restoration.

At present the airframe's corrugated skin is in a poor condition and could prove extemely difficult to repair. The upper surfaces of the wings and tail are sprayed in random patches of light green and lilac with the lower surfaces in a pale yellow. 568/18 bears the constructor's number 252 and is fitted with its original powerplant, a 200 hp high-compression Mercedes Benz IV (No. B252974).

A fuselage of another J.4 is currently displayed in Italy at the Museo Nazionale della Scienza e della Technica in Milan. Its origins are unknown and one of the wooden panels attached to it carries the serial 68.03, which belongs to a Hansa Brandenburg C.I shot down by Francesco Baracca! Several more authentic serials remain on the J.4, however, including 'Leergewicht kg 1690', 'Fab. 8–6–1918', 'NR R.97' and 'Z.A.K.' the latter being the acronym for *Zentrale Abnahame Kommission* (Central Acceptance Commission).

The metal-skinned Junkers J.4 (J.I) armoured biplane is currently stored at Rockcliffe. The condition of the metal skinning and complex form of construction makes full restoration an unlikely prospect. (NAM 15147)

Close-up of Rockcliffe's J.4 when displayed at Ottawa in the early 1980s. The state of the lower wing structure and covering is readily apparent. (Don Connelly, CAHS)

The world's sole surviving Junkers J.9 (D.I) all-metal monoplane fighter preserved at Le Bourget. It was restored in the early 1970s. (Stuart Howe)

Junkers J.9 (D.I)

D5929/18. Musée de L'Air et de L'Espace, Le Bourget Airport, France

The Junkers J.9 (Military Designation D.I) followed a natural development of Professor Hugo Junkers' revolutionary all-metal cantilever monoplane designs initiated with the 1915 J.I. The corrugated skinning of most of these designs was a characteristic feature of Junkers aeroplanes that would continue for many years, to culminate in the classic Ju 52 trimotor transport which saw service throughout World War II and

well beyond, several examples of which are still air-worthy today and in regular use.

The final development of the Junkers J.7, intro-duced in February 1918, so impressed the German authorities that Junkers were rewarded with a pro-duction order and, redesignated J.9, the first pre-production examples began to appear in April. The machines differed from the prototype in being fitted with a 185 hp BMW III engine and strengthened airframe. Production J.9s had lengthened fuselages to counter lateral stability problems.

By mid-1918 the Allies were in the ascendancy in the air war and *Kogenluft* (General in command of the German Army Air Service) was becoming concerned about shortages of equipment and so the J.9 entered production before a full flight testing programme could be completed. Only a handful of J.9s (D.Is) were at the front before the Armistice, most of the aeroplanes not being completed until after 11 November. Approximately 41 were built and the only 'active' service they saw was immediately after hostilities had ceased, operating on Germany's eastern borders and into 1919 with the *Flugpark Kurland*.

One example of a J.9 survives. This is D5929/18, which is displayed at Le Bourget airport, part of the magnificent Musée de L'Air collection. It was restored by museum staff during 1973, its present colour scheme of mottled mauve and 'Forest Green' uppersurfaces and pale blue undersides being based on the original colours. The full history of this particular J.9 is obscure, but it is in excellent condition as any visitor to *La Grande Gallerie* will readily testify.

Knoller C.II (Lo) 119.15 at the Prague Technical Museum prior to recent removal and restoration. The original hand-painted multi-coloured camouflage pattern is clearly seen. (Albatros/P. L. Gray Archive)

Knoller C.II

119.15. National Technical Museum, Prague, Czechoslovakia

In late 1915, following the failure of Austro-Hungarian aeroplane manufacturers to provide a reliable C-type two-seater design, the Government of the Dual Monarchy decided to choose its own design and designate certain factories to produce the type. Their final choice was the compact design by Professor Richard Knoller of the Vienna Technical University, and Lohner, Phönix, Aviatik and WFK were selected to produce the aeroplane. Sadly the basic design was flawed, but, not unnaturally, the Government were strongly opposed to abandoning the programme and as a result a moderate number of C.IIs were constructed. Despite this, none were ever used in action

and the few examples that were flown ended their days as mail carriers, test aeroplanes and trainers.

An example of a Lohner-built Knoller C.II was for many years suspended in Prague's Technical Museum until its removal to Kbely in 1987 for restoration. This machine, serialled 119.15, was donated to the museum in 1919 by the Ministry of National Defence. Originally it lacked a powerplant, but subsequently a 185 hp Austro-Daimler engine was donated to the museum, where it was later installed.

Until its restoration the Knoller was the only source for the painted multi-coloured hexagonal camouflage adopted by the Austro-Hungarians in World War I. Several students have faithfully recorded the machine's complex scheme as well as matching the various colour shades adopted, important and vital work, since the museum's repaint does not appear to match the original in terms of either colour sequence or position on the airframe! The

Prague's Knoller C.II photographed in the 1950s. The arrangement of engine cowlings and their fasteners is noteworthy. (Albatros/P. L. Gray Archive)

The Knoller fuselage in the Kbely workshops during September 1987 for restoration. (Stuart Howe)

The 185 hp Austro-Daimler engine out of the Knoller for refurbishment. Kbely, September 1987. (Stuart Howe)

The recently restored Knoller in late 1988 with repainted camouflage pattern which does not, surprisingly, exactly duplicate the original finish ... (Via P. M. Grosz)

serial number has also been repositioned further aft and the metal nose cowlings, originally camouflaged, are now bare metal. Why the scheme of the original has not been reproduced exactly is a mystery and one hopes the original fabric has been preserved.

LFG Roland D.VIb

D2225/18. Polish Museum Lotnictwa i Astronautyki, Krakow, Poland

Despite the poor marks awarded them by pilots at the Second Fighter Competition in 1918, the Roland D.VIa and D.VIb were placed in limited service, arriving at the Front in May-June 1918, where they were distributed to squadrons for evaluation pur-

An example of the Roland D.VIb. The remains of one of these machines is part of the Krakow Collection now in Berlin for restoration. (Albatros/P. L. Gray Archive)

poses. *Jasta* 35b received five Roland D.VIa fighters on 14 May, 1918, but three months later, these and remaining Albatroses and Pfalzes, were replaced by Fokker D.VIIs. Sharing the airfield with *Jasta* 35b was *Jasta* 23b, which, similarly equipped, operated in concert with a handful of Albatros D.Va fighters, although, by July, the Fokker D.VII was already replacing the Rolands. A report concerning the Roland D.VIa submitted by *Jasta* 23b in June 1918 stated:

'The performance does not differ much from the Albatros D.Va and Pfalz D.IIIa; the rate of climb is a bit less but the speed slightly greater and the manoeuvrability better. It is possible to fly quick turns (corners) with this machine. At higher altitudes it falls off rapidly in a curve; at lower altitudes it climbs.'

As the superior Fokker D.VII began to equip the German squadrons in ever-increasing numbers, the Rolands were relegated to training units and naval base defence flights, serving in such capacities up to the Armistice. Post-war, the D.VIa and D.VIb soldiered on, a number being delivered to the emergent Czechoslovakian Army Air Service. Several D.VIb fighters were also taken by the Allies; France, Japan, Canada and the United States all acquired examples of the type as war booty and at least 13 D.VIs, two D.VIIs and seven Roland 'spares' were listed on the 'Inventory of Enemy Material in the US' on 27 August, 1919.

Of all the many and varied Roland designs built only one, a D.VIb, is known to have survived. This particular machine is D.VIb 2225/18, which had actually taken part in the Second Fighter Competition and was part of the pre-war DLS collection in Berlin. Its present condition is far from perfect and only the fuselage, engine, airscrew and undercarriage remain. Plans for an eventual restoration/rebuild are being considered.

Lloyd

40.01. Kozlekedesi Muzeum, Budapest, Hungary

The Lloyd Company, located in Arzod, about 15 miles north-east of Budapest, Hungary, produced licensed versions of the Austro-Hungarian Aviatiks C.I and D.I as well as the Phönix C.I. Until late 1917, however, the manufacturer was heavily involved in the production of its own two-seater designs, the C.I to C.V biplanes. Among them were 13 prototypes and the first of these was 40.01, which in 1917 set an altitude record and, soon after, was donated to the Hungarian Museum of Transport in Budapest. The museum, which was founded in 1896, still exists (despite suffering severe bomb damage during World War II) and so does the Lloyd, one of very few surviving WWI Austro-Hungarian designs.

Lohner L.I

L.127. Museo Storico AMI, Vigna di Valle (Rome), Italy

This flying boat is one of 24 built under licence by the *Ungarische Flugzeugfabrik A.G.* (UFAG) with serials L.120–143 and equipped with Hiero, Austro-Daimler, Rapp, Mercedes or Benz engines in the 150–160 hp range. Delivered to the *KuK* naval air service on 3 June, 1916, two years later L.127 was at Lussino (now Losinj) air station in Dalmatia, about 50 km south-east of Pola, with L.113.

On 3 June, 1918, two *matrosen* (sailors) of Italian origin, Spilirato and Foresti, destroyed L.113 and flew to Italy in L.127, despite the fact that neither was a pilot. A few days later *guardiamarina* (sub-lieutenant) Alberto Briganti, then with the Venice naval air station, ferried the aeroplane south.

L.127 was not the first Lohner to fall into Italian hands. That 'honour' belongs to L.40, forced down by engine trouble during the night of 27/28 May, 1915, near Porto Corsini (Ravenna province). L.40 was despatched to the Nieuport-Macchi works at Varese, where an exact copy was built and flown in just 33 days. Following successful testing by Captain De Roberti, it was ordered as the Macchi L.1, with the 150 hp Isotta Fraschini V-4, a 'straight six' despite the designation. 140 were built before switching to the L.2 (ten built) and then to the L.3/M.3 (200 built).

In the mid-seventies the fuselage of L.127 was in Bari's city museum, where the aeroplane was wrongly claimed to have put down in front of the city in 1917. Engine, wings and tail unit were long lost. With the opening of the Vigna di Valle museum in the early 1980s the flying boat moved to Lecce for restoration by the 3° RTA team. The rebuild was carried out following Macchi-supplied L.I drawings. By summer 1985 the Lohner was complete except for the engine, for it had proved impossible to trace an original Austrian powerplant. After three years of struggle between the Air Force, who wanted the boat at Vigna di Valle, and Bari, which insisted the Lohner be returned, L.127 went to Vigna di Valle in March 1988 for display in the World War I hall – fittingly housed in an Austro-Hungarian hangar!

The splendid restoration is marred by a tall rudder: the Macchis had an extra rib, and this was wrongly incorporated in the rebuild. The hull is in its original colours, thanks to pressure by the Italian national aeroplane preservation society *Gruppo Amici Velivoli Storici*, who insisted that there was no need to repaint it. The name 'Mani' appears in black above the cross on the bow.

LVG C.VI

7198/18. Shuttleworth Collection, Old Warden, Bedfordshire, UK

The *Luft Verkehrs Gesellschaft* C.VI was a twin-seat reconnaissance and artillery observation machine of which some 1100 examples were built during 1918. It was a natural successor to the Johannisthal company's C.V, from which it differed little, although it was lighter and more compact, the accent being on utility and serviceability. Powered by the 200 hp Benz BzIV engine the LVG C.VI was armed with one fixed forward-firing machine gun and a flexible-mounting on the rear cockpit bearing a single Parabellum machine gun. A light bomb load of up to 250 lb could also be carried.

The Shuttleworth-based LVG C.VI as it appeared during the 1937 Hendon Air Display and where it performed mock air battles with an SE5a and Bristol Fighter. (Via John Garwood)

During the 1950s, the LVG reappeared on the display circuit dazzle-painted in vivid patches of yellow, green and rust red! (Via John Garwood)

The twelve-year restoration of the LVG by the Shuttleworth Trust was one of their most ambitious projects at the time. Completed in 1972 the aeroplane has performed at many displays since. (Author)

Shuttleworth's LVG is currently the world's only airworthy genuine WWI German two-seater. Modern pilots have likened its performance to a 'heavy Tiger Moth'. (Author)

The C.VI served alongside its predecessor until the Armistice, but never entirely replaced the more numerous C.V. Before the peace treaty prevented further German aeroplane construction the LVG Company manufactured the civilian P.I and W.I versions, the former being a three-seat version of the C.VI.

Of the three surviving LVG C.VIs the best known is the Shuttleworth Collection's machine, which was superbly restored to full flying condition during the 1970s and continues to enthral visitors to summer air displays, the only genuine airworthy WWI two-seater in the world. 7198/18 was forced down on 2 August, 1918, by two SE5a pilots of No. 74 Squadron RAF. After shipment to England it was exhibited at the White City, London, in support of a charity drive and subsequently passed into the hands of the Imperial War Museum, remaining in their care until 1925, when it was taken over by the RAF and placed into storage at Cardington. 1936 saw a complete restoration being undertaken. Over the years deterioration and the loss of various components called for the rebuilding of much of the airframe, expecially the metal cowling panels. In 1937 the now airworthy LVG appeared at the Hendon Air Display, where it was flown in mock dogfights with a Sopwith Triplane, SE5a and a Bristol Fighter Mk. IV. The LVG appeared with a plain varnished fuselage and brightly coloured camouflaged wings 'dazzle-painted in the correct manner' as *Flight*, somewhat erroneously, noted.

During World War II the LVG was placed into storage and then in 1945 the Historical Branch of the

The Brussels LVG C.VI still in original finish and complete with wooden wheels. The unrestored machine was minutely documented by enthusaists of the SVAS when restoration of the Shuttleworth machine was taking place. (Brussels Air Museum)

Air Ministry took charge and transferred it to RAF Kemble, thence to Colerne in 1950, where it was renovated yet again in time for the RAF display at Farnborough for static exhibition. It arrived at Colerne crated, minus most of the bracing cables and some engine panels. The machine was somewhat hastily restored with makeshift replacement parts, its fuselage sprayed in a 'pseudo lozenge' to match the wings. The service serial had then long vanished, but the number of the engine was confirmed as 3788.

In 1959 the Shuttleworth Collection took over the aeroplane on extended loan from the AHB and six years later began the slow painstaking restoration, culminating in its return to flying status on 20 September, 1972. All credit must be given to the Collection's engineering staff and specialist members of the Shuttleworth Veteran Aeroplane Society for the magnificent result which many enthusiasts believe to be among the finest restorations of any surviving WWI aeroplane.

The Royal Army Museum in Brussels, Belgium, currently displays LVG C.VI 3141/18, still in its original finish, complete with wooden 'Swiss cheese' wheels, the aeroplane proving an invaluable guide to the Shuttleworth engineering staff during restoration of their machine. The third surviving C.VI, 9041/18, was discovered in a Belgian barn some years ago, but has subsequently been swapped by the Royal Army Museum for a Caudron G.III and a Voisin nacelle from the Musée de L'Air.

LWF Model V

Serial unknown. National Technical Museum, Prague, Czechoslovakia

The Lane, Willard and Fowler Engineering Co. Ltd. (nicknamed 'Linen, Wood and Fabric'!), of Long Island, New York, began to build their own aeroplanes during 1915 and are best known for their development of monocoque-type fuselages. The LWF Model V was produced in 1916 as a training machine for home use, although a small number of them reached France during the war. Powered by a 135 hp

Thomas engine the aeroplane's maximum speed was a modest 93 mph and its gross weight was 2500 lb. Fewer than two dozen examples were built.

During the Russian Revolution the Czechoslovakian Army received a number of aeroplanes for its short-lived air force in Siberia, including, incredibly, an American LWF. Its previous history and subsequent service is unrecorded and all that is known for certain is that the machine was donated to the Prague

Close-up of the LWF at Prague during the 1950s reveals the smooth fuselage contours and wide-chord wings. (Albatros/P. L. Gray Archive)

The unique American-built LWF Model V in Prague's Technical Museum. Its history is, regrettably, not known. (John Garwood)

Museum during 1920 and it has been there ever since. The sole remaining LWF still bears its original clear-doped finish complete with late-style five-pointed star insignia with a large black figure '4' on each side of the fuselage.

Martinsyde F.4 Buzzard

MA-24. Air Museum of Central Finland, Tikkakoski, Finland

With its superb climb, speed and manoeuvrability the Martinsyde F.4 was undoubtedly the finest British single-seat fighter aeroplane in production by the end of the war. Developed from the F.3 of 1917 the Buzzard was powered by the 300 hp Hispano-Suiza 8Fb eight-cylinder engine and it was intended to field the first F.4 squadron by April 1918 with another following a month later. It was not to be. Delays in production and engine delivery denied the type's introduction into service before the Armistice and it was never to prove itself in combat. Some examples lingered on in post-war service for a few years, but the F.4 was unjustly passed over by the RAF in favour of the inferior Sopwith Snipe.

The Finnish Air Force purchased F.4 MA-24 from the Aircraft Disposal Company on 11 February, 1927, along with 13 others. When the machines arrived in Finland they entered full-time operational service in the fighter unit at Utti AFB on 30 March, MA-24 becoming the personal aeroplane of Sergeant (First Class) Urho Heiskala. During its time at Utti, MA-24 was used for aerobatics, combat and dive-bombing practice. On 12 October, 1929, the F.4 was transferred to the Finnish Air Force Flying School at Kauhava, where it was frequently flown until a landing accident on 24 February, 1930, when it was sent to the State Aircraft Factory at Santahamina for repairs. A year later MA-24 suffered another accident, necessitating further repairs, and was transferred back to Utti on 13 May, 1932.

On 4 April, 1934 Sergeant Unttu was making a test flight with MA-24 when its port lower wing struck a tree top. The resulting damage was soon repaired, but some time later the F.4 was dismantled and sent back to the Kauhava Flying School, where it was reassembled and flown several times before its last flight was made on 7 July by Lieutenant Backberg. By that time

Finland's Martinsyde F.4 Buzzard is the sole surviving example of this remarkable and powerful late-war fighter. MA-24 flew for many years after the Armistice and was fully restored in the early 1970s. (Air Museum of Central Finland)

the Buzzard had logged 492 hours in 1320 flights. On 19 November it was handed over to the 'Mekaanikkokoulu' (Air Mechanics' School) for preservation and the aeroplane was eventually restored by the personnel of Luonetjarvi Air Force Base at Tikkakoski during 1970–72, a project taking over 3000 man hours. MA-24 is currently displayed with skis originally fitted to a VL Viima biplane.

Morane Saulnier AI

MS1591. Old Rhinebeck, New York, USA

The Morane Saulnier AI parasol monoplane was introduced during the summer of 1917 and was almost as revolutionary in its own way as the Sopwith Triplane had been the previous year. A test of the prototype AI was made on 11 September, 1917, by Lieutenant R. Labouchère, whose report was highly favourable. Although the new monoplane's take-off was comparatively long, this was amply compensated for by the fighter's supreme agility. The test pilot reported that the aeroplane was extremely responsive and manoeuvrable as well as having good stability. The view from the cockpit was considered excellent, unequalled, in Labouchère's opinion, by any other contemporary French fighter.

The Morane Saulnier AI appeared at the same time as the 150 hp Gnome-powered Spad 15.C1 and Nieuport 28.C1. It was undoubtedly superior to both of them and in fact the parasol compared so favourably with the Spad 13.C1 that the official decision to order

Palen's completed MS AI parasol restored to airworthy condition. (Leo Opdycke/WWI Aero)

it in quantity must have been more or less inevitable, especially since considerable problems were being encountered with the geared Hispano-Suiza motors in the Spads. Well over 1000 Morane Saulniers were built, production aeroplanes becoming available in early 1918, new *Escadrilles* being especially formed to receive them.

The operational career of the AI, however, proved to be a brief one, all of the machines having been withdrawn by mid-May to be replaced by the Spad 13.C1. Several sources have opined that the aeroplane was either withdrawn because of structural deficiencies or that its temperamental 150 hp Gnome Monosoupape proved too tricky to handle in operational service.

Following the A.1's front-line withdrawal, it was used as an advanced trainer, most of the aeroplanes being powered by either the 120 hp Le Rhône 9Jb or the 135 hp Le Rhône 9Jby and redesignated MoS.30.EI.

A post-war-built AI (F-ABAD) is currently displayed in the Musée de l'Air's Hall A at Le Bourget, but to examine a genuine wartime machine the enthusiast must travel to Cole Palen's famous Old Rhinebeck aerodrome near New York in the USA. Palen bought two original AI Parasols from the 'Wings and Wheels' Museum auction in 1981. One of these, MS1591, was in reasonably good condition and has now been restored to airworthy condition. Its partner was incomplete and the decision was made to use the remains as a basis for a replica Morane Saulnier Type N 'Bullet'. Although beautifully constructed and finished this particular hybrid cannot really be considered an authentic survivor.

One of two Morane Saulnier AI monoplanes bought by Cole Palen in 1981. It is seen here at Kermit Weeks's Miami workshops in 1985 during restoration. (Stuart Howe)

Morane Saulnier BB

A301. Royal Air Force Museum, Hendon, London, UK

The Morane Saulnier BB (MS.7) first appeared in 1915 and was supplied to British forces only. The BB had a Le Rhône rotary of 80 or 110 hp, fitted with a circular cowling, the airscrew boasting such a large spinner that only a small gap was left for cooling air. The wings were of fairly short span with single bays of struts; ailerons were carried on the top wing, which had a large rectangular cut-out in its trailing edge. A Lewis gun was carried on a spigot-mounting behind the headrest of the rear seat, and occasionally another fixed to fire over the top wing.

The BB never formed the sole equipment of any unit. Nos. 1, 3 and 60 Squadrons, RFC, had a flight of BBs each by 1 July, 1916; besides their reconnaissance work they sometimes acted as escorts, as on 2 August, when four No. 1 Squadron machines accompanied six BE2cs on a raid to Brussels. The type also served in No. 4 Squadron, RFC, and No. 4 Squadron, RNAS, but very few were built.

At Hendon, the RAF Museum displays the restored fuselage frame of an ex-BEF Morane Saulnier BB complete with its original undercarriage unit. The Morane's discovery was bitter sweet, for just two or three years prior to its rescue from a garage loft at Ware in Hertfordshire, the original owner had put a match to the airscrew and wing panels!

Maurice Farman Serié 11 (Shorthorn)

VU-UBC. National Aviation Museum, Rockcliffe Airport, Ontario, Canada

It is as a primary trainer that the Maurice Farman 'Shorthorn' is best known and it served in this capacity with all Allied air services. This classic French design was also known as the 'Rumpety' in RFC service and operated not only in home-based and front-line units but also in Mesopotamia, where No. 30 Squadron performed important photo-reconnaissance duties.

More examples of the Serié 11 'Shorthorn' were built than its predecessor, the Serié 7 'Longhorn', those for the RFC being constructed by The Aircraft Manufacturing Co. (Airco) under the seemingly

The nacelle of the Aeroflex Museum's Maurice Farman Serié II before acquisition by Wings and Wheels and subsequent purchase by Canada's National Aviation Museum in 1981. (John Garwood)

Fully restored, Rockcliffe's MF11 is one of their most prized exhibits. (NAM 16063)

never-ending Contract 87/A/109. Practically every training squadron was equipped with Shorthorns and the type survived well into the last year of the war. One example of a Shorthorn is now displayed in Canada at Rockcliffe as part of the National Aviation Museum.

Although the original serial of the aeroplane is not recorded, it was one of many Shorthorns manufactured in 1915–16 by Airco of Hendon for the Royal Flying Corps. By 1917 the machine was in Australia, one of four sent to Point Cook for training use. In 1919 it was sold at auction to Messrs R. G. Carey and A. Fenton of Essondon, Victoria, and subsequently registered G-AUBC and later VU-UBC – the second aeroplane to be entered on the Australian register. Placed into storage during the 1930s, the Farman was rebuilt during the 1950s using several components from another S11 machine, VU-UCW.

In 1956 the machine was purchased by Frank Tallman of California and re-registered N96452. It remained in Tallman's collection for 12 years, when, coming under the hammer once again, the Farman was purchased by the Aeroflex Museum in New Jersey. In 1922 Dolf Overton of the Wings and Wheels, Museum, Santee, South Carolina/Orlando, Florida, acquired the machine and on 6 December, 1981, at a Christie's auction it was purchased by the National Aeronautical Collection. The NAC's S11 bears the constructor's number 25 and is fitted with a Renault 80 hp engine (No. 1505).

Several other examples of the Maurice Farman Shorthorn have survived. One of these belongs to the Royal Army Museum in Brussels and was acquired by the museum during the 1920s. The aeroplane was suspended from the roof of the main gallery for many years until 1980, when it was taken down and completely restored by Koksijde BAFB and is once more on display.

Another Shorthorn (JA 7201) emerged in Japan during 1953, when it was placed on exhibition as part of a static aeronautical display at Hibya Park in Tokyo. As displayed it bore it constructor's number, 266, and was in a rather sorry state. A placard revealed that the aeroplane took part in a raid on the

The Royal Army Museum in Brussels acquired a 'Shorthorn' in 1920 which is seen here prior to its 1980 restoration. (John Garwood)

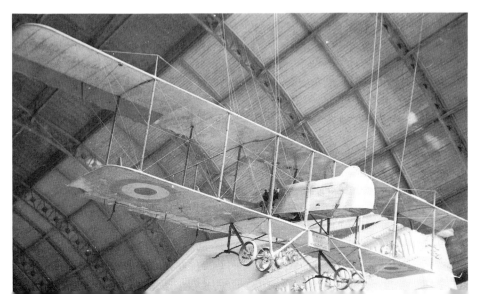

The Maurice Farman used by the Japanese in 1914 to bomb the German-held port of Tsingtao. It now resides in Tokyo's National Science Museum. (John Garwood)

German-held base at Tsingtao. In 1963 it was in storage at the Tohoku University's Engineering Department, but has been restored in recent years. Fitted with a 100 hp Daimler motor, the Shorthorn is now owned by the Kotsu Transportation Museum in Tokyo.

A second MF11 of Japanese origin was shipped to America following World War II as part of the US Technical Air Intelligence effort and in 1958 was restored by the USAF Museum at Wright Patterson AFB and returned to Japan for commemorative ceremonies during the establishment of the Japanese Self Defence Air Force. It is currently at the JASDF Museum in Hamamatsu City.

Currently dismantled for renovation is the Musée de l'Air's Maurice Farman MF Serié 7 'Longhorn'. It is seen here at Chalais Meudon in 1975. (Stuart Howe)

Nieuport 10

15179. Museo Nazionalle della Scienza e della Technica, Milan, Italy

The basic design of the distinctive Nieuport sesquiplane 'Vee-strutters' of the early war years may be attributed largely to the gifted Gustave Delage, who joined *Société des Establissements Nieuport* in January 1914. His initial design was the Type 10, which appeared in two forms, the Nie.10AV (*avant*) in which the observer occupied the forward seat and the Nie.10AR (*arrière*) in which he occupied the rear.

Nieuport 10s were issued to observation units of the *Aviation Militaire* during the summer of 1915 and were mainly of the 10.A2 type, but these were gradually converted to 10.C1 form (with a single seat) for use as fighters. The alterations were straightforward and consisted of fairing the front seat over and installing a Lewis machine gun to a rudimentary overwing mounting. Those aeroplanes in the reconnaissance role carried armament similarly mounted, operated by the observer, who was compelled to stand with the upper half of his body through an upper wing cut-out fully exposed to the elements. French-manufactured Nieuports were issued to the RNAS/RFC, Belgium, Russia and Italy, where today at least two original examples may be found.

The Nieuport was also built in Italy by Nieuport-Macchi and in July 1916 the 1ª and 2ª *Squadriglia* operated the single-seat fighter version. Production totalled 240 examples, many of which survived until after the war in training roles. It is recorded that the Macchi machines were better built than the French originals.

The ex-NASM Nieuport 10 as it appeared during the 1950s when it wore a dubious colour scheme. Captain Charles Nungesser brought the Nieuport to the USA in 1924 for film and air display work. (John Garwood)

Milan's example was purchased after the war by a *signor* Strafelini, known in Rovereto as the *Asen d'oro* (Golden Ass) because of his wealth. In the summer of 1922, the Nieuport was damaged on landing in Rovereto's military field (Piazza d'armi) while being flown by Galletto Lualdo and with Strafelini as passenger. Both port wings suffered considerably and the aircraft was never repaired, eventually being donated to the *Museo della Guerra* being established in the Rovereto fortress.

In spring 1984 Gino Piccoli, who as a young boy had witnessed the crash, obtained financial backing from Renato Fornaciari, then president of the Trento Aero Club, to restore the wings. Work was carried out by Umberto Venturini in his fifth-floor apartment, the wings being lowered out of the windows when work was completed. They are now displayed alongside the aeroplane, which is in an overall green scheme of dubious accuracy. A long-term plan exists to make the machine airworthy, but no work has yet been undertaken to this end.

The museum owns another Nieuport 10. This is 15179 and is a late production machine. After the war it was acquired by Piero Magni, a great Italian pioneer and inventor, who used it with the civil registration I-BORA for experimental and training work.

It was donated by Magni to the museum together with the Magni PM 3/4 Vale prototype and much other material and currently sports rather rough and impersonal representative Italian colours.

The National Air and Space Museum held an example of a Nieuport 10 in storage for several years until quite recently, when it was exchanged for Cole Palen's Nieuport 28. The Type 10 was brought to the USA in 1924 by Captain Nungesser along with a Hanriot and Potez and the French ace flew it in the film *The Sky Raider* as previously described. Following Nungesser's death the Nieuport was purchased by Aero Brokerage Services, who replaced the original 130 hp Clerget rotary engine with an 80 hp Le Rhône. After several years the aeroplane became one of a group of veterans at Roosevelt Field, Long Island, New York, from which, coincidentally, Palen started his famous collection in 1951. It was during that same year that NASM acquired the Nieuport, photographs taken at the time showing it finished in an irregular camouflage pattern and bearing French roundels. Following the trade of the two Nieuports Cole Palen embarked on a full restoration of the Type 10 and it took to the air for the first time since the 1930s on 20 June, 1987. It is currently in French colours with Nungesser's wartime insignia somewhat incongruously adorning the fuselage sides.

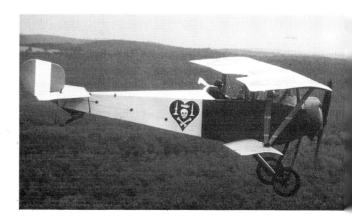

Cole Palen exchanged his Nieuport 28 for NASM's Nieuport 10 in recent years and has since restored the latter to flying condition. (Barry Dowsett)

Nieuport 11

'N976'. Musée de l'Air et de l'Espace, Le Bourget Airport, Paris, France

It was the Nieuport 10 that initiated the well-known sesquiplane configuration which was to remain the standard pattern for most of the Nieuport biplane designs of World War I. Not far behind came the 1915 Nieuport 11, a smaller version, a single-seat fighter powered by the 80 hp Le Rhône engine.

In the French *Aviation Militaire*, the 11 joined the 10 in service, many units operating both types, and there were at least 90 Bébés at the Front by February 1916. The Royal Naval Air Services also received examples serving with No. 1 Wing in France and No. 2 Wing in the Aegean, deliveries taking place in January 1916. Although it was planned, no transfer of the type to the RFC was ever made; this fell instead to the Nieuport 16, a more highly powered version but outwardly virtually indistinguishable from the Type 11.

The Bébé was built in Italy under licence by Macchi; Russia and Holland also built and used the type. During the troubled period when the 'Fokker Scourge' reigned over the Western Front, the Nieuport 11 proved its worth. Most of France's more celebrated aces flew the type, including Guynemer, Nungesser and Navarre, not to mention the American pilots of the *Lafayette Escadrille*. When superseded by the Type 16, some Bébés were usually armed with a single Lewis gun mounted on a bracket above the upper wing and clearing the arc of the airscrew. Eight 'aerial torpedoes' (Le Prieur rockets) could also be carried, four apiece to each interplane strut.

The Musée de l'Air have owned their Nieuport 11 since the end of WWI. For many years it was displayed in an overall aluminium scheme with French markings and the serial N976 on the rudder. The cowling was highly polished, as were the varnished interplane struts, and no armament was fitted. Prior to its recent reappearance the Bébé underwent extensive restoration and is now covered in clear-doped linen and sports a new serial, N556. The cowling and metal panels are now even more highly polished, but a Lewis machine gun and its mounting have been fitted to the upper wing.

The Musée de l'Air's Nieuport 11 is the only known survivor of this classic fighter. It is seen here in its original finish. (John Garwood)

In the mid-1970s the Musée Nieuport was in need of renovation and extensive work was carried out before the aeroplane's reappearance in La Grande Gallerie, Le Bourget. *(Stuart Howe)*

Nieuport 12

'A4737'. National Aviation Museum, Rockcliffe Airport, Ontario, Canada

The Nieuport 12 first appeared in 1915 as an uprated version of the French manufacturer's N.10. Outwardly the two types were indistinguishable except for their interplane strut configurations: vertical to the line of flight on the Nieuport 10, splayed outwards on the N.12. As well as service with French forces at least 169 RNAS serials have been recorded for the N.10/12 series, 50 of the latter being built by the Beardmore Company of Dalmuir, Scotland, some with fixed fins and fully circular cowlings.

The example currently owned by the NAM is thought to have been manufactured in 1915–16 by Nieuport, although neither its original serial nor constructor's number have been discovered. It is fitted with a fixed fin, and although this is a feature normally associated with Beardmore-built machines, neither fin nor rudder conform to Beardmore standard and it may have been fitted in a post-war restoration.

The early history of the museum's machine is not known. Their earliest record dates back to 1936, when a note in the National Research Council Aero-

nautical Museum recorded that the War Trophies Board was seeking storage space for a 'Nieuport donated by the French Government'. During 1958 the Nieuport was restored by RCAF No. 6 RD Trenton, Ontario, and finished in RFC scheme with the spurious serial A4737. In May the following year it went on display at the RCAF Station at Trenton and was subsequently displayed at Rockcliffe between 1963 and 1964. It is currently in storage awaiting restoration.

Currently awaiting its turn in an extensive restoration programme is the National Aviation Museum's Nieuport 12. The aeroplane's original identity is not known. (John Garwood)

Nieuport 23.C1

N5024. Musée Royal de l'Armée, Brussels, Belgium

Undoubtedly one of the finest French fighter aeroplanes of the war, the Nieuport 17.C1 served with all Allied air services and the leading air aces of Belgium, Great Britain, France and Italy scored many of their victories on this nimble machine. Developed from the earlier Nieuport 11 and 16, the type 17.C1 was a somewhat more refined version; powered by the Le Rhône 9Ja rotary it was provided with increased wing span and area. The new fighter retained the principal Nieuport design characteristics, being a single-bay sesquiplane with single-spar lower wing, V-form interplane struts and typical Nieuport rudder. Fuller (asymmetric) fuselage flank fairings behind the fully circular engine cowling blended its cross-section smoothly into the flat sides of the rear fuselage.

Many Nieuports in French service were armed

For many years the Brussels Nieuport 23 carried an overall aluminium finish and Aviation militaire belge markings. (John Garwood)

In recent years the Belgian Nieuport has had roundels added to the lower surface of the upper wing and the red/white comet marking of the 5e Escadrille applied to the fuselage. The machine is currently under restoration. (Brussels Air Museum)

with a single fixed Vickers gun synchronized to fire through the airscrew arc and on occasion Le Prieur rockets were carried in electrically operated tubular launchers mounted on the interplane struts. On RFC Nieuports the standard armament was a Lewis gun fitted to an overwing Foster mounting.

In service many Nieuports suffered from structural problems. Mostly the incidents were as a result of the lower wing single spar twisting in the unsatisfactory collar attachment at the foot of the interplane struts. Several pilots were killed when complete wing panels came away in mid-air. nevertheless the Nieuport 17.C1 became to be highly regarded by Allied airmen and the basic sesquiplane layout of the earlier Type 11 so impressed the Germans that many carbon copies were constructed, and the Albatros DIII and DV/Va and Pfalz DIII fighters were designed on Nieuport principles.

Another unique Nieuport is the Royal Army Museum's 23.C1. A development of the famous type 17, this is the only original example known to have survived. (John Garwood)

The offset Vickers gun, the result of improved interrupter gear, confirms the identity of the Brussel's Nieuport as a Type 23 rather than a 17 as originally thought.

Nieuport 28.C1

N8539. US Air Force Museum, Wright Patterson AFB, Ohio, USA

The 28.C1 was intended to replace earlier Nieuport designs, but having been largely rejected by the French authorities it was put into production for the American Expeditionary Force, who had arrived in France with no fighter aeroplanes. Nieuport 28s were delivered to four AEF units, the 27th, 94th, 95th and 147th Pursuit Squadrons, and it was the 94th who mounted the first armed combat patrols on 14 April, 1918. The second patrol that day saw the first combat victories by an operational American unit when Lieutenants Alan Winslow and Douglas Campbell each brought down an enemy fighter.

Many American aces flew the Type 28.C1 in combat, managing to maintain a favourable ratio of victories to losses despite widely differing opinions on its performance. Agreement was universal, however, on the aeroplane's frailty. The Nieuport had an unfortunate, frequently fatal, tendency to shed its upper wing fabric in long dives, while problems with engine fuel lines led to several fires in mid-air.

The Type 28.C1 was the first Nieuport design to feature a two-spar lower wing with a chord nearly matching the upper as opposed to previous sesquiplane configurations. It was also the first Nieuport production aeroplane to be armed with two synchronized machine guns, both offset to port on the fuselage sides.

After the Armistice several Nieuport 28s were shipped to the USA. At least 12 were operated by the Navy in 1919, flown from platforms mounted over the forward gun turrets of battleships, some of these aeroplanes being fitted with flotation gear and hydrovanes. Nieuport 28s also served the Army as trainers for a while and many found their way into civilian

The sole known remaining Nieuport '17.C1' is actually a 23 as evidenced by its offset Vickers gun, the only visible difference between the types, and was acquired by the Royal Army Museum during the 1920s and is currently under restoration. For many years it was displayed in its original condition finished overall in aluminium dope with Belgian markings, although in recent years have these been applied to the lower surfaces of the upper wing. Wartime stencilling included the part numbers 742 beneath the upper wing leading edge and the trailing edges of both ailerons with a post-war 'serial' VIII/5452 painted beneath the cowling.

The USAF Museum's Nieuport 28.C1 has passed through many hands and its most recent restoration took place during the early 1980s. It is the museum's intention to fully restore the Nieuport to more authentic configuration in the near future. (USAF Museum)

Switzerland boasts two examples of the Nieuport 29.C1. This is 607 at Dubnendorf. (Michael Schmeelcke)

ownership for both racing and to 'star' in Hollywood war films such as *The Dawn Patrol* and *Men with Wings*.

At least seven Nieuport 28s have survived, and with the exception of the ex-Tallmantz 'N5246' now in the UK, and two in Switzerland, are all to be found in the USA. Although not entirely authentic in all respects, one of the best-preserved examples is currently displayed by the USAF Museum. N8529 was built in 1917 and although details of its early career are obscure it may have seen wartime service and is likely to have appeared in one of the popular post-war films.

For many years N8529 formed part of the Tallmantz collection, most of which was acquired in recent years by enthusiast Kermit Weeks of Miami, Florida, for his growing air museum. In 1985 the Nieuport was transferred to the USAF Museum as part of an exchange and is currently displayed pend-

ing an eventual, thorough restoration. the aeroplane had been refurbished by the Weeks Museum, but after so many years of modifications and rebuilds it is not 100 per cent authentic. At present the machine is covered in 'Ceconite', the cockpit coaming and seat covered with vinyl and aluminium pop rivets have been used to secure certain panels. The engine cowling is of glass-fibre, while the outline shapes of vertical tailplane, rudder and undercarriage fairings are dubious. The colours and markings are also inappropriate. Museum staff have discovered, however, that most of the metal fittings *are* original and that at least part of the wooden structure dates from the aeroplane's earliest origins. The engine appears to be a genuine Gnome 9N, although all leads, pipes, etc., are modern. At some time the wings have been clipped (probably for film use, where the modification improved roll rate for aerobatics) then returned to original configuration during one of the Nieuport's more recent restorations.

It is normal practice for the USAF Museum to display exhibits in as near perfect, authentic appearance as possible, but since it may be many years before their skilled specialists can include the Nieuport in the schedule it is being displayed in its current state. Eventually the veteran will be restored to its original condition.

Nieuport 28.C1

'N4123A'. National Air and Space Museum, Washington DC, USA

An example of the Nieuport 28 well known to American enthusiasts is another of the ex-Tallmantz machines owned by Cole Palen, who in recent years exchanged it with NASM's Nieuport 10/83, the latter, now fully restored, currently flying from

Cole Palen's well-known Nieuport 28.C1 was a regular weekend performer at Old Rhinebeck for many years. It was exchanged recently for the NASM Nieuport 10. (Via John Garwood)

Nieuport 28.C1 688 in pristine condition. (Swiss Museum of Transport and Communications, Lucerne)

One of the stars of the 1938 remake of The Dawn Patrol *was this Nieuport 'N5146', now in the UK for restoration by Vintage Aero Ltd.* (Author)

The condition of the ex-Tallmantz 'N5246' is poor, but the present owners are confident of an early restoration. (Author)

Palen's Old Rhinebeck aerodrome. The NASM 28.C1 was one of the original 1919 US Navy aeroplanes with a steel tube rudder and was used until 1926 in launching tests from the battleship USS *Arizona*.

Later that year, together with three others, it was purchased by the First National Vitagraph Company for use in the original (1930) version of the classic film *The Dawn Patrol*. All four machines remained airworthy, appearing in numerous productions, and several guises, including *Hell's Angels*, and later moved on to Warner Brothers during 1936 for *The Story of Vernon and Irene Castle* and *Men with Wings*, thence to Paramount, in whose employ they all underwent drastic modifications. Two of them were fitted with single 'I' interplane struts and the others with 'N'-type struts to speed rigging adjustments. Three of them had their wing spans reduced by about one metre and all four were fitted with shallow non-standard cowlings probably from Thomas-Morse trainers. By 1938 the aeroplanes were extensively renovated for the Warner Brothers remake of *The Dawn Patrol* starring Errol Flynn, David Niven and Basil Rathbone. Only one of the Nieuports flew in the remake, most of the flying scenes being taken from the 1930 version, the others performing as 'authentic' stand-ins. In the film's several line-up shots the NASM 28.C1 appears with the serial '34S' on the rudder and bearing 'O' on its fuselage. Although fitted with 'I' struts this Nieuport apparently did not have its wing area reduced.

Following the Nieuports' film career they became the property of Paul Mantz, who bought them from Paramount during World War II. In 1957, when Mantz was collecting aeroplanes for use in the Charles Lindbergh 'biopic' *Spirit of St Louis*, he exchanged one of his Nieuports for Cole Palen's Curtiss JN-4C. Palen subsequently restored the Nieuport to flying condition and until 1972 it performed for many years at air displays.

Packard Le Père Lusac II

SC42133. USAF Museum, Wright Patterson AFB, Dayton, Ohio, USA

The Packard Motor Car Company of Detroit, Michigan, played an important part in creating the Liberty 8 and 12 aero engines, their engineer, J. G. Vincent,

Packard's Le Père Lusac II two-seat fighter, the sole-surviving example of which was displayed in the Musée de l'Air for many years. (John Garwood)

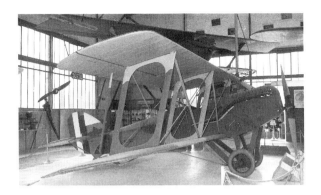

The refurbished Packard seen at the Musée in 1974. It has since been exchanged with NASM for a Lockheed F.5. (Stuart Howe)

being among the chief designers. The eight-cylinder version was abandoned in December 1917, and development work concentrated on the bigger engine, which after modification proved to be a first-class power unit.

The company obtained the loan from the French Government of an experienced aeronautical engineer, Capitain G. Le Père, and began to design their own aeroplanes. A two-seater fighter biplane the Lusac (Le Père US Army Combat) II, was the first and best of these. In September 1918 the prototype was handed over to the US Army Air Service. Its power unit, naturally, was the big 400 hp Liberty 12. Twin Marlin synchronized machine guns, both situated on the starboard side of the fuselage, fixed to fire through the airscrew arc, were provided for the pilot. The observer had twin Lewis guns, mounted on a Scarff ring.

The Lusac II was strong, manoeuvrable, heavily armed and fast (132.2 mph), which would have made it very useful had the war continued. By the Armistice the Packard company had supplied 30 machines, two of these, 42130 and 42131, both of greater span than the original model, undergoing official service trials in France.

For many years the world's only remaining Packard Lusac was displayed in the Musée de l'Air, but the Museum recently exchanged it for one of the NASM's Lockheed F-5s. If the significance of this is lost to readers, it should be noted that the much celebrated and beloved French pilot and writer Antoine de Saint Exupery disappeared flying an F-5.

Pfalz D.XII

'7511/18'. Champlin Fighter Museum, Arizona, USA

After the D.III and D.IIIa the only other Pfalz fighter design to enter quantity production was the D.XII, two of which appeared at the June 1918 fighter trials at Adlershof. The design was, outwardly at least, influenced by its more famous contemporary the Fokker D.VII, but in construction it could not have differed more. The main differences were the typical Pfalz semi-monocoque wooden fuselage and double-bay, fully braced wing cellule; the latter, whilst producing an extremely strong structure, was unpopular with ground crews due to the additional maintenance work involved.

Rudolph Stark, commander of the Bavarian *Jagdstaffel* 35, would record after the war that when his unit received examples of the Pfalz D.XII in early September 1918 they were intially regarded with suspicion by most pilots. However, once the members of his squadron had familiarized themselves with the new fighter they were able to combat SE5as, Sopwith Camels and Dolphins on more or less equal terms. There is little doubt that the Pfalz D.XII was a sound machine, well designed and engineered. Had the war continued into 1919 it would probably have emerged from the shadow of the mercurial Fokker D.VII to play a major part in the air war. The D.XII was supplied to 11 front-line *Jastas* as well as several home defence units and by October 1918 there were 180 machines in active service.

Four examples of the D.XII survive, two of them in the USA. The latter were part of a large number of captured machines shipped out to the USA during 1919 for evaluation at McCook Field. They were subsequently sold off as government surplus and acquired by Hollywood for filming purposes, including both versions of *The Dawn Patrol*. Stills from the 1930 First National-Vitagraph production show both machines with black-painted fuselages and two diagonal white stripes behind the cockpits. For the 1938 remake the fuselages of both aeroplanes had been overpainted with broad horizontal black and white stripes fore and aft. Once filming work was completed both Pfalz were put up for sale at Venice Park near Los Angeles. One of the machines was bought by Colonel G. B. Jarrett for display at his Moorestown, New Jersey, museum, who cleaned off the old film company 'warpaint' to uncover the original finish. When Colonel Jarrett re-entered army service during World War II, his prized WWI aeroplane collection, which as well as the D.XII included an Avro 504K, DH4, Fokker D.VII, Nieuport 28.CI, Sopwith Camel, Spad 7.C1 and Thomas Morse S-4C, were dismantled and placed into storage until 1946, when it

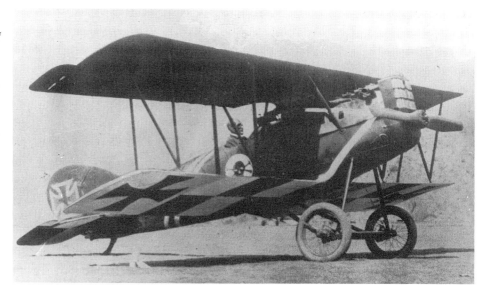

Pfalz D.XII '7511/18' seen here during the filming of the original 1930 version of The Dawn Patrol *at Newhall, California. Markings are typically Hollywood! This aeroplane was later acquired by Colonel Jarrett and subsequently owned and restored by Frank Tallman. (Harry Woodman)*

The restored Tallman Pfalz D.XII registered N43C. Rebuilt to flying condition in 1959 it was later sold to the Wings and Wheels Museum in Florida. (John Garwood)

Current owner of the ex-Tallman Pfalz is the Champlin Fighter Museum, Arizona. Since 1984, when this photograph was taken, the machine has been repainted and re-covered in more authentic finish. (H. Van Dyk Soerewyn)

The NASM Pfalz D.XII 7517/18 seen prior to painting for Buck Kennel before WWII. (John Garwood)

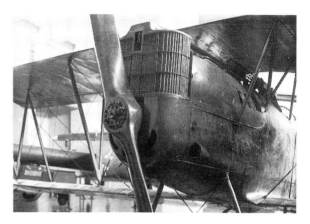

Pfalz D.XII 2600/18 is owned by Australia's War Museum and is seen here during the 1950s prior to restoration. (John Garwood)

was discovered that they had suffered badly over the intervening years. Sadly the DH4 was burnt, the 504K and Thomas Morse sold off, and when Colonel Jarrett moved the rest of his collection to Maryland the D.VII was subsequently destroyed. During the following years some restoration work took place on the four surviving machines, but in 1950 these too were sold. The new owner was Mr Frank C. Tallman, who, in turn, passed two of the aeroplanes to other enthusiasts. The Camel was rebuilt for Tallman by Ned Kensinger of Illinois, who received the Nieuport in lieu of payment, while in exchange for the Spad 7, Robert Rust of Atlanta, Georgia, undertook restoration of the Pfalz to flying condition.

By the time Mr Rust took charge of the German fighter it was in a very sorry state with much of the woodwork so badly rotted that it had to be replaced. Restoration began in April 1955 and since the wings had deteriorated so badly they served merely as patterns for new panels to be made. At one stage it was thought feasible to fit a modern engine, but when the original 180 hp Mercedes was stripped down and examined it was found to be in such good condition that it was overhauled and put into running order. During the restoration, the airscrew, radiator, water

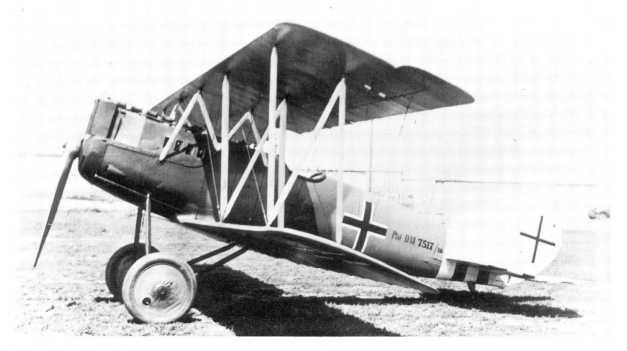

The Jarrett/Kennel D.XII in the finish it wore for many years. (John Garwood)

Restoration of the Australian War Memorial Pfalz D.XII took several years and the result is one of the most authentic examples of a WWI German aeroplane anywhere in the world. (Via Colin A. Owers)

The Musée de l'Air's D2690/18 photographed at Chalais Meudon in the late 1950s. It is currently displayed at La Grande Gallerie, Le Bourget. *(John Garwood)*

pipes, petrol tanks, fuel lines and about a third of the many small metal fittings were replaced. Finished in a pseudo-wartime camouflage and bearing the registration N43C, the Pfalz took to the air once more in January 1959 from Futton County Airport in Atlanta, Frank Tallman himself at the controls. It was subsequently taken by road to Los Angeles to join the Tallman collection and flew at air displays for several years, logging about ten hours.

During 1968 the Tallman collection came under the hammer and the Pfalz changed hands once more, this time to the Aeroflex collection. It was subsequently displayed at the Wings and Wheels Museum in Orlando, Florida, until the end of 1981, when another auction resulted in another move, this time to Doug Champlin's Fighter Museum in Arizona. Once there it was dismantled and, with the help of Jim Appleby, restored in authentic finish, including proper 'lozenge' fabric, much needed assistance coming from Australian War Museum staff at Canberra, who had, at that time, just completed a restoration of their D.XII, 2600/18. Champlin's Pfalz D.XII remains unique as the only example of the type in a private collection.

The other American-based Pfalz is owned by the National Air and Space Museum. This aeroplane was sold to Mr Buck Kennel, a property man at Paramount Studios, in 1938. With Colonel Jarrett's assistance Kennel restored the Pfalz to airworthy condition and flew it regularly until 1939. The machine, since restored, is currently loaned out by NASM to the Experimental Aircraft Association Museum at Oshkosh, Wisconsin.

A fourth example of a D.XII is displayed in *La Grande Gallerie*, Le Bourget. This is D2690/18 and was partially restored by M. Jean Salis in post WWII years. The 'lozenge' fabric on the wings is original.

Royal Aircraft Factory BE2c

4112. National Aviation Museum, Rockcliffe Airport, Ontario, Canada

The RAF BE2c was the result of Edward Busk's extensive experiments in automatic stability. At that time, in 1914, this highly desirable quality was thought to be of prime importance, providing stable platforms for reconnaissance and spotting operations; the military had yet to realize the full potential of the

RAF BE2c 4112 seen here at Suttons Farm in 1916. This historic aeroplane was flown by Lieutenant Frederick Sowrey (third from left) when he shot down Zeppelin L32 during the night of 23/24 September, 1916. (AM Sir Frederick Sowrey)

Sowrey's 4112 was displayed at Rockcliffe for many years wearing this inappropriate finish and replacement fin. It is currently being restored to its original 1916 appearance. (CFPU PL 140900)

aeroplane in wartime. The BE2c was put into large-scale production and performed its intended tasks admirably until the advent of greatly improved German fighters, against which BE2c crews had little hope of effective opposition.

As a home defence machine, however, the BE2c proved successful, for its inherent stability was a distinct asset for night-flying duties. Five German airships fell to BE2c pilots flying their machines converted to single-seat fighters armed with an upward-firing Lewis gun. On the Western Front BE2cs were operated by a dozen RFC squadrons and also by No. 1 Wing RNAS and units of the Belgian *aviation militaire*. Apart from home defence and training units in the UK, BE2cs also saw service in the Aegean, Africa, Australia and India. Over 1300 BE2cs and BE2ds were eventually delivered to the RFC and RNAS, a number from which only three BE2cs have survived.

For many years an unrestored BE2c was suspended from the roof of the Imperial War Museum aeronautical gallery at Lambeth. This was 2699, which saw service with No. 50 Home Defence Squadron at Dover and was flown on several nocturnal operations. In its original finish it displayed dark-painted upper-surfaces with its fuselage doped in the standard PC10 khaki camouflage. 2699 was built by Ruston, Proctor and Co. of Lincolnshire during 1916 and after its service with No. 50 HDS passed to No. 190 Night Training Squadron in April 1918 and in October was transferred to No. 192 NTS. Its last two months of service were spent with No. 51 Squadron and in May 1918 it was withdrawn, following a forced landing, and subsequently placed in the care of the Imperial War Museum. 2699 remained at Lambeth until 1979, when it was taken down and sent to IWM Duxford for restoration and display. Now back at Lambeth, in the recently refurbished main exhibition gallery, it currently bears a rather dubious 'clear-doped' finish; in fact the overall standard of the restoration leaves

An ex-50 HDS BE2c is 2699 as displayed at The Imperial War Museum for many years until 1979, when it was removed to Duxford for renovation. (Stuart Howe)

much to be desired.

The Musée de l'Air workshops at Meudon val Fleury first overhauled their BE2c in 1957. This machine (9969) was one of a batch built for the RNAS by Blackburn. Recently the BE was the subject of a complete overhaul before being displayed alongside the DH9 and Sopwith 1½ Strutter in the museum's new *La Grande Gallerie* at Le Bourget.

BE2c 4112, preserved by Canada's National Aviation Museum, has a dramatic history, having been involved in one of the war's great events, the destruction of a Zeppelin over London. Built by the British and Colonial Aircraft Co. Ltd., in 1915 (Constructor's number 663) it served with B Flight of No. 39 Home Defence Squadron at Suttons Farm, Essex, in 1916. It was flown by Captain Arthur T. Harris (later 'Bomber' Harris of WWII RAF Bomber Command) during the night of 25/26 April to attack Zeppelin *LZ97* without result. On the night of 23/24 September 4112 was being flown by Second Lieutenant Frederick Sowrey when he successfully attacked the German Zeppelin *L32* commanded by Werner Peterson.

It took three drums of ammunition before Sowrey's tenacious attack proved conclusive and was rewarded

with the awesome spectacle of a red glow deep within the Zeppelin. Seconds later the vessel was rocked with explosions and slowly slid out of the sky. Sowrey watched the blazing wreck as it plunged past his aeroplane and finally neared the ground in a river of fiery orange which turned vivid green on impact. Sowrey was awarded a DSO for his night's work.

The IWM BE2c at the new IWM exhibition gallery opened in 1989. (Author)

The Musée de l'Air BE2c 9969 as displayed in 1974 sans rudder. (Stuart Howe)

A more intimate view of 9969 shows its Blackburn Aeroplane and Motor Co. Ltd, factory trademark. The aeroplane was one of a batch built for the Royal Naval Air Service. (Stuart Howe)

Somehow 4112 survived the war and was acquired for Canada by Lieutenant Colonel Arthur Doughty as part of a number of war trophies and arrived in June 1919. It was initially displayed at the Canadian National Exhibition in Toronto, Ontario, and subsequently stored in the Trophy building until 1936, when the aeroplane was repaired and reconditioned at No. 1 Aircraft Depot at RCAF Ottawa and put on display once more, this time at the Aeronautical Museum of the National Research Council. 4112 remained on exhibition until 1940, when it was returned to storage for many years. In the late 1950s the aeroplane was completely restored by No. 6 RD, RCAF Trenton, obtaining a new engine from the Science Museum and making up various parts that were missing. In 1962 the original airscrew was donated to the Canadian War Museum, where 4112 was displayed, by the British Air Ministry at the sugges-

tion of Wing Commander F. B. Sowrey, the son of the machine's victorious pilot. In 1983, 4112 was removed from display to be completely restored to its original 1916 configuration. As originally exhibited this BE2c was painted in black with simple white rings in the usual positions, the 1957–8 restoration team faithfully following the original finish of the aeroplane as it appeared in 1919. Such a scheme was used as night-fighter camouflage for the latter war years, a distinct contrast to the finish worn by 4112 when Frederick Sowrey matched it against a Zeppelin over seven decades ago.

Royal Aircraft Factory BE2e

A1325. Mosquito Museum, London Colney, Hertfordshire, UK

The Royal Aircraft Factory created two developments from the successful BE2c – the BE2d and BE2e. The former was externally very similar to the 2c but was fitted with dual controls and featured a revised fuel system that incorporated an external gravity tank under the port upper wing linked to a tank in the fuselage top decking. By the autumn of 1915 four batches of BE2ds were on order, two from the British and Colonial Aeroplane Co. and one apiece from Vulcan and Ruston, Proctor. Considerable numbers of these aeroplanes were to be modified, either during production or after, to have the unequal-span mainplanes introduced with the BE2e.

The prototype BE2e was flying before any of the production BE2ds became available and initial results were considered promising and it showed a modest improvement over its immediate forebears. As a result the machine's slightly better performance prompted large-scale production, more so than any other BE variant. Deliveries to the Western Front commenced in June 1916 and continued well into

RAF BE2e A1325 currently housed at the Mosquito Museum in London Colney is soon to be restored to its original configuration. (Stuart Howe)

The Imperial War Museum RAF Reconnaissance Experimental No. 8 F3556, built by Daimler in 1918. It never saw combat service. (John Garwood)

The Norwegian BE2e arrives at the Mosquito Aircraft Museum. (Stuart Howe)

1917, by which time aerial warfare had advanced to a marked degree, but the BE2e was little match for the speedy, well-armed Halberstadt and Albatros fighters. The BE2e also saw operational service in Aden, Africa, India, Macedonia and Palestine as well as in Great Britain for home defence duties against German airships and bombers, where its performance proved unequal to the task. The BE2e continued in service up to the Armistice, although by then it had been relegated to the training schools, where it performed valuable work.

The example preserved at the Mosquito Museum was originally purchased along with nine others from RFC surplus stocks in 1917 by the Norwegian Army Air Force. Altogether some 17 machines had been acquired by 1921 along with many spare parts. One of these (A1380) was eventually earmarked for preservation and was recently fully restored by Captain John Amundsen for the Royal Norwegian Air Force collection at Gardenmoen near Oslo. A second BE2e airframe (A1325) has also survived and was donated to the Mosquito Museum by the RNAF in September 1982. At the time of writing little information on the aeroplane's early service career has been discovered other than that it was from the second batch of BE2es built by Napier and Miller of Old Kirkpatrick.

A1325 is by no means complete. The fuselage frame, uncovered at present, appears to be intact, with cockpit floor, seat, controls, rear decking, tail-skid, fin (from A1379), three bottom wings, all interplane struts, flying cables, oil tank, gun mountings, bomb rack and sundry fittings. Some restoration work has already been carried out following receipt from the RNAF and as currently displayed a complete undercarriage has been installed along with engine bearers, while castings for a dummy RAF 1a

Preserved in Norway is this magnificently restored BE2e 131 (ex-F1380) for the Royal Norwegian Air Force Collection at Gardenmoen. (IPMS Norway)

engine have also been fabricated. In recognition of its long service in Norway and of the generosity of the RNAF in donating the machine it is intended that A1325 will eventually be restored in Norwegian Army Air Service colours, but a great deal of work remains to be done before covering and finishing can be undertaken.

Royal Aircraft Factory RE8

F3556. Imperial War Museum, Duxford, Cambridge, UK

Designed as a replacement for the out-dated BE2c the RE8 – the initials stand for 'Reconnaissance Experimental' – was produced in considerable numbers, some 3000 being built, of which about 67 per cent saw action on the Western Front, the most widely used reconnaissance machine to be fielded by the RFC. In combat situations the RE8 proved to offer scant improvement over the BE2c. Once again its inherent stability, whilst an advantage in artillery spotting and reconnaissance work, was offset by a lack of manoeuvrability, which made the machines frequently vulnerable to fighter attack. Early operational use was marred by a number of accidents. Many RE8's spun in at low altitude and fire often followed as a result of the engine being pushed back into the fuselage, rupturing the fuel tanks. Subsequent investigations were conducted and it became clear that the main cause of the tragedies lay in the inadequate training given to RFC airmen at the time, probably aggravated by

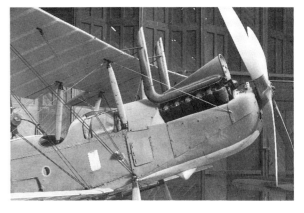

Restoration of the IWM RE8 was completed in 1980, but its new finish is not particularly authentic. (Author)

frequent failure of the RAF 4a engine. As 1917 passed, the 'Harry Tate', as it became known to its crews, equipped more and more front-line units. Various modifications were introduced throughout the year and both the pilot's and observer's armament installations were greatly improved. By October 1918 the RE8 was in service with 19 squadrons and despite its shortcomings the type did sterling service, enabling British artillery to silence enemy gun positions in many significant battles. The RE8's successes are usually overlooked and on many occasions experienced and resolute crews were to prove that the aeroplane was more than able to defend itself in combat.

The Imperial War Museum's RE8 was built by Daimler Ltd. in 1918, but never saw action, being delivered to the RAF after the Armistice. Painted on

During 1974 the IWM RE8 was transferred to Duxford for restoration and displayed at one of the IWM air displays with the port side of the fuselage uncovered. (Stuart Howe)

The 150 hp Hispano-Suiza of the Brussels RE8 gives an unusual aspect to this classic WWI warhorse. (John Garwood)

the port side of the nose is the presentation inscription 'A Paddy Bird From Ceylon', this legend originally borne by BE2c 4073, which was paid for by subscriptions in Ceylon under a scheme sponsored by the newspaper *The Times of Ceylon*. After this BE2c was lost on 8 March, 1916, the name passed, on 1 January, 1919, to F3556. The aeroplane logged only a few hours' flying time before being transferred to the IWM. It was initially displayed at the Museum's first home at the Crystal Palace during 1920 and was partially renovated in 1950. During 1974 the RE8 was moved from the IWM's Lambeth headquarters to Duxford for thorough restoration, a task completed in 1980.

During 1917, 22 RE8 airframes were supplied to the Belgian Army Air Service, which, on delivery, fitted the aeroplanes with the 150 hp Hispano-Suiza 4a engine, necessitating a drastic redesign of the forward fuselage. One of these unusual machines is exhibited by the Royal Army Museum in Brussels, having been there since the 1920s. Bearing the service number '8' it has recently been restored by the Belgian Army's No. 17 Squadron Light Aviation Section.

The remains of a third RE8 are believed to be in storage at the Musée de l'Air in France, but thus far no confirmation of this has been forthcoming.

Royal Aircraft Factory SE5a

F904. Shuttleworth Collection, Old Warden, Bedfordshire, UK

Together with the Sopwith Camel the SE5a was perhaps the finest British fighter to see service in World War I. Originally powered with the 150 hp Hispano-Suiza the aeroplane could be easily flown by pilots with limited experience as it incorporated the traditional inherent stability of previous RAF designs. While that meant it was less manoeuvrable than the Camel it proved to be a steady and reliable mount. Later models were fitted with the geared Hispano, which proved extremely troublesome and was subsequently replaced by the 200 hp Wolseley Viper, a British-built derivative. Nevertheless, the problems were not over. The direct-drive Viper had been created by Wolseley's as a result of misinterpreting an order for 400 direct-drive powerplants of the basic 150 hp Hispano-Suiza 8Aa already built in Britain as the Python. Production Vipers suffered various troubles which were eventually overcome, a great deal of development work being necessary to achieve a reliable radiator installation.

The SE5a underwent further modifications to cure structural problems of both fin and mainplanes and the inadequate steel tube undercarriage struts. Once these various defects were eradicated the SE5a soon acquired its fine reputation for strength and stability as a gun platform and became a firm favourite with many leading fighter pilots, airmen such as Beauchamp-Proctor, Dallas, Jones, Mannock and McCudden scoring a large number of their victories on the type.

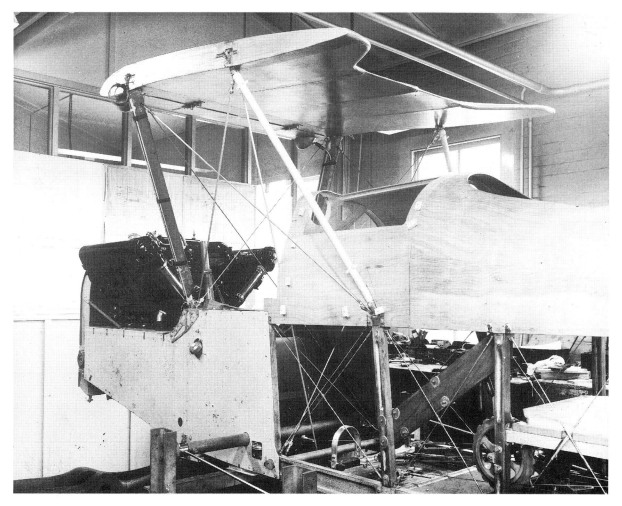

The Shuttleworth Trust's SE5a F904 whilst undergoing restoration at Farnborough during 1958–9. The wood fairings have yet to be fitted to the rear centre-section struts. (P. J. McDonagh via J. M. Bruce)

During the war various attempts were made to improve the SE5a's manoeuvrability, but despite experimental armament installations, changes in elevator and aileron areas and redesigned tail surfaces, the classic fighter ended the war not significantly different from its original 1916 design.

After the Armistice, when the Aircraft Disposal Board were selling hundreds of war surplus machines at bargain prices, Major John Savage purchased 45 SE5as and began converting them for commercial use. A large fleet of the ex-fighters was then used by Savage and Parsons for skywriting, crop-spraying and other purposes during the 1920s and 1930s. Major Savage more or less invented skywriting and was the founder of Skywriting Ltd., most of whose pilots were ex-RAF men and readily familiar with the SE5a. During the early days of the Savage Company, much of the work was done in Great Britain, where the

aluminium-doped aeroplanes became a familiar sight. Three of these former skywriting SEs have survived to this day. Formerly bearing the civil registrations G-EBIA, G-EBIB and G-EBIC, all three were, for a time, being flown in the USA, but were brought back to the UK by Major Savage. One of them (G-EBIA) has been maintained in an airworthy condition and is currently displayed at the Shuttleworth Trust's Old Warden aerodrome.

One of the earliest records of this now famous machine is a magazine photograph published in January 1939, showing an airframe, without engine and covering, beneath the wing of an Armstrong Whitworth Ensign. The SE5a had become the property of the Coventry-based AW Company in 1939 and remained in their flight shed at Whitley until 1955, when it was acquired by the Shuttleworth Collection, who passed it to staff and apprentices of the Royal

F904 at a Shuttleworth air display during the 1970s when fitted with the 200 hp Hispano-Suiza engine. (Author)

Aircraft Establishment – the former Royal Aircraft Factory – for restoration to airworthy condition.

The RAE found very little of the original airframe left to build, for the engine, most of the cowling and metal panels, radiator and smaller components were all missing. G-EBIA was originally powered by a Wolseley Viper, but since a replacement could not be found the Shuttleworth Collection provided a 200 hp Hispano. RAE's own files provided a complete set of original drawings, and several senior staff members, who had experience of building SEs some 35 years previously, found themselves in great demand! De-

spite many of the smaller components being discovered on dusty, long-forgotten shelves and others donated from a number of private sources the RAE had to fabricate a large number of new parts.

In the autumn of 1959 the SE5a emerged from the workshops in authentic wartime configuration but painted in overall aluminium with the bogus serial 'D7000' and red 'squadron' markings adorning the fuselage sides. The restored machine was test flown by Air Commodore Wheeler and commander K. R. Hickson, RN, both reporting that the aeroplane flew superbly and was a pleasure to fly.

In later years the machine was stripped and re-painted in No. 56 Squadron markings as 'F904' and further work was undertaken in 1975 when problems with the Hispano led to installation of a Wolseley Viper.

Royal Aircraft Factory SE5a

'F938'. Royal Air Force Museum, Hendon, London, UK

Another Savage skywriter, G-EBIC, was sold to R. G. Nash in 1937 to become part of his well-known pre-war collection of historic aeroplanes and vehicles – obviously a man of foresight. By the following year the SE5a had been generally restored to its original configuration, being painted in olive and with RAF markings applied. During World War II the Nash

One of three extant ex-Savage Skywriters, G-EBIC is currently displayed in the Royal Air Force Museum marked as 'F938'. (Author)

Royal Aircraft Factory SE5a

'F939'. Science Museum, South Kensington, London, UK

G-EBIB was converted to skywriting configuration during 1922 and became the 'flagship' of the Savage fleet. When its flying days were over the aeroplane was presented to the Science Museum on 27 July, 1939, in its existing overall aluminium finish. Before exhibition it was stripped of all its skywriting equipment and restored, more or less, to a wartime appearance, but lacked armament. In about 1940–41 the museum gave the aeroplane a quick coat of 'muddy brown' together with a set of roundels and rudder stripes; at the same time the long exhaust pipes were either cut back or replaced altogether.

In 1961 the former skywriting SE5a was re-covered and the brown colour and markings were carefully matched. The then curator, Mr Brian Lacey, and well-known aviation writer Bruce Robertson strove to discover the aeroplane's original serial number and, based on the assumption that constructors' numbers and RAF serials ran in parallel, arrived at F939 – they were out by one figure, it should have been F938, that number being used by the RAF Museum when restoring their SE5a! The current Science Museum's curator, J. A. Bagley, does not accept his predecessor's assumptions and the aeroplane is currently being restored back to its former G-EBIB guise. All things considered this should result in a most impressive exhibit. Without Major Savage there would probably be no SE5as in the UK today and such a restoration is a fitting tribute to his memory. . .

The Shuttleworth SE5a as originally restored in 1950, wearing a spurious overall aluminium finish. (John Garwood)

collection was placed into storage and emerged after cessation of hostilities to make a number of public appearances, including displays at Farnborough in 1950 and Hendon in 1951. By then a spurious serial, 'B4563', had been added to the SE5a's fin, a number originally used on a *BE2e*.

In 1955 Mr Nash sold the SE5a to the Royal Aeronautical Society, who added No. 56 Squadron markings to its fuselage sides. Three years later the entire RAeS collection was placed in a hangar at Hendon and renovation work started. Progress was slow and although the SE5a was dismantled and partially uncovered, little else was done before the collection was on the move again, this time to London Airport to be placed in a BEA hangar for further attention. Once there the aeroplanes were offered on loan to other museums, but no offers were forthcoming until the emergent RAF Museum took charge of them in March 1963 for eventual complete restoration.

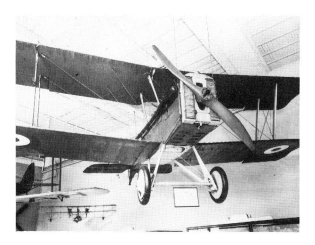

The Science Museum's SE5a as displayed during the 1950s. It is being restored to its original skywriting configuration. (John Garwood)

This SE5a, whose identity is not confirmed, is currently displayed at the South African National War Museum at Saxonwald. (John Garwood)

The world's fifth surviving SE5a may be found in Australia. Fitted with a 200 hp Wolseley Viper, the machine is serialled A2–4. (John Garwood)

Royal Aircraft Factory SE5a

'F7781'/'F7783'. South African National War Museum, Saxonwald, Johannesburg, South Africa

At the end of the war, the British Government resolved that the major Empire countries should be assisted to form their own air forces and South Africa received 110 aircraft under this programme – the so-called 'Imperial Gift'. Of these, some 22 were SE5as, which formed the fighter/ground attack element of the fledgling air force. The Saxonwald museum's aeroplane is one of these 22 and although its original RAF serial number has not been traced with certainty, it is believed to be either F7781 or F7783, which were built by Wolseley Motors. Suspended from the roof of the Brink Hall the SE5a is fitted with a 200 hp Wolseley Viper engine (No. 4210R-F 74723), as appropriate to late production machines, it being a high-compression development of the Hispano-Suiza of the earlier version.

SE5as were gradually phased out by the SAAF from 1922 onwards, being eclipsed as a fighter by the *M'pala* I (a version of the DH9 powered by a Bristol Jupiter eight-cylinder engine), and were relegated to training duties.

The museum's example was given to the Durban Technical College prior to World War II where it was used for technical training. At the end of the war, with the assistance of Professor J. H. Neal, Professor of Mechanical Engineering at Howard College, Durban, it was donated to the Museum after repairs had been undertaken by 69 Air School SAAF. The

aeroplane is currently doped overall in aluminium.

A fifth SE5a survives and belongs to the Australian War Memorial in Canberra, Australia. This particular machine is believed to have seen service with No. 2 Squadron AFC on the Western Front during 1918. It was one of the Imperial Gift aeroplanes sent to Australia after the Armistice and was declared surplus by the RAAF in 1929 and presented to the War Memorial. The aeroplane is silver-doped and serialled A2–4, this scheme being applied in 1927, and is fitted with a 200 hp Wolseley Viper. It appears to be in its original configuration apart from an oleo-type undercarriage of distinctly post-war origin.

Rumpler C.IV

'310?/17'. Deutsches Museum von Meisterwerken der Naturwissenschaft und Technik, Munich, West Germany

The Rumpler C.IV, one of a successful series of reconnaissance machines from the Rumpler Flugzeug Werke GmbH, was regarded by most Allied airmen as a formidable adversary. Its tremendous ceiling (for those times) of 21,000 feet enabled the aeroplane to fulfil its role of long-range spotting, well out of range of the majority of contemporary Allied fighters. Blessed with a splendid overall performance in speed and climb to lofty altitudes, the Rumpler was more than adequate for its designed purpose.

The C.IV went into quantity production during 1917, and by the standards of the time was a very

One of Germany's most efficient and numerous two-seater designs was the Rumpler C.IV. A recently restored example is preserved by the Deutsches Museum in Munich with its port side exposed to reveal the structure. (Christian Emrich)

'clean' aeroplane. Powered by the 260 hp Mercedes D.IVa six-cylinder motor and armed with a forward-firing LMG 0.8 gun and free-mounted Parabellum in the rear cockpit, the C.IV could give a good account of itself. As opposed to the earlier C.III, which had horn-balanced ailerons, the C.IV was fitted with plain ailerons on upper wing only. Lower wings were of 'Libellen' form (Dragonfly) shape designed by F. Budig, and the efficiency of this wing coupled with a thin rib section went a long way to give the machine its splendid performance.

The Rumpler's tail unit was very neat in design and fitted with either plain or balanced elevators, braced above and below with a total of four airfoil-shaped struts. The C.IV was also built under licence by Germania as well as Bayru (*Bayerische Rumpler Werke*) and a modified version by Pfalz, who added some extra struts to the tailplane and wings and labelled it the 'Pfalz C.I'.

German units in Italy and Palestine used the machine, and it did sterling service over the Western Front during the later years of the war.

The Rumpler C.IV now displayed in the Deutsches Museum may have been a survivor of the former Deutsche Luftfahrt Sammlung (German Aviation Collection), which was situated near the Lechte railway station in Berlin. In 1943 the museum fell victim to an Allied bombing attack, but before the exhibition halls were destroyed over 100 aeroplanes had already been moved into the eastern region of the Reich for safety except for, it seems, the C.IV.

For many years the Rumpler languished in a Berlin allotment garden, but during the 1960s, in an extremely poor state of repair, it had been dismantled and displayed at the Lilienthal *Fliegerberg* (Flyer's Mountain) at Lichterfelde. By 1976 the remains had been recovered by MBB Ottobrun Masterbau (MBB Ottobrun Reconstructions) for a complete restoration, although the task was a daunting one. Years of neglect had taken their toll: crumpled wood, rotting fabric, a confused tangle of struts and spars, the reconstruction of which proved even more difficult owing to the lack of original archive material. Sieg-

The Munich Rumpler was fully restored in the late 1970s, but lacks armament. (Christian Emrich)

fried Bergner, head of the Messerschmitt-Bolkow-Blöhm assembly shop team, began work on the Rumpler in February 1977 with 'great idealism and much love, in order to preserve this rare object for future generations'. In May 1978 the result of their labours was first displayed to an admiring public at an open day held by the *Fliegerhorst* (Pilot's Eyrie) before eventual removal to the Deutsches Museum. The restoration team deliberately omitted sections of both wing and fuselage covering to reveal parts of the original structure.

Rumpler 6B.1

5A1. Hallinportti Ilmailumuseo, Halli, Finland

The Rumpler 6B.1 of 1916 was a manoeuvrable single-seater floatplane developed from the Rumpler C.I reconnaissance machine and used for seaplane station defence purposes. Construction was virtually identical to that of the C.I, and a later version, the 6B.2, differed only in adopting the same tailplane profile to that of the later Rumpler C.IV. The German Naval Air Service operated at least 37 examples of the 6B.1. Powered by a 160 hp Mercedes D.III engine and armed with a single fixed, forward-firing machine gun, the Rumpler 6B.1 had an operational endurance of about four hours.

The first two 6B.1s, Nos. 787 and 788, were delivered in July 1916 with the prototype (751) arriving

Radiator and engine detail of the Finnish Rumpler 6B.1. (Wahlstrom via P. M. Grosz)

Finland's unique Rumpler 6B.1 floatplane following recent restoration at Hallinportti. It is the sole remaining example of a WWI German fighter seaplane. (Wahlstrom via P. M. Grosz)

the following month. Although quite a large aeroplane for a single-seat fighter, the Rumpler 6B.1 gave a good account of itself in combat whilst operating from the Ostend and Zeebrugge seaplane stations. 6B.1 pilots operating over the Black Sea have been recorded as shooting down several Russian flying boats. A total of 36 Rumpler 6B.1s and 50 6B.2s were eventually constructed.

One example of a 6B.1 has survived, in circumstances yet to be discovered, in Finland during 1918 and was flying there as late as 1926. During the early 1980s this unique aeroplane was fully restored, the only non-original item being a reproduction float. It is currently on display at the Hallinportti Ilmailumuseo at Halli and is doped an overall pale greyish buff with Finnish Air Force markings. The restoration is an excellent one and the aeroplane itself is historically important as the sole remaining example of a WWI German fighter seaplane.

Short 184

8359. Fleet Air Arm Museum, RNAS Yeovilton, Somerset, UK

The Short 184 gained its name from the quaint system adopted by the Admiralty in taking the first serial number allocated as a type designation, but the aeroplane was also known as the 225, the horsepower rating of its Sunbeam engine. The 184 was developed before the war as a torpedo carrier and its first successes were in the Dardanelles campaign, when a

The battered front cowling of the FAAM Short 184 at RNAS Yeovilton. (Author)

Short from HMS *Ben-my-Chree* in the Gulf of Xeros sank an enemy ship on 12 August, 1915. Piloted by Flight Commander C. H. K. Edmonds, a Whitehead torpedo was launched from an altitude of 15 feet at

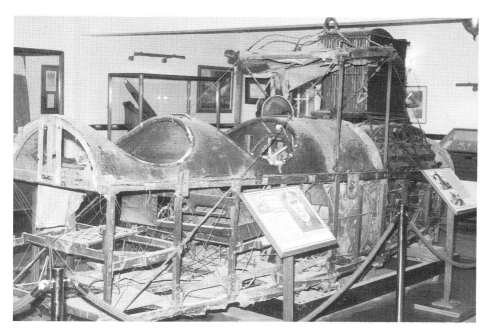

All that remains of Short 184 8359 is preserved by the Fleet Air Arm Museum at RNAS Yeovilton. It is seen here in late 1988 displayed in the museum's new WWI display area. (Author)

300 yards. Similar successes were achieved. Night-bombing attacks were made by 184s when Ostend and Zeebrugge were attacked in the early morning of 10 November, 1916; one Short 184, No. 8016, lost on this raid, was captured by the Germans.

Large numbers of Shorts were produced with a proportionately large number of sub-contractors, many introducing improvements. In all, over 900 184s were produced. Changes of engine resulted in the installation of the 240 and 260 hp Sunbeams and the 240 Renault, whilst the 275 hp Sunbeam Maori III was introduced in August 1918.

Although the 184 was still in production when the war ended, it had been replaced in seaplane carriers by Fairey Campanias, except for N9069 in HMS *Pegasus*, and during October 1918 the 184s of No. 229 Squadron were being replaced by Fairey IIIBs. No. 237 at Cattewater and No. 239 at Torquay were the only squadrons to have Short 184s as their sole equipment by the Armistice, but some 20 other squadrons operated one or two flights.

During the Battle of Jutland in 1916, a Short 184 became the only seaplane to take part in the great naval clash. The machine in question, 8359, was one of a pair carried aboard HMS *Engadine* and was hoisted out soon after 15.00 hours on 31 May with Flight Commander Rutland piloting with Assistant Paymaster Trewin acting as observer. Their subsequent reconnaissance patrol, however, did not have any bearing on the battle.

After the war 8359 was donated to the Imperial War Museum, where it was severely damaged during the Blitz, the wings and most of the fuselage being destroyed. The forward fuselage section of this historic Short 184 is currently displayed at the Fleet Air Arm Museum, who have long-term plans to produce a replica 184 to partner their Sopwith Baby.

Sopwith Baby

'N2078'. Fleet Air Arm Museum, RNAS Yeovilton, Somerset, UK

The Sopwith Baby was a somewhat more powerful version of the famous Schneider, fitted with the 110 hp Clerget rotary in place of the Gnome Monosoupape of 100 hp. An initial production order of 100 Babies was delivered by Sopwith between September 1915 and July 1916, while production of a further 71 was made by the Blackburn Company, most of these machines being powered with the 130 hp Clerget.

The Sopwith floatplanes operated from seaplane carriers in the North Sea and Mediterranean on anti-Zeppelin patrols and for bombing operations, others mounting fighter patrols from Dunkirk until replacement by RNAS Sopwith Pups in July 1917.

Yeovilton's Sopwith Baby is a hybrid based on the remains of two originals married to a non-typical steel tube fuselage. It is currently displayed with an original Baby float alongside. (Author)

Although the Sopwith Baby displayed in the Fleet Air Arm Museum may be unique, it is not 100 per cent original, being carefully constructed from the remains of two original Babies (8214 and 8215) married to a steel tube fuselage, the latter being quite untypical.

The remnants of the original machines were once part of the old Nash collection and consisted of a fuselage, wings, some tail parts and one float. In 1955 the remains passed into the hands of the Royal Aeronautical Society and were stored at Hendon Aerodrome until 1960, when they were removed to a hangar at London Airport. Study of the components in 1960 revealed that the fabric-covered areas were mostly clear-doped with the rudder striped in red, white and green. The port wing tip was doped red and the starboard wing tip in green, which tended to support the claim, made by several writers, that at least one of these machines was Macchi-built in Italy.

In the late 1960s, work began to make something of the Babies and three years of work by craftsmen at the

Royal Naval Aircraft Yard, at Fleetlands, Gosport, in Hampshire resulted in an extremely authentic-looking exhibit.

Lieutenant Commander C. A. Cox, then curator of the FAAM, enjoyed the close co-operation with many informed sources to ensure that the rebuild/reconstruction would appear as authentic as possible and a vigorous search was made for original parts and fittings. At least one ex-RNAS pilot came forward with pieces of a Baby airscrew brought back after the war as an authorized souvenir from Mesopotamia. Authentic PC10 dope was re-created as were many metal parts; the controversial steel tube fuselage was produced purely for expediency. Few drawings were available to the Fleetlands craftsmen and many new drawings had to be initiated before the project was finally completed in May 1970.

Sopwith LCT (1^1/$_2$ Strutter)

S85. Musée Royal de l'Armée et d'Histoire Militaire, Brussels, Belgium

The unusual W-form of cabane bracing initiated with the Sopwith 'Sigrist Bus' of 1914 reappeared the following year on a somewhat larger, military two-seater, its unusual strut arrangement leading to the aeroplane's unofficial name, the 1^1/$_2$ Strutter. To Sopwith's the new aeroplane was the LCT, the initials possibly signifying Land Clerget Tractor, its engine being the Clerget 9Z of 110 hp. Although the LCT was regarded as a fighter, as originally designed it was armed with a single flexibly mounted machine gun to be mounted in the rear cockpit, which was positioned well aft. The apparent reasoning for this was to provide the gunner with a clear field of fire, enabling him to fire almost dead ahead above the upper wing. Presumably the expected superior performance of a conventional tractor aeroplane, as opposed to a pusher, where the view forward was unobstructed, would be more desirable. At the time reliable interrupter gears were still under development.

The LCT was an unusually compact aeroplane and rather small for a two-seater. It employed several new and interesting features, including a variable-incidence tailplane that could be controlled by the pilot. The machine was also fitted with air-brakes in the trailing portions of the lower wing centre-section and when an interrupter gear did become available, the LCT became the first British aeroplane to be so equipped.

First deliveries of the type went to the Royal Naval Air Service, many examples of which were completed as single-seat bombers, and during April 1916 a number of naval 1^1/$_2$ Strutters were transferred to the RFC to increase the number of squadrons at the front. The first RFC unit to receive the new Sopwith

In a rather dilapidated state Sopwith LCT S.85 hangs from the roof of the Royal Army Museum in Brussels during the 1950s. (John Garwood)

was No. 70 Squadron, who arrived in France between May and July 1916, but by the time other units had been deployed in the field it was found that the aeroplane was already outclassed by its adversaries, even though most 1^1/$_2$ Strutters that were sent to France after May 1917 were fitted with the more powerful 130 hp Clerget. Replacement of the two-seater Sopwiths began in July, when No. 70 was re-equipped with the Camel, and by September all 1^1/$_2$ Strutters had been withdrawn from the front line. The type had given good service with the RFC, while it also did valuable work with the RNAS and later RAF, some 40 being embarked at sea with the Grand Fleet.

Small numbers of the 1^1/$_2$ Strutter were delivered to the Belgian and French air services, the type actually entering large-scale production in France, where it was known as the Sop. 1.A2 (fighter-reconnaissance form); Sop. 1B.2 (bomber) and Sop. 1B.1 (single-seat bomber). At least three Belgian squadrons were also known to have been equipped with the 1^1/$_2$ Strutter and one of these machines is preserved in the Royal Army Museum. Fitted with a 110 hp Le Rhône the aeroplane has been with the museum since the 1920s and in recent years was fully restored by the Elementary Flying School at Goetsenhoven. It is displayed without armament.

At Le Bourget the superbly restored example of a Sopwith 1A.2 (1263) is suspended in *La Grande Gallerie* alongside Guynemer's Spad 7. The machine's origins are unclear, but it may have seen civil use, for the rear cockpit has been modified to accept a forward-facing seat. No armament is fitted. A third 1½ Strutter is currently owned by the Kermit Weeks Museum in Florida. The complete airframe was purchased from Mr E. A. Jurist of Vintage Aircraft International in Nyack, New York, who had acquired it from Hector Mendizabal in South America.

Sopwith Pup

N5195. Museum of Army Flying, UK

Undoubtedly the Sopwith Pup is one of the classics of WWI. In its day this tractable little biplane inspired more genuine affection among pilots than any other contemporary aeroplane and set new standards in flying control response. The prototype (3691) went to the RNAS in early 1916 and saw initial service with No. 5 Wing at Dunkerque. Naval pilots took to the aeroplane with enthusiasm and neither the Admiralty nor the Royal Flying Corps were slow to order the type in quantity. Early in its career the Sopwith acquired its unofficial name, probably the result of a remark by Brigadier General W. Sefton Brancker,

who, on seeing the aeroplane for the first time, exclaimed: 'Good God! Your 1½ Strutter has had a pup!' The RFC knew it officially as the Sopwith Scout; to the RNAS it was the Type 9901, but to airmen of both services it was, and always would be, the Pup.

Production was brisk and the Pup saw widespread service in France with both British air arms and proved a formidable opponent to the heavier Albatros fighters. Pups were also used by the RNAS in deck-flying experiments, where the aeroplane's superb controllability was a great advantage. Various types of skid undercarriages and arresting apparatus were tried using Pups alongside 1½ Strutters and much useful work was accomplished.

By autumn 1917 the operational front-line career of the Pup was on the wane and the type was gradually replaced by the more powerful, twin-gun Camel. Pups served on Home Defence duties in the UK and latterly became the favourite mount of instructors at training squadrons, where the aeroplanes could be seen in a variety of exotic colour schemes. Pups served in the trainer role right up to the Armistice, production being sustained until as late as October 1918, when the last standard-built Pup was delivered.

The Sopwith Pup will always hold a hallowed place in WWI aviation lore and its reputation has made it a natural favourite with replica builders the world over. Yet despite the Pup's long and successful service no completely genuine example has survived. The well-

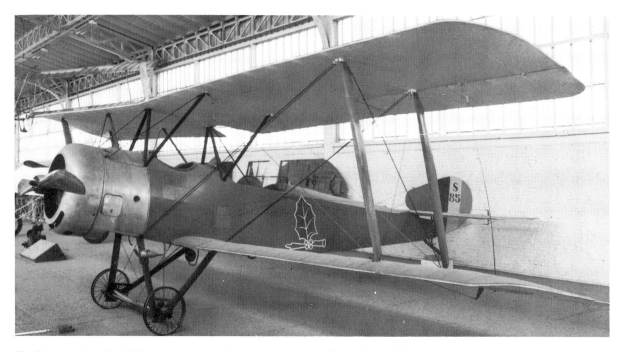

The Brussels Sopwith 1.A2 has been restored in recent years by the Goetsenhoven Elementary Flying School. (Brussels Air Museum)

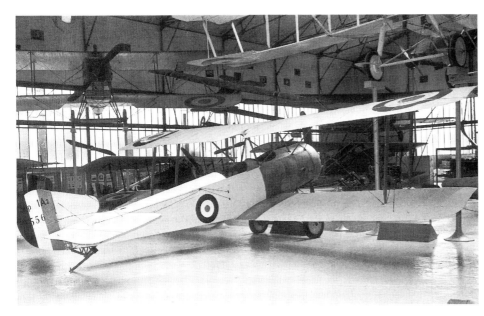

Displayed at Chalais Meudon in 1974 is the Musée de l'Air Sopwith 1.A2 now at Le Bourget. (Stuart Howe)

known airworthy 'Pup' owned by the Shuttleworth Collection is actually converted from a two-seat Dove built in 1919 while the aeroplane in the RAF Museum is a replica incorporating a number of components from several Pup airframe remains. This machine was constructed by Desmond St Cyrien of Redhill, who also built a second, more authentic, Pup using a substantial number of parts from an original Pup which had been sold as war surplus to a Mr John Halkes of Lincoln in 1919. Mr St Cyrien located the remains in 1963 and paid £25 for them! Registered as G-ABOX the Pup re-emerged in airworthy condition during 1985 fitted with an 80 hp Le Rhône rotary acquired from RAF St Athan. It is currently on loan to the Museum of Army Flying at Middle Wallop and in 1988 took part in the celebrations for the late Sir Thomas Sopwith's 100th birthday with a memorable formation flypast with a GR.5 Harrier at the Biggin Hill Air Fair.

Sopwith Triplane

N5912. Royal Air Force Museum, Hendon, London, UK

Like its contemporary stablemate, the superlative Pup, the Sopwith Triplane was a single-seat fighter armed with a single Vickers machine gun. It was fitted with the more powerful 110 hp Clerget, the first example of the new aeroplane being completed in May 1916. By that time enough experience of air combat had been gained by designers to appreciate the essential requirements for a successful fighter aeroplane: speed, manoeuvrability and a wide field of

view for the pilot. The radical triplane configuration was adopted to achieve these ideals and it met them all. General performance of the aeroplane was extremely good, its climbing performance phenomenal and its rate of roll remarkable.

Although ordered for both RFC and RNAS use, the naval service almost exclusively operated the type, having exchanged their Spad 7s for Triplanes in early 1917 to increase RFC numbers at the front. Naval Squadrons Nos. 1 and 8 had been re-equipped with the Triplane by February followed by Nos. 9, 10 and 12. B Flight of 'Naval 10', the famous 'Black Flight' led by Canadian Flight Commander Raymond Collishaw, scored many victories during May and July, Collishaw himself accounting for seven enemy machines and driving down at least another 17. The work of the naval units during the Battle of Arras earned the Triplane a considerable reputation although its operational life was brief and as early as July 1917 it was being replaced by the Camel. Nevertheless, few Allied designs made such an impact on the Germans as did the Sopwith Triplane fighters that appeared during 1917 after the Sopwith had made its startling début over the Western Front.

The RAF Museum exhibit was one of 25 Triplanes ordered from Oakley and Co. of Ilford in 1917, but only three examples were completed before the contract was cancelled – N5912 being the third and, as it transpired, the last of the batch. Although it was the intention that the Oakley triplanes would be armed with *twin* Vickers guns, contemporary photographs of the machine show it without armament, at least for a time, during its service at the School of Aerial Fighting, Marske, in 1918. The triplane was retained by the Air Ministry after the Armistice and it was displayed at the Imperial War Museum during the

The ex-Air Ministry Sopwith Triplane N5912 seen here at Hendon in 1951 for the Daily Express *Royal Aero Club Jubilee Display.* (John Garwood)

fully flew the Sopwith at the Pageant on 27 June and the following year the aeroplane participated at Hendon once more, its sprightly performance drawing favourable comment from several aeronautical correspondents.

During 1945 the Triplane re-emerged at No. 5 Maintenance Unit, RAF Kemble, along with many other aeroplanes, to be offered for public sale. Not surprisingly there were no takers in that immediate post-war economic climate and the Triplane languished for another five years. As a preliminary to the 1950 RAF Display at Farnborough a number of vintage aeroplanes were gathered at No. 39 RAF Maintenance Unit, Colerne, for restoration. Most of these were from the Nash Collection, but also included the RAE's LVG C.VI and Triplane N5912. The latter had arrived crated to be reassembled, but was found to be incomplete. There was no engine, no airscrew, the interplane struts, various fittings and bracing wires were also missing, and the fabric was shredded.

There was little time to locate original drawings and parts so corners were cut. The Nash Collection contributed a Clerget engine, while a cowling based on Camel design was produced. The latter proved to be of greater chord than the Triplane's original and the replacement airscrew – an incongruous 1929 Armstrong Siddeley Lynx – had to be packed out with washers. It still rubbed the front of the cowling, however, but at least it could be turned. Struts were carved from builders' planks, the rigging cut and welded from Tiger Moth spares, and the lower wings connected to the fuselage with suitably modified rifle-

early 1920s before being removed to Cardington aerodrome, where it lay, forgotten, until the mid-1930s.

During preparations for the 1936 Hendon Air Pageant the Triplane was retrieved by RAF Flight Lieutenant Buckle and moved to Hendon, where reconstruction was undertaken. Apart from the wing struts, N5912 was more or less complete, which was just as well, for the rebuild had to be done without the aid of drawings. Flight Lieutenant Buckle success-

Since completely restored, but not in original wartime markings, N5912 is now displayed at The Royal Air Force Museum, Hendon. (Author)

Sopwith Triplane N5486 went to Russia and never returned. It is probably the aeroplane preserved by the 'Red Banner Academy' in Monino, near Moscow. (Harry Woodman)

cleaning rods. Like the previous restoration, the pseudo-RAF markings were inappropriate to N5912, but the overall effect was considered satisfactory.

The Triplane was subsequently exhibited in the *Daily Express* Royal Aero Club Jubilee Display at Hendon in 1951 before being placed in storage at RAF Fulbeck until 1959, by which time it had acquired an authentic airscrew. The following year the Hawker Aircraft Company obtained permission from the Air Ministry to restore N5912 and it was moved to Dunsfold, where it received a new colour scheme. Following completion the Triplane was subsequently displayed at Earls Court for the 1962 Royal Tournament, thence to RAF Biggin Hill's museum hangar and then loaned by the Air Historical Branch to the Royal Naval Air Museum (now Fleet Air Arm Museum) at Yeovilton, where it was displayed for several years before being removed for a complete restoration and subsequently destined for the new RAF Museum.

Substantial work was necessary to bring the Triplane up to the required high standards. Additions included a complete instrument panel, correct cowling, metal fuselage side panels, and twin Vickers guns. Complete restoration of the airframe took place and after re-covering an authentic PC10 khaki and clear-doped scheme was applied and all metal panels brightly polished. Thus renewed, Sopwith Triplane N5912 made its first public appearance at the Science Museum in connection with the 1968 RAF Golden Jubilee celebrations before moving to its present location.

Only one other Sopwith Triplane exists and this one is in the Air Force's 'Red Banner Academy' in Monino, near Moscow. On 4 May, 1917, N5486 left the RNAS depot at the White City destined for

Russia. It was flown on the Eastern Front and by the winter of 1917–18 it had been fitted with skis in place of its original wheels. Although not confirmed, one may assume that N5486 is the Monino Triplane.

Sopwith F1 Camel

F6314. Royal Air Force Museum, Hendon, London, UK

Without doubt the Sopwith Camel was the most famous British fighter to see service in World War I and accounted for 1294 enemy aeroplanes and at least three airships, the greatest number of machines to be brought down by a single type on either side during the war.

This classic fighter appeared towards the end of 1916, designated Sopwith F1; it was powered by a 110 hp Clerget 9Z and armed with two Vickers machine guns synchronized to fire through the airscrew arc. It was in the armament that the new machine represented the greatest improvement over its predecessors, enabling British fighter pilots the means of matching opposing Albatros single-seaters on equal terms. The guns were partially enclosed in a hump-like fairing that gave rise to the 'Camel' nickname, a soubriquet that was immediately popular and eventually officially recognized. Various engines were fitted in Camels and the type entered quantity production with several sub-contractors.

In its flying qualities the F1 proved to be completely different from its more docile and tractable forebears. The Camel, in the hands of a competent pilot, was incredibly manoeuvrable, but was totally unforgiving of the kind of mistakes made by many of

The ex-Nash/Royal Aeronautical Society Sopwith F1 Camel at the 1951 RAC Jubilee display at Hendon. It wore somewhat unusual fuselage and rudder markings at that time. (John Garwood)

the poorly trained young men who were required to fly it after only a few hours of instruction. Once its idiosyncrasies could be mastered, the Camel became one of the deadliest 'dog-fighting' aeroplanes in the Allies' inventory.

Camels saw service not only on the Western Front but also, in modified form, as UK-based home defence fighters, while others were used for experimental work in flying from towed lighters at sea. From a total of almost 5500 Sopwith F1 and 2F1 Camels eventually built, six complete, genuine examples are known to have survived.

The best known British-based F1 is currently displayed at the Royal Air Force Museum and it has an interesting history which begins in April 1923, when ex-Camel pilot and journalist Grenville Manton acquired an unused, war-surplus Camel from the Aircraft Disposal Company. The log book accompanying the Camel – which did not have an engine – revealed it to have been built by Boulton and Paul Ltd. of Norwich and that it had logged barely two hours in the air. Mr Manton eventually purchased a 45 hp six-cylinder Anzani radial to power his Camel and necessary conversion work to mount the new engine took place, much of the aeroplane's fabric being replaced at the same time. Only two flights were

Re-marked F6314, the ex-RAeS Camel as displayed at the Royal Air Force Museum, Hendon. (Author)

The Camel was restored during the early 1960s and on 27 October, 1963, was rolled out of the BEA hangar at London Airport and the engine run up for the first time in many years. (John Garwood)

made, enough to show that the Camel was woefully underpowered, and this, coupled with the rather inadequate rudder area, made it a dangerous prospect. Before long an advertisement appeared in the columns of *Motor Sport* offering the Camel for sale and attracted a builder from North Wales, who collected it from Mr Manston at Tring in Hertfordshire and towed it all the way home behind his Fiat! By 1935 it had changed hands once again to become the property of a Mr D. C. Mason of Hornchurch, Essex, and the following year was taxied during the RAF Pageant at Hendon, soon after which it was bought by the Nash Collection.

After wartime storage the Camel joined Sopwith Triplane N5912 and other veterans at 39MU Colerne for 'renovation' purposes. At that time F6314 was fitted with a sub-standard cowling and its instrument panel was incomplete, and aside from a little token repainting and fitting of Dunlop motorcycle tyres, the Camel was displayed at the 1950 Farnborough Display as received. When Mr Nash decided to dispose of his valuable collection in 1953 it was purchased by the Royal Aeronautical Society, most of the aeroplanes being displayed at various events, the first of these being the 1954 Garden Party of the Society at London Airport.

The final public appearance of the Camel in its old colours was at the RAeS function held at Wisley in September 1957 and the following year saw the machine removed to Hendon, where a group of enthusiasts began long-term restoration. Little work had been done by 1960 when the Nash Collection was moved to London Airport and work was revived while the removed fabric and original airframe was minutely scrutinized in an effort to confirm the machine's original identity.

On 27 October, 1963, the fully restored Camel, now finished in 'authentic' markings, was wheeled out of its shed and the engine run up. The rotary required some fine-tuning and following minor adjustments the Camel was placed under cover at London Airport with the airscrew removed and its guns carefully wrapped. Its restored finish was representative of a No 43 Squadron Camel and became the subject of some controversy, it later transpiring that the chosen scheme was at one time worn by wartime Camel B2510. As a result of this the markings were changed to represent those of a No. 65 Squadron Camel, retaining the serial but the individual letter 'A' was replaced by 'B'. After these cosmetic changes the Camel was passed on permanent loan to the then embryo RAF Museum for eventual display.

The first public appearance of F6314 in its final form was at Abingdon in June 1968 for the RAF Golden Jubilee and subsequently at Horse Guards Parade, London, during September along with many other superbly restored veterans. After a week of fine weather a violent downpour so damaged the Camel's

new fabric that at one time a partial re-covering was considered. The Camel remained in storage thereafter until 1972, when the RAF Museum opened its doors to the public for the first time.

In October 1989, the UK's second Camel joined the Museum of Army Flying at Middle Wallop. B6291 has been loaned by restorer Desmond St Cyrien who acquired its remains in 1962. After five years' work the '70% original' Camel is destined to fly before retirement in the museum. Restoration was undertaken jointly by British Aerospace and British Caledonian – now part of British Airways.

Sopwith F1 Camel

B5747. Musée Royal de l'Armée et d'Histoire Militaire, Brussels, Belgium

This example of a Belgian Air Service Camel was donated to the museum during 1920, one of six manufactured by Clayton and Shuttleworth for use by the

Sopwith F1 Camel B5747 as originally displayed in Brussels with years of dust and grime over its original fabric well in evidence. (John Garwood)

Recently restored, the Royal Army Museum's Camel now wears the Cocotte emblem of the 11ᵉ Escadrille. (Brussels Air Museum)

Aviation militaire belge. The final number of Camels diverted for such use has been reported as 36 or 62 according to various sources. Whatever the figure, all of them had been withdrawn from use by 1922. When the Royal Army Museum's example was handed over it arrived without documentation and so its wartime history, if any, is unknown, although the white thistle marking of 9ᵉ *Escadrille* adorned the Camel's fuselage at one time.

For many years B5747, bearing the legend 'Scll' on its rudder, was displayed suspended from the museum's roof and it was possible to note the original British serial number and that a non-standard semi-circular windscreen was installed. The Camel, while somewhat grimy and weathered in general appearance, was nonetheless the only example remaining in wartime condition. In recent years the Camel, like most others in the Brussels museum, was taken down for restoration. The work was undertaken by Bierset AFB, who overhauled the 130 hp Clerget and re-covered the airframe, which now bears the insignia of 11ᵉ *Escadrille*.

Another F1 Camel survives and this is B7280 built by Clayton and Shuttleworth in 1918 and owned by the Polish Museum Lotnictwa i Astronautyki. The Camel served with No. 210 Squadron and was forced down in German territory on 15 September, 1918, exhibited post-war in Berlin's Deutsche Luftfahrt Sammlung and transferred to Poland during World War II to avoid the air raids. Currently the Camel's fuselage is devoid of fabric and the wings are in stor-

age, but its engine still forms part of the official exhibition. It is currently being restored.

America's only genuine Camel is 'N6254', currently displayed at the USMC Museum in Virginia. It was flyable until the mid-1950s, when this photograph was taken. (John Garwood)

Sopwith F1 Camel

'N6254'. US Marine Corps Museum, Quantico, Virginia, USA

One genuine Sopwith F1 Camel survives in the USA and has enjoyed a long and varied career. Although its wartime service is unknown the machine would appear to have been built by the British Caudron Company and was brought to America in 1920 by Clarence Chamberline, who had purchased the war-surplus Camel. The aeroplane became a personal 'hack' for Chamberline, who flew it regularly along the East Coast during the early 1920s. During that time a second seat was added to the rear fuselage for passenger use, but the scheme proved to be a commercial failure and the second cockpit was clumsily faired over. The Camel's existence soon became known to Colonel G. B. Jarrett, who was then collecting exhibits for his private World War I museum at Steel Pier, Atlantic City, which he formed in 1915. After some negotiation, Colonel Jarrett bought the Camel at Jersey City Airport in 1931 for just 100

dollars. Around the time of the machine's purchase its true identity was lost to posterity when the maker's plate was 'souvenired' by a New England schoolboy. Why the original serial was never recorded previously remains a mystery.

When Jarrett moved his collection to Moortown the Sopwith was repainted to represent a wartime machine and given the spurious serial of a Ruston and Proctor-built Camel, B7301. Jarrett attempted to reconstruct the markings of the 209 Squadron Camel flown by Captain A. R. Brown during his combat with Manfred von Richthofen, but due to insufficient reference material available at the time he merely painted two vertical stripes aft of the cockpit. Two Vickers guns from the Colonel's war trophy collection were fitted at this time, but sometime later the serial number was changed to A-1171 (that of a Henry Farman!).

During WWII the Jarrett collection was stored while its owner was serving in the armed services and in 1946 what remained of the exhibits, including the Camel, were transferred to Aberdeen, Maryland. In 1948 the Camel was loaned to the US Air Force, which displayed the now somewhat ravaged veteran

Another UK-based Camel is this F1 rebuilt by enthusiast Desmond St Cyrien and currently displayed by the Museum of Army Flying. (British Aerospace 8800 410 via R. Chesneau)

at the Newark Air Force Day celebrations in New Jersey. Following Colonel Jarrett's decision to sell off his collection, the Camel was bought by Frank Tallman in 1950. It was taken to Logan airport in Boston at first, where it was displayed in connection with Armed Forces Day, before moving to the New England School of Aviation for a complete restoration.

Original Camel drawings were obtained from Hawker's in the UK, spares were collected, including a pair of wheels and a number of turnbuckles, while a quantity of seasoned ash and spruce was purchased to replace many rotted, broken and missing parts of the airframe. Metal parts that were either corroded or rusted were sandblasted and the original 110 hp Le Rhône was put into running order, with two others being acquired, including a 9J located by Ed Maloney of the Claremont Air Museum. Progress was painfully slow and after four years the assistance of Ned Kensinger, who offered to rebuild the Camel in exchange for Tallman's Nieuport 28.C1, was welcomed.

Initially the Camel was destined to be completed as a static exhibit, but Kensinger became more ambitious as time passed and airworthy status became the ultimate goal. This was finally realized in 1955, when the aeroplane took to the air once more. For safety's sake the Camel was fitted with a non-standard hand-pumped fuel system in place of the original pressure tank. The old system was considered a fire hazard and so the restored Camel's engine was fed from a small 15-gallon wing-mounted gravity tank, which was supplied by the main fuselage tank. More obvious as a deviation from standard was the steel tube undercarriage, while the airscrew was a copy of an authentic specimen loaned by a museum. The Camel made its first public appearance at the 1955 National Air Show in Philadelphia, although it was not allowed to fly during the event, officials considering it a danger to the crowd. Since that time, however, the Camel has flown many times without incident.

In more recent years the Camel has passed through several hands and was used in several films, including Warner Brothers' *Lafayette Escadrille* and *Hell Bent for Glory* before its purchase by the Aeroflex Museum for $40,000. When this organization closed the Camel passed, on extended loan, to the US Marine Corps Squadron in Virginia.

Sopwith 2F1 Camel

N6812. Imperial War Museum, Lambeth, London, UK

The prototype F1 Camel was, as has been related, completed in late 1916 and the aeroplane was soon ordered in quantity by the RNAS and RFC. At the same time the Sopwith design staff were working on a replacement for the Sopwith Baby single-seat seaplane. The result, prepared under the company type designation FSI, was known as the Sopwith Improved Baby and serials N4 and N5 were allocated to two prototypes ordered in January 1917. In the event the seaplane fighter was not proceeded with, but a landplane version was ordered in large numbers. The new fighter boasted a detachable rear fuselage (for ease of stowage aboard ships) with special control runs to the tail unit, one off-set fixed Vickers gun mounted on the fuselage, a Lewis gun on an overwing mounting and steel tube interplane struts. Sopwith gave the aeroplane, in its final form, the designation 2F1 and in service it became known as the 'Ship's Camel' or 'Split Camel'.

First deliveries began in late 1917 and many of the naval Camels were allotted to battleships, battle cruisers, cruisers and early carriers such as HMS *Manxman, Furious* and *Vindex*. 2F1s operating from capital ships had to fly from minuscule platforms, employing techniques pioneered by the RNAS with Sopwith Pups. Somewhat more hazardous experiments involved taking off from a towed platform (lighter) behind a destroyer. Camels using skids instead of wheels proved troublesome, but conventional machines were more successful.

Seven Sopwith 2F1 Camels made aviation history on 19 July, 1918, by mounting the first true carrierborne air strike. Taking off from HMS *Furious* to bomb the Tondern Zeppelin base they destroyed *L54* and *L60* in their sheds. Only two of the seven Camels managed to rejoin their naval task force after the action, but it was a portent of what would follow in another world war.

Of the four WWI aeroplanes originally displayed at the Imperial War Museum only two remain, the others having been removed to Duxford. One survivor is Sopwith 2F1 Camel N6812, the only example anywhere in the world fitted with a 150 hp Bentley BR1 rotary and an aeroplane that shares a rare distinction with only one other extant machine, for this Camel was responsible for the destruction of a Zeppelin in 1918 and the story is sufficiently well documented that anything other than the brief résumé that follows would be superfluous.

Flown by a Canadian pilot, Lieutenant Stuart Douglas Culley, Camel N6812 was being towed by lighter into the vicinity of the Heligoland Bight with

Lieutenant Stuart Culley's famous Sopwith 2F1 Camel N6812 at Felixstowe in 1918 and seen in the configuration it appeared in when Culley shot down Zeppelin L53. (Albatros/P. L. Gray Archive)

the Harwich Force on 10 August, 1918. Three destroyers towed lighters carrying flying boats, and HMS *Redoubt* towed Culley, his Camel armed with two Lewis machine guns fixed to a special mounting above the upper wing. In support, three or more Curtiss H12 flying boats flew from Great Yarmouth to accompany the fleet, under the command of Major Robert Leckie.

At 08.30 hrs a Zeppelin, *L53*, was sighted and in turn the Harwich Force had been spotted by a flotilla of German torpedo-boats, which were quick to alert their seaplane stations in the Bight. Thus was the stage set for a battle royal. The commander of the Harwich Force, Rear Admiral Tyrwhitt, ordered his ships out to sea, a deliberate attempt to draw the Zeppelin away from the coast and, ultimately, the range of protective German seaplanes. Smoke screens

completed the illusion.

Culley took off safely from *Redoubt*'s lighter (No. H5) at 08.58 hrs, running only five feet before the 30 kt speed of the destroyer gave sufficient headwind for the Camel to become airborne. It took over 30 minutes for Culley to reach 18,000 feet, with the enormous black airship still beyond reach. A further 28 minutes and Culley was in range, just, and stalling the Camel, which was now at its maximum ceiling, he opened fire. His subsequent report was typically brief:

'08.58 hours, flew from lighter to attack Zeppelin from 300 feet below. Fired seven rounds from No. 1 gun which jammed and a double charge from No. 2. Zeppelin burst into flames and was destroyed.'

Meanwhile Stuart Culley found it necessary to switch over to the Camel's gravity tank as the main one was empty and he was experiencing some difficulty in re-locating the flotilla. With only 20 minutes' fuel remaining it was impossible to make landfall, so the pilot considered ditching beside some Dutch fishing vessels. However, almost immediately he sighted his own force and at once made a descent onto the waves beside HMS *Redoubt*, which not only plucked him from the water but also salvaged the machine and returned it to its lighter. Subsequent examination showed that the fuel tank contained a mere pint of petrol. Culley was later awarded the DSO for his action, although the VC had been recommended.

The subsequent wartime career of N6812 has not been recorded, although at some stage its armament was returned to original configuration before being handed over to the Imperial War Museum in the early 1920s. The Camel probably owed its preservation to a 1917 Air Council decision to establish a National

N6812 as displayed in the Imperial War Museum at Lambeth for many years. (John Garwood)

Fully restored in the late 1980s by Skysport Engineering. Culley's N6812 now comes within a whisker of its original 1918 configuration. (Author)

Aeronautical Museum, for which exhibits were being set aside during the last year of the war. Almost immediately after the Camel had been donated by the Air Ministry it passed to the Science Museum at South Kensington, being temporarily stored there since the War Museum was in course of moving from Crystal Palace. 1924 found N6812 still in a series of crates marked with the identification number and date of acquisition, 1923–683, and it remained so until 1932, when a shortage of space demanded its removal to RAF Cardington.

When the Imperial War Museum had established itself in its third home, the former Royal Bethlehem Hospital at Lambeth opened up to the public for the first time in 1935, Culley's Camel was one of three aeroplanes displayed in the Air Services Rooms. The machine on view had obviously been repainted since 1918, and incorrectly at that, while other anomalies included the absence of both cable and quick release clip under the undercarriage spreader bar and an airscrew about nine inches less in diameter from standard. This is the one still fitted, which bears the inscription 'Manufactured by Humber Ltd., England, B.R.1 150' with a suffix of figures '893' and '37133' both boxed. It was in this guise that Camel N6812 entered another war and on 31 January, 1941, a German bomb made a direct hit on the IWM building. Among the items damaged was the Camel, which was removed for storage. When the Imperial War Museum re-opened after the end of hostilities the Camel was not among the exhibits and it was not until

1953 that it was displayed again, this time at the Royal Tournament at Earls Court.

A considerable amount of 'restoration' had been undertaken by Cardington engineers for the Camel's Earls Court début, but the result was far from admirable. The 2F1 tubular struts had been replaced by F1-style *wooden* ones, while the entire uppersurfaces had been doped in a bright 'Peacock' green and the undersides, including metal areas, *painted* light cream. The serial number had been changed, inexplicably, to F3043, which was that of a Vickers Vimy bomber! This was corrected in 1955.

During 1963 the IWM was visited by Major Stuart Culley himself, then resident in Milan, who gave the museum's curator a photograph of N6812 at the time of its engagement with *L53*. Major Culley also revealed that his Camel had its undersurfaces doped in a light blue. When some of the bogus cream paint near the undercarriage was scraped away, the original blue was revealed.

The author would be interested to know whether the covering removed in the early 1950s was the *original* material of 1918 merely re-doped, in which case a layer of blue would have been seen under the khaki of the fuselage undersides. Unfortunately it appears the Cardington team failed to preserve the fabric. Since the wings were clear-doped when the Camel was presented to the IWM in 1923 one must assume they were either re-covered after 1918 or were from another Camel altogether.

Today the Camel hangs in the IWM's new exhibition hall, following a thorough overhaul and recovering by Skysport Engineering of Bedfordshire. It now carries the correct armament and wears a more authentic finish with correct tail striping, serial presentation and PC10 colour scheme with clear-doped linen undersurfaces as opposed to the pale blue the Camel wore when Culley destroyed *L53*. N6812 does now however carry the correct steel tube centre-section struts and twin Lewis guns over the upper wing, and all the particular features of the 2F1 Camel.

Sopwith 2F1 Camel

N8156. National Aviation Museum, Rockcliffe Airport, Ontario, Canada

One must travel to Canada to examine the only other surviving 2F1 Camel, an ex-RAF machine manufactured by Hooper and Co. in 1918. N8156 was one of eight Camels purchased in 1924 from war-surplus stock with the purpose of entering them into service with the newly formed Royal Canadian Air Force.

Although 2F1 Camels, all the machines were powered by 130 hp Clerget motors instead of the Bentley normally associated with the variant. Four were part of a contract placed with Arrol-Johnston Ltd. of Dumfries: N7357, N7364, N7367 and N7369, the latter being the last delivered. A single example of a Clayton and Shuttleworth Camel was N8204, again a

final delivery, while the three others were Hooper-built N8151, N8153 and N8156.

The Canadian 2F1s were among the longest survivors of the type, since four years later N7356 was still in use by the RCAF Exhibition Flight at the principal station of the time, Camp Borden, and it gave a flying demonstration at Toronto in 1928.

It is known that N8156 was at Camp Borden in August 1925 for ground training and 11 years later the Camel was displayed at the National Research Council's aeronautical museum in Ottawa, Ontario, until 1940, when it was stored except for occasional display purposes. The aeroplane was loaned to the Canadian War Museum in November 1957, who passed it on to RCAF No. 6 RD Trenton for restoration. When it emerged the Camel had been painted in pale khaki and as a tribute to then Chief of Air Staff finished with the 'dumb-bell' insignia of No. 210 Squadron. Although the original serial number was retained the new scheme was obviously intended to give the impression of an F1 Camel, but thankfully no structural changes were made, the single Vickers gun was still in place, this having been the armament since Camp Borden days; none of the 1924 purchase had Lewis guns fitted.

Perhaps due to the highly polished metal fuselage panels it was noted that the cockpit appeared to have been enlarged fore and aft with the ply-covered area at the front deleted. This feature dated from the machine's earliest years and was shared by at least one other of the original eight, N7367.

Sopwith 2F1 Camel N8156 went to Canada in 1924 and is the sole survivor from a group of eight. It is seen here in the early 1960s after its first restoration.

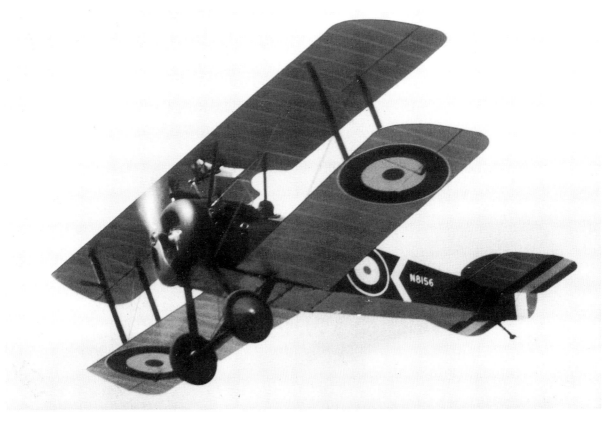

N8156 makes one of its final flights in 1967, piloted by Wing Commander P. A. Hartman. (NAM via J. M. Bruce)

In 1966 the Camel was transported to Sycamore, Illinois, USA, where master craftsman Carl Swanson had been contracted to restore the machine to an airworthy condition. After a year the work was complete and the result was an authentic-looking 2F1 built to exacting standards thanks to a complete set of over 200 drawings purchased from Hawker Siddeley. Anomalies in armament and cockpit fittings had all been corrected and the final work had been a finish representative of a Camel flown by Lieutenant William S. Lockhart, RNAS, from the turret of HMAS *Sydney* during 1919. Photographs lent by Mr Lockhart, then resident at Parsippany, New Jersey, provided reference for the markings.

Following its return to Canada, N8156 made its last flight on 10 June, 1967, in the hands of Wing Commander P. A. Hartman, during the Armed Forces Day at Rockcliffe, Ontario. The Camel was subsequently put on display at the Canadian War Museum in Sussex Drive during 1984.

Sopwith 7F1 Snipe

E6938. National Aviation Museum, Rockcliffe Airport, Ontario, Canada

The Snipe was designed in mid-1917 as a successor to the Sopwith Camel and the intention was to use those engines standardized for the earlier type and 150 hp Bentley BR1, 150 hp Gnome Monosoupape, 130 hp Clerget 9B and 110 hp Le Rhône 9J rotaries were all regarded as suitable power units. Six prototypes were ordered in various configurations and the fourth, B9965, was the first to feature the two-bay wing cellule which would become standard for production machines.

Test reports on the new aeroplane were guarded, but despite this the Snipe was placed into large-scale production and the first examples began to appear in the summer of 1918. Production Snipes were substantially similar to B9966 – the fifth prototype – but the fin and rudder areas were further increased. The design of certain internal components and members had also been revised, the original Lewis gun replaced by twin fuselage-mounted Vickers guns, while electrical heating equipment and oxygen apparatus were

Sopwith Snipe E6938 seen at Los Angeles Airport in 1953 for a USAF air display. At that time it belonged to the County Museum. (John Garwood)

fitted as standard. Steel tube undercarriage members replaced the wooden versions of the prototypes. The Bentley BR2 remained the standard powerplant and although the 200 hp Clerget 11Eb was an alternative it appears only one Snipe, E2340, was fitted with one.

No. 43 Squadron was the first RAF unit to receive the type, their first patrol with the new machines being made on 23 September, 1918. The following month No. 4 Squadron Australian Flying Corps and No. 208 Squadron RAF received Snipes, although the war ended before the aircraft could make any significant contribution. Had hostilities continued any longer, Snipes would have replaced Camels on shipboard duties and in home defence units, several examples of the latter equipping four such squadrons after the Armistice.

The Snipe remained the RAF's standard single-seat fighter for several years after WWI, serving in Egypt, India, Iraq and Turkey. For training purposes a two-seat version of the Snipe was developed and the type was not withdrawn until 1927.

During 1923 the Hawker Aircraft Company overhauled a large number of Snipes for despatching overseas to Middle East RAF stations. A change in Air Ministry planning resulted in several machines being surplus to requirements and they were put up for sale. Former RFC pilot Reginald Denny, the well-known film actor, purchased three of the Snipes in 1926 and shipped them to Hollywood for use in motion pictures. The Snipes first appeared in *Wings*, made in 1927, while stills from *Hell's Angels* show them lined up together on the 'Allied aerodrome'. Hollywood did not treat its 'stars' very kindly; by the time the depression years arrived they were in a sorry state and the City of Los Angeles subsequently became their new owners. One of them, E6938, was placed in the County Museum, while the others were presented to the Educational Department of the City of Los Angeles and were presented to local schools.

E6938, which also carried the US Civil registration 6638, was one of 100 Snipes built by the Nieuport and General Co. Ltd., but its RAF history is obscure. After many years the Snipe was loaned to the USAF, arriving at the Norton Air Base in California during 1942. The aeroplane formed part of a display held at the National Orange Show, Bernardino, California,

The state of E6938 was poor indeed when engineer Jack Canary took it over for complete restoration in late 1953. (John Garwood)

125

A photograph of E6938 during restoration work undertaken by Jack Canary. The engine is a Bentley BR2. (John Garwood)

in March 1950 and three years later exhibited at both the Los Angeles International Airport and North American Aviation, one of whose engineers, Jack Canary, offered to rebuild the airframe if it was turned over to him.

Stripping down of the airframe began in September 1953 and most of the following year was spent cleaning, repairing and replacing various parts. Possibly the biggest job of all was the enormous amount of correspondence Canary undertook to uncover information on rigging, instruments, cockpit fittings, engine and a number of other items. During 1955, as more data began to arrive, assembly of the airframe began in earnest. The original airscrew was missing, one from a Curtiss Jenny having been a temporary fitting, and a company was sought who could manufacture one from scratch with only scanty reference material. The machine's Bentley BR2 was found to be in fair condition, but required extensive re-bushing and the replacement of several missing parts. Two magnetos were built by a UK firm who had bought out the company that originally produced the wartime magnetos for Bentley. Few instruments had survived and drawings of the originals were obtained from S. Smith & Sons in London so that exact replicas could be made of the missing items.

As Canary's project progressed more and more individual enthusiasts and various manufacturers became interested and offered assistance. The Northrup Aeronautical Institute rebuilt the wing panels and covered them with fabric donated by the Flightex Company, while the Dunlop Company re-rimmed the wheels and fitted them with the correct smooth-surface tyres. Many other people offered helpful advice and gradually throughout the 1950s the Snipe took on its original appearance.

By 1960 most of the restoration work was complete and the machine was finished in the correct PC10 colour and bearing the markings of No. 208 Squadron, which included a bright red cowling which may, or may not, be authentic. Initially the Snipe was fitted with dummy Vickers guns, but original weapons acquired from individual collectors were subsequently fitted. The restored Snipe was flown once at California's Torrance Municipal Airport before being loaned to the USAF Museum at the Wright Patterson AFB, being displayed there for the first time in June 1961. Ownership then passed to the Canadian War Museum, who purchased the Snipe on 7 February, 1964. On 21 May that year the aeroplane made its first flight at Rockcliffe piloted by Wing Commander P. A. Hartman. It was last flown in June 1967.

During 1970 British enthusiasts were treated to the appearance of the Snipe, on loan, first to the RAF College, Cranwell, and then the Science Museum in London. It is currently on display at the National Aviation Museum.

Although, as noted, the Snipe arrived too late in the war to see much action, E8102 earned its place in aviation history on 27 October, 1918, as the aeroplane in which the Canadian airman Major W. G. Barker, then attached to No. 201 Squadron, fought the outstandingly courageous combat for which he was awarded the Victoria Cross. This action took place over Foret de Mormal against a large formation of Fokker D.VIIs, and although badly wounded in one arm and both legs, Barker shot down three German fighters in flames, the flight ending with Barker crashing his Snipe behind Allied lines. The remains of the machine were salvaged and preserved as a war memento by the Canadian government.

The fuselage of E8102 has been in the possession of the Canadian War Museum since the war. It still has a few instruments, but the wings, undercarriage, engine and tail are all missing. The centre-section and struts remain, however, and the port side bears the original fabric doped in PC10 complete with RAF roundel, five vertical white stripes and the serial number.

Sopwith 7F1 Snipe

Serial unconfirmed. National Air and Space Museum, Washington DC, USA

Of the three Snipes brought to the USA by actor Reginald Denny, one is currently preserved in Canada, as already described, one was wrecked by vandals in the late 1920s and the third, based for many years

Major Barker, VC's, famous Snipe E8102, or what is left of it, is currently on loan to the Canadian War Museum. (NAM 13852)

with Cole Palen at Old Rhinebeck, is now with the NASM collection. Following film use, the latter machine was purchased by J. M. Romberger of Endicott, New York, from Clarence Chamberline for $75. In 1930 Romberger soloed the Snipe, after only four hours of instruction in a Waco 9, and continued to do so until October 1931, when he presented the aeroplane to the Roosevelt Field Museum. It was displayed there until the airport had to close in order to make way for a new shopping centre. Cole Palen

successfully bid for six of the Roosevelt Field aeroplanes, including the Snipe, which was in fairly good shape although unrestored and apparently still covered in its original fabric. A complete overhaul was made and an engine-starting problem was cured when the oil and fuel lines were interchanged and fitted to their correct locations on the engine. Powered by a 130 hp Clerget the Snipe first flew from Old Rhinebeck in 1962 and was a regular part of the museum's air shows until 1966, when its flying career was curtailed as engine failure compelled pilot Paul Richards to make a forced landing. The Snipe was badly damaged, but was subsequently rebuilt by Gordon Bainbridge, who installed a 230 hp BR2 Bentley and the machine was 'retired' to Old Rhinebeck's museum building. At the end of the 1987 flying season, 'E8105' was dismantled and moved into one of the collection's flight hangars and is being restored by Carl Schneide for the museum's new WW1 gallery.

Spad 7C.1

S.254. Musée de l'Air et de l'Espace, Le Bourget Airport, France

Much of the design geometry and form of wing bracing employed by Frenchman Louis Bechereau for his

Sopwith 7F1 Snipe 'E8105' seen at Old Rhinebeck in 1983. It is now with NASM in Washington DC on long-term loan. (H. Van Dyk Soerewyn)

Guynemer's famous Spad 7.C1 S.254 was displayed in Paris during 1917 before and after the ace's death in September 1917. (John Garwood)

Guynemer's Spad S.254 as displayed in the Court of Honour, Les Invalides, Paris in 1960. (John Garwood)

alarming mid-engined Spad A-2 of 1915 were incorporated into the Spad 7, a conventional single-seat fighter of exceptional neatness. It was powered by the Hispano-Suiza 8A, a water-cooled V-8 designed by the Swiss engineer Marc Birkigt. The 'Hisso' would become recognized as a milestone in aero engine design and Bechereau designed his new aeroplane around it – the result was a WWI classic.

The general performance of the new Spad (an acronym of the *Société anonyme pour l'Aviation et ses Dérivés*) was promising and it entered production in 1916 with the official designation of Spad 7.C1. Deliveries of the new aeroplane were impeded by problems in radiator manufacture and only 495 had been delivered by 1 August, 1917. More than 50 *Escadrilles de Chasse* were operating the type by then, however, and the Spad had already acquired an excellent reputation. About 3500 were eventually built and the type served long after the arrival of the

twin-gun Spad 13, which suffered initial problems with its 200 hp geared Hispano-Suiza powerplant.

The success of the Spad 7 is a matter of record. Two British contractors built the type for RFC use, while the aeroplane fought on until the Armistice with French, Belgian, Italian and American units; examples were also built in Russia. Many of the Allies' leading airmen flew the Spad 7 with aplomb and perhaps its greatest exponent was the French ace Georges Guynemer, who scored 54 victories before his death in September 1917, many of them on Spad machines.

Following an amazing restoration which included reinstating the original fabric, Guynemer's Spad now takes pride of place at Le Bourget. (Jon Guttman)

Preserved in Czechoslovakia is Spad 7, 11583. It is seen here as originally displayed in Prague's National Technical Museum (Albatros/P. L. Gray Archive)

Guynemer flew several Spads throughout his career and one of them has survived, possibly one of the most historically important of all extant WWI aeroplanes. Following Guynemer's death, S254, which he last flew in July 1917, was taken to the Musée de l'Armée at the Hotel des Invalides in Paris and exhibited to a mourning public. A year later it was placed in the Court of Honour at the Invalides, and over the next 58 years the machine suffered badly. It was not until 1975 that the new director of the Musée de l'Air *Vieux Charles* should at last receive the restoration it demanded. The Spad was transferred to the museum's workshops at Meudon, where work began in 1981, the full restoration taking some four years.

As currently displayed at *La Grande Gallerie* the Spad is a superb example of restoration for it still bears its *original* fabric covering with all markings intact. The Musée de l'Air has set a precedent for all future aeronautical renovations by removing the original fabric, treating it chemically with assistance from technicians at the Louvre, re-covering the restored airframe with muslin and then carefully pasting the original linen back in place *on top of the new material* and with colours retouched where necessary. The results are extraordinary. Future generations can now study the Spad secure in the knowledge that its markings are original as opposed to a reconstructed scheme. Although many museum specimens have been carefully painted to match original specifications, which method is more historically important, indeed, desirable?

At least five other Spad 7s survive in Europe. 11583 has recently been restored in Czechoslovakia and is owned by the Vojenske Museum (Expozicé Letectvá a Kosmonautiky) at Kbely Airport in Prague. Powered by a 180 hp Hispano-Suiza this Spad served with the Third Air Regiment at Nitra between 1919 and 1935 and was subsequently based at the Westczech Aeroclub Plzen until 1930. The National Technical Museum exhibited the machine from 1937 to 1980, when it was dismantled and transferred to Kbely in November for full restoration. The Spad is now painted in four-colour French camouflage with Czechoslovakian military markings and its powerplant is in running order.

An ex-Tallmantz Spad with the constructor's

The Czechoslovakian Spad 7 as now exhibited at Kbely following restoration in the early 1980s. (Stuart Howe)

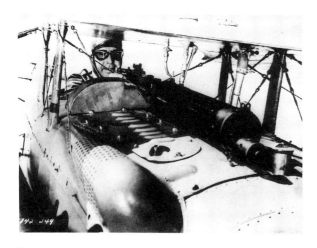

number 248 is currently displayed at the Imperial War Museum's Duxford facility near Cambridge in the UK. Fitted with an original 220 hp Hispano-Suiza, the machine's true identity is unclear, although the wings are known to have been built by Mann Egerton, so the machine would, fittingly, appear to have returned to its roots. What *is* known is that the Spad served with the AEF during the war and was shipped to the USA following the Armistice. It was later sold to Paramount for film use and became a regular air show participant during the 1950s until acquisition by the Aeroflex Museum, thence to the now defunct Wings and Wheels collection. At the Christie's auction held on 6 December, 1981, it was purchased by a member of the Blériot family, who generously made it available on loan to IWM Dux-

Veteran film actor Fred McMurray 'flies' the ex-Tallmantz Spad 7 for the Hollywood movie Men With Wings *made in 1938. Note the spurious ammunition 'feed box'.* (Via John Garwood)

The Spad 7 painted realistically to resemble a French Air Force machine for use in Men With Wings. (John Garwood)

Some 'Great War' relics formerly owned by the late Paul Mantz for film work. Seen here in 1957 are a Spad 7, a brace of Nieuport 28 fighters (one of which is believed to be the machine currently with Vintage Aero Ltd.) and, in the background, a DH4. (John Garwood)

The ex-Tallmantz Spad as currently displayed at IWM, Duxford. (Author)

The Paul Mantz Spad 7 was flown by Major K. S. Brown during the 1957 Eglin Air Force Base display. By then it had been painted to represent Eddie Rickenbacker's famous Spad 13, 'Old No. 1'. (John Garwood)

ford, where it arrived during February 1982. It is currently displayed in pseudo-French camouflage and spurious 94th AS markings.

Spad 7.C1

S.1420. Museo Storico AMI, Vigna di Valle (Rome), Italy

The *Aeronautica del Regio Esercito* (Royal Army's Air Service) received its first Spad 7s in March 1917, initially equipping 77ᵃ, 91ᵃ *Squadriglia*, followed by 71ᵃ and 72ᵃ and others. The Spad became the mount of three of the top five Italian aces: Francesco Baracca (34 victories), Pier Ruggiero Piccio (24) and Fulco

Ruffo di Calabria (20). Less manoeuvrable than its competitors, the Spad was highly regarded because of its excellent engine and sturdy airframe. The last Italian Spads were retired in 1926.

S.1420 belonged to Ernesto Cabruna, a non-commissioned officer of the *Carabinieri* promoted to officer status through his fine performance. Flying this actual machine on 29 March, 1918, Cabruna fought alone against 11 enemy aeroplanes. By the end of the war, Cabruna was credited with eight aeroplanes and two balloons.

The Spad was first exhibited at the Genoa war trophies display in 1921 and on 25 March, 1923, it was donated to Cabruna's hometown Tortona, in the Alessandria province. In October 1934 it was placed at the entrance of the fabulous Milan Aviation Show but by then it lacked its lower wing panels and the overall condition was very poor. Returned to Tortona after the show, S.1420 was eventually walled up in a cellar to protect it during the stormy summer of 1943 which saw Mussolini's downfall, the Armistice and the beginning of the civil war. Around 1968 the ace's sister, Fillide Cabruna, and Countess Maria Fede Caproni persuaded the town to donate the aircraft to the Italian Air Force, so S.1420 was removed from its hiding place and taken to Vigna di Valle, where it was completely restored.

It is currently on display at the Museo Storico AMI at Vigna di Valle. It bears the red heart insignia of the 77ª *Squadriglia* and the Tortona badge on the fuselage sides, and 'kill' markings on the fuselage. Several inaccuracies include a very strange paint scheme (hand-brushed brown over buff), no serial, machine gun or tyres. It is also likely that at some point during its service S.1420 carried a large Roman numeral XIII (for 13th Gruppo to which 77ª *Squadriglia* belonged), but this is not currently carried.

The museum owns another Spad 7, but this remains in storage at the time of writing. It has an interesting history, however.

Fulco Ruffo di Calabria, descended from the famous 18th-century soldier-cleric Cardinal Fabrizio Ruffo, became Italy's fifth highest ace. After Baracca's death, Ruffo succeeded him as CO of 91ª *Squadriglia*, the élite fighter outfit known as *la squadriglia degli assi* (the aces' squadron) because of the high proportion of outstanding scorers in its ranks. Ruffo adopted the *testa di morto* (skull and crossbones) as his personal insignia.

In April 1919, the Italian government decided to present a number of aces with the machines they had flown during the war and Ruffo was among those thus honoured. In 1923, Ruffo donated his Spad to the Royal Aero Club of Naples and it is recorded that it was exhibited, still sporting its lugubrious insignia, at the Grand Hotel for a ball held on 3 May. The Spad

Displayed at the Italian Air Force Museum in 1986 was Spad 7, S.1420, flown during 1918 by Ernesto Cabruna. The red heart insignia of the 88ª Squadriglia is prominent on the fuselage sides. (Stuart Howe)

was later on show at Naples' Capodichino airfield until requested by the *Regia Aeronautica* (Royal Air Force) for the great show held in Turin in 1928 to celebrate the tenth anniversary of the victory in World War I. From Turin, the Spad travelled south again, joining the embryo historic collection being gathered at the *Accademia Aeronautica* (Air Force Academy), then housed in the royal palace at Caserta. In 1934 Ruffo's aeroplane was among those displayed in Milan. In 1935 its condition was described as 'Spad aircraft with engine, without instruments, of Ruffo di Calabria'.

In 1943 the Accademia moved to Forli, leaving the collection at Caserta, and in 1944 the royal palace housed Alexander's headquarters. Part of the collection, however, survived on site until the late 1960s, when, with the Italian Air Force making an effort to establish its museum, substantial remnants were recovered. Ruffo's machine, its identity forgotten, was thus rebuilt into an anonymous Spad 7 and is used today as a travelling exhibit at air shows, ceremonies and other public events. It is painted in completely false colours and bears Baracca's prancing horse. When not mobile, it is stored at Vigna di Valle.

Described as a replica, it is instead an *original*. The wing ribs still bear factory inspection stamps, the metal parts all have original part numbers stamped, and the cockpit is far more complete than that of Gabruna's S.1420. Setting aside the markings question, it is a national shame that the very existence of an ace's aircraft should be jeopardized by repeated dismantling, transporting and temporary display.

Spad 7.C1

S2489. Museo Baracca, Lugo di Romagna, Ravenna, Italy

Francesco Baracca, a cavalry officer, gained his wings on 9 July, 1912. His first operational machine was the two-seater Nieuport 10, known as '18 mq' in Italy because of its wing area. As the war progressed, Baracca flew the Nieuport 11 and 17, receiving a Spad 7 in mid-1917 and he liked this so much that he turned down the Spad 13 after a test flight. Baracca's long career ended on 19 June, 1918, when he did not return from a ground-attack mission over the Montello. He had scored 34 victories. The engine of the Spad in which Baracca was shot down is displayed at Vigna di Valle. His prancing horse insignia was presented years later by his mother to a young racing driver named Enzo Ferrari: it became the official insignia of his team's Alfa Romeos and, later, of his own racing cars.

A complete Spad 7, serialled S.2489, is displayed at the Museo Baracca in the ace's hometown of Lugo di

Spad 7.C1 S.2489 was once flown by the revered Italian air ace Francesco Baracca and is preserved at Lugo di Romagna. It has recently been fully restored. (Museo Baracca)

Romagna. An inscription on the fuselage proclaims this to be the Spad flown by Baracca when he scored his 30th victory on 17 December, 1917, and the camera porthole on the lower left fuselage is noteworthy. Its history is unknown, but the aeroplane was restored in 1967 by the then Historic Aircraft Centre at Vigna di Valle. According to the technicians, its condition was so good that it could have been made flyable.

The markings are original and consist of the 91ᵃ *Squadriglia*'s Griffon on the right rear fuselage, together with the large Roman numeral X, indicating Baracca's status as CO of 10th Gruppo, and the ace's prancing horse on the left fuselage.

Spad 7.C1

'AS-94099'. USAF Museum, Wright Patterson AFB, Ohio, USA

This Spad was purchased for training use by the US Government in August 1918 and transferred to the McCook Field Museum in 1922. Re-engined in 1924 with a 180 hp Wright-built Hispano-Suiza, Model E.2, it was loaned to the Museum of Science and Industry, Chicago, Illinois, during 1932, where it remained until 1953, when it passed into the hands of the Air Force Museum. Restoration to an airworthy condition began in 1962 by the 1st Fighter Wing at the Selfridge Air Force Base in Michigan.

The work was completed on 18 June, 1965, when the aeroplane was successfully flown. The restoration proceeded slowly but steadily, with some delays incurred because of difficulty in getting proper types of wood, parts for the engine and fittings. New timber was needed for the fuselage, lower right wing and upper left wing, the latter being reconstructed by a former civilian worker at Selfridge who had a half-century of wood-working experience. It was also found necessary to change many fittings, nuts and bolts in the airframe and engine from the metric system to the Imperial system.

Restoration work required the volunteer efforts of many technicians at Selfridge. These included experts in aircraft maintenance, engine maintenance, sheet metal repair, welding, machinists and pneudraulics (bending of oil and fuel lines). Although the Spad was restored to as authentic a condition as possible, some exceptions were made to increase safety and durability. The original Spads were covered with cotton muslin, but the museum's example was re-covered with Irish linen, which should last much longer. In addition, the fabric was coated with Butyrate dope because it is fireproof; the original machines

The USAF Museum Spad 7 as now displayed at Dayton, Ohio. (USAF Museum)

The Spad 7.C1 owned by the USAF Museum was restored to airworthy condition in 1962 when this photograph was taken. (John Garwood)

At Kermit Weeks's Air Museum in Miami is another ex-Tallmantz Spad seen here in 1958 after renovation by Peter Bowers. The aeroplane was originally built by Mann Egerton & Co. and serialled B9916. (John Garwood)

bears a camouflaged finish and features, inappropriately, a 103rd AS Indian head insignia on the fuselage sides. The rudder serial, 3733, is similarly spurious.

The San Diego Aerospace Museum at Balboa Park in California displays a rebuilt Spad 7. Originally displayed at NASM it was later acquired by the Wings and Wheels Museum in Florida, thence to San Diego following the 1981 Christie's Auction. The third American-based Spad 7 is displayed at the Weeks Air Museum in Miami and was originally owned by Tallmantz. Its true identity is unconfirmed, but the number B9916 has been quoted by several sources, which would place it among a batch of 20 Spad 7s built in the UK by Mann Egerton & Co. Seven of these Spads went to the USA, B9916 among them.

Spad 13.C1

'S16541'. Old Rhinebeck Aerodrome, New York, USA

The Spad 13.C1 was designed to exploit the standard 200 hp Hispano-Suiza 8B powerplant and was fitted with twin machine guns as opposed to the single weapon carried on the Spad 7. The prototype is believed to have been S392, which was flown by *Sous Lieutenant* René Dorme at Buc on 4 April. Towards the end of the following month, the first production machines began to emerge, the initial contract being for 250 machines. However, production was slow to gather momentum and by 1 August only 17 examples had been delivered and six more were at Villacou-

were coated with cellulose nitrate dope and potentially highly flammable.

During the restoration, the Spad was checked out by Federal Aviation Agency (FAA) inspectors and the final inspection was conducted by Sgt Alfio Sapienza, project chief, and a qualified FAA inspector. The first public flight of the machine was made on 18 June, 1965, with the 1st FW Wing Commander, Colonel Converse B. Kelly, piloting the craft. On hand as an intensely interested witness was Captain Eddie Rickenbacker, 75, who had commanded the 94th Pursuit Squadron during World War I, and flying Spad 13s scored 26 victories, the highest total of any US pilot during the war.

As now displayed at Wright Patterson the Spad

The business end of the NASM Spad 13.C1, Raymond Brooks's famous 'Smith IV', which has now been fully restored. Taken in 1983 this photograph shows the aeroplane still in its original finish. (NASM 83–2241–32)

Another angle on S.7689. Note original 'iron cross' patches covering bullet holes in tail surfaces. (NASM 83–2241–37)

blay's experimental station.

As early as April 1917, and before the prototype was fully evaluated and approved, it was confidently estimated that over 2200 Spad 13s would be delivered by March the following year. This somewhat optimistic forecast was made before the almost continual problems of the 200 hp Hispano-Suiza became apparent. As it transpired only 764 examples of the new Spad had been completed by the target date and of that number fewer than 300 were in operational service by 1 April.

As soon as they became available Spad 13s were issued to the *escadrilles de chasse* either as new equipment or to replace the earlier Spad 7s. Production of the latter did not cease, however, and during the first quarter of 1918 some 1220 Spads 7 were built compared with 630 of the later type.

Problems with the 200 hp Hispano worsened. In early 1918 mechanical faults had rendered almost 60 per cent of operational Spad 13s unserviceable. It was indeed fortunate that production of engines with improved reduction gears, coupled with independent work by Marc Birkigt on the lubrication system, remedied the situation. By March the parent Spad company was producing their Type 13.C1 at the rate of 11 machines per day, while eight contractors were also turning them out. By the time full-scale production had ceased in 1919 over 8470 Spad 13s had been built. The aeroplane saw service with the air services of Great Britain, Italy and Belgium, but second only to France in terms of numbers used was the US Air Force, which bought a total of 893.

The Spad was generally well-liked by the American squadrons and was flown with considerable success by many leading fighter pilots such as Frank Luke and America's 'Ace of Aces' Eddie Rickenbacker, who once told the author he regarded the Spad as 'one of the finest planes of that era'. The 13.C1 also featured in an ambitious programme that was getting under way when the Armistice was signed and thus the three contracts for 6000 American-built Spads never materialized. Had these aeroplanes been built they would most probably have been armed with two Marlin guns as opposed to the standard Vickers; a handful of Spads in US service were so armed.

Although the Spad 13 has acquired a somewhat inflated reputation over the years it was never really the operational success it should have been. In French service the Spad 7 remained in use well into the last year of the war to plug the gaps that would have otherwise appeared in the *Escadrilles* had they relied exclusively on its intended successor.

The Spad 13.C1 that for many years has been flying regularly at Cole Palen's Old Rhinebeck aerodrome was to move to the USAF Museum at Dayton. Built in 1918, nothing is known of the Spad's immediate post-war history until 1921, when it was reported at Kelly Field. The aeroplane was subsequently owned by Colonel Benjamin Kelsy of Bethany, Connecticut, who flew it to Roosevelt Field in 1930 for repair work. Unaccountably the Colonel never returned for his machine and all communications to him from Roosevelt field were returned unanswered with no clues as to his whereabouts. After a period of time Roosevelt Field took over the aeroplane in lieu of hangar rent and placed it in their museum, where the Spad remained until 1951, when Cole Palen purchased it for $200.

The only military marking featured on the Spad at any time during its known history is the inscription 'Lt Strickland' on the port side of the cockpit. At the time Roosevelt Field took the aeroplane over, some components were missing, including the radiator, cowling, exhaust pipes and airscrew. It was obvious that at one time these items had been removed while work took place on the engine and were never replaced, being either lost or stored elsewhere.

Some time after Cole Palen had purchased the Spad he decided that the aeroplane could be restored to flying condition. The long-overdue engine repairs were made, the missing parts replaced or fabricated and minor repairs carried out. During October 1956 the Spad, more or less in the same condition as it was in 1930, took to the air once again and became a regular performer at Old Rhinebeck until 1971, when it was temporarily retired. The Spad was restored again in 1989.

Spad 13.C1

S.7689. National Air and Space Museum, USA

This particular Kellner-built Spad was one of over 890 machines purchased by the USA from France in 1918 and was fitted with a Peugeot-built 220 hp Hispano-Suiza (No. 119436) and armed with a pair of 0.30 Marlin machine guns. The Spad has recently been the subject of a thorough overhaul and restoration by the NASM team and is currently displayed with its original fabric alongside for comparison and historical interest; and S.7689 does indeed have an interesting history.

First Lieutenant A. Raymond Brooks had already served with distinction in the 139th Aero Squadron in 1918 before transfer to 22 AS of the 2nd Pursuit Group, American Expeditionary Force. Brooks's 'personal' aeroplane number was 20 and this was applied to his first three Spads in the 22nd, marked respectively: 'Smith II', 'Smith III' and 'Smith IV' ('Smith I' was his aeroplane in the 139th). The name referred to Smith College, attended by his fiancée, Ruth M. Connery. While many other pilots named their machines after wives and girlfriends, Brooks could not bring himself to say things like 'Ruth had got her tail shot off', hence the use of the college name. When Brooks was hospitalized in October 1918, 'Smith IV' was inherited by Lieutenant Clinton Jones, who scored victories with it on 27 and 30 October.

After the Armistice Ray Brooks, who had ended the war with six confirmed victories, was selected to bring back to the USA a pair of Spads for evaluation and chose Nos. 1 and 20, his beloved 'Smith IV'. Within a few years No. 1 had disappeared, presumably scrapped or sold, but No. 20 was acquired by the Smithsonian, and Paul Garber, who subsequently became the driving force behind what is now NASM, ensured the Spad's survival.

During 1985 the decision was made to fully restore Brooks's Spad and many months of painstaking work was rewarded on 12 November, 1986, when the machine was unveiled in NASM's place of honour. Invited to this special event was the Spad's original pilot, former Captain A. Raymond Brooks, once again reunited with the aeroplane he had flown operationally 68 years previously.

Cole Palen's well-known Spad 13.C1 flew at Old Rhinebeck for many years until its 'retirement' in 1971. (John Garwood)

Spad 13.C1 'S.16541' restored by Gordon Bainbridge. The fighter was destined for the USAFM but the deal fell through and it should be staying at Old Rhinebeck. (Barry Dowsett)

S6789 has been meticulously restored to its original finish and is among the finest examples of extant Spads. One of its most interesting aspects concerns the wing configuration, for the machine has the blunt wing tip shape of late Spads, but the lower tips were rounded, as per initial Spad 13 production batches, and incorporate the somewhat alarming plywood 'pocket' extension pieces.

Spad 13.C1

'S1420'. Museo Storico AMI, Vigna di Valle, Rome, Italy

Pier Ruggiero Piccio, born in Rome on 27 September, 1880, took his pilot's licence on 12 July, 1913. Already a major when Italy entered the war in May 1915, he immediately became CO of 70ª *Squadriglia*. Even when promoted to lieutenant colonel, commanding a full *Gruppo*, he continued flying operational sorties and at the Armistice ranked third amongst his country's aces with 24 victories. In 1923 he was appointed first Commandant-General of the newly independent *Regia Aeronautica*, becoming Chief of Staff when the position was created in 1925. Until 1939 he was Air Attaché in Paris.

In April 1919 Piccio was presented with a Spad 13 by the government, which, until 1928, was XIII Gruppo's gate guardian at Turin's Mirafiori field. After taking part in the 1928 Turin victory celebrations, it joined the Caserta collection, which it briefly left in 1934 for the Milan show. In 1976, Angelo Lodi listed as Item 79 of his catalogue of the Italian Air Force Museum, 'wreck of Spad 13 (engine, landing gear, parts of wings, tail assembly). Belonged to Piccio. At Vigna di Valle.' Colonel Aldo Rampelli, first director of the museum, confirmed that the engine cowlings carried a crude 'Piccio' inscription when recovered.

However, despite clear knowledge of its identity, the precious aircraft, one of the few Spad 13s known to survive, was rebuilt in the late 1970s into a replica of Cabruna's Spad 7. The so-called replica was intended for the budding collection of the *Servizio Aereo dei Carabinieri* (Carabinieri's Air Service), but delivery has been repeatedly postponed and the machine is used often for temporary displays. Normally the Spad is stored at Vigna di Valle. As in the case of Ruffo's Spad 7, something must be done to save this unique and historic aircraft. A full replica should be produced for the Carabinieri and Piccio's machine saved for posterity.

Four other examples of the Spad 13 remain in Europe, three of them in the type's country of origin. In the Musée de l'Air's new *La Grande Gallerie*, their well-known Spad 13.C1, originally thought to be 15295, is now displayed in René Fonck's colours with

Originally displayed at Chalais Meudon in the 1950s was one of the Musée's two Spad 13s. (John Garwood)

The Musée de l'Air Spad 13 in 1960 wearing its controversial camouflage scheme. (John Garwood)

At La Grande Gallerie in 1988, the Musée de l'Air Spad 13 now repainted in the Spa 103 markings of Lt René Fonck complete with light green radiator cowling. Suspended above the Spad are the Museum's 1½ Strutter, Pfalz D.XII, Junkers D.I and DH9. (Jon Guttman)

the spurious serial 'S5925'. For many years this aeroplane was displayed in a most unusual camouflage pattern before its recent renovation. Recently restored (in early 1990) to airworthy status is another French Spad 13, 4377, on long-term loan from the Jean Salis Collection at La Ferté Alais. Operated by the Meudon Memorial Flight Association, the Spad has been restored and finished to an extremely high standard. The Musée owns the remains of a third Spad 13, the fuselage and fin of a machine recorded as being 8340.

Belgium's Royal Army Museum houses SP49, which has been in the museum since the 1920s. It was restored in 1975 at the Goetsenhoven Air Force Base and currently bears the comet insignia of 10ᵉ *Escadrille* on its fuselage sides.

Spad 16.A2

A59392. USAF Museum, Wright Patterson AFB, Ohio, USA

Designed by Louis Bechereau the Spad 11 two-seater appeared in September 1917 and was powered by the troublesome 200/220 hp Hispano-Suiza motor. In general the graceful S.11 resembled a scaled-up Spad 7, although the enlarged wings featured positive stagger and pronounced sweepback. A particularly strong undercarriage unit was fitted and the machine was armed with a single forward-firing Vickers machine gun for the pilot and a single Lewis on a ring mounting for the observer.

Production of the Spad two-seater was temporarily held up by the unreliable Hispano-Suiza motors, but by January 1918 the aeroplanes were rolling off the assembly line. Although the control system of the

The Royal Army Museum's recently restored Spad 13.C1 in the markings of 10ᵉ Escadrille. (Brussels Air Museum)

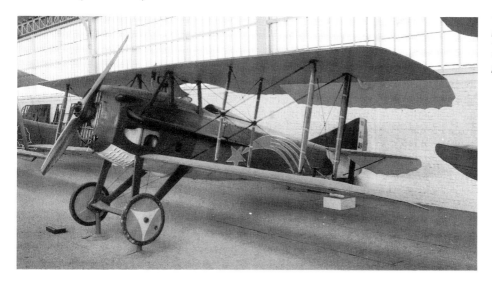

Spad 11 was found to be unsatisfactory in view of the inadequacies of contemporary Sopwith and AR types which then equipped most of the *Corps d'Armée*, it was intended to employ the Spad as a stop-gap until sufficient numbers of the superior Breguets and Salmsons became available. On 15 March, 1918, an explosion at the Bernard factory at Courneuve held up S.11 production for almost two months.

In service the Spad 11 proved disappointing with a poor climb rate. The type's high stalling speed, fully loaded, also made it difficult to fly and it was withdrawn from French service by July 1918. The *Aviation militaire belge* was less fortunate and their 4e, 5e and 6e *Escadrilles* remained equipped with their Spads right up to the Armistice. The AEF purchased 35 Spad 11.A2s to partially equip the 1st and 99th Aero Squadrons in mid-1918. They also acquired six examples of the later Spad 16.A2, which proved to be equally unsuccessful. This version was powered by the 220 hp Lorraine and one of these rare machines, 959, was flown in the war by General Billy Mitchell and was displayed in Washington DC as part of the National Air and Space Museum's collection until September 1988, when it was moved to the USAF Museum at Wright Patterson AFB for full restoration.

Billy Mitchell poses with his Spad 16.A2 two-seater in 1918. Suspended from the NASM roof until 1988, the aeroplane is now at Dayton, Ohio, with the USAF Museum. (John Garwood)

The historic Spad 16, having been suspended for many years, now has wings with a permanent droop! (H. Van Dyk Soerewyn)

Major K. S. Brown climbs into the newly restored Standard E–1 trainer for a flight in the late 1950s. This machine is now at Dayton.
(John Garwood)

Standard E-1

AS41928. USAF Museum, Wright Patterson AFB, Dayton, Ohio, USA

The Standard Aircraft Corporation of Elizabeth, New Jersey, began to supply aeroplanes to the US Signal Corps in 1917, when three Standard H-2 (formerly Sloane H-2) reconnaissance biplanes were delivered, and by late 1918 the company had become the second largest producer of aeroplanes in the USA. In addition to the manufacture of Allied types such as the DH4, Handley-Page 0/400 and Caproni, the firm designed its own types, such as the Twin Hydro, the JR-1 and 1B, and the E-1.

The first two machines of the E-1 type were delivered in January 1918. A single-seater biplane its power unit was the 80 hp Le Rhône 9C rotary engine, and a heavier version of the E-1, intended as an advanced trainer, was supplied from August 1918 onwards. This was powered by the 100 hp Gnome B-9 rotary engine, manufactured by the General Vehicle Company. Provision was made for installation of a .30 Marlin gun on the port side of the fuselage top to fire through the airscrew arc, while a camera gun could be mounted to starboard, parallel to the machine gun.

By the time the E-1s were coming off the production lines the war had already ended, but the type saw extensive use in post-war years. The US Air Service purchased 128 Standard E-1s, 30 of which were powered by the Gnome B-9 and 98 by the C-9. Two examples of the Standard E-1 survive, that in the

41928 is on permanent loan to the USAF Museum from Mr. J. B. Petty. (USAF Museum)

USAF Museum known to have been in US Signal Corps service until at least 1930. This aeroplane was placed on indefinite loan to the museum in 1959 by Mr J. B. Petty of North Carolina. A second machine, formerly marked B-123, is owned by the Virginia Aeronautical Historical Society and currently displayed in the Virginia Museum at Richmond.

Standard J-1

'22692'. USAF Museum, Wright Patterson AFB, Dayton, Ohio, USA

The Standard J-1 was a two-seat primary training machine developed from the earlier Sloane and Standard H-series designed by Charles Healey Day. When the United States entered World War I the Army ordered the aeroplane (then designated SJ) to supplement the Curtiss JN-4 Jenny, which was already in production. Concurrently Standard introduced an advanced SJ version – the JR. Although the Army bought only six of the new aeroplanes, some features of the JR were incorporated into SJ production aeroplanes, the resulting variant being known as the J-1.

Four companies, Standard, Dayton Wright, Fisher Body and Wright-Martin, built 1601 Standard J-1s before production ceased, 2700 further orders being cancelled when the Armistice was signed. The most commonly used powerplant was the Hall Scott, although some J-1s were fitted with 150 hp Hispano-Suiza and 90 hp Curtiss OX5 engines. Somewhat similar in appearance to the JN4 the Standard was

Work on this superbly restored Standard J–1 was completed in 1981 and is perhaps the finest of the many surviving specimens. (USAF Museum)

Built in 1916, Standard J–1 823H is now displayed in the Henry Ford Museum at Dearborn, Michigan. (John Garwood)

This Standard J–1 N62505 now owned by Ray Fulsom was used in the film The Great Waldo Pepper and is seen here in 1984 at the now defunct Mantz Movieland of the Air Museum in Santa Ana, California. (H. Van Dyk Soerewyn)

reported to be more difficult to fly and never gained the popularity of its more numerous and well-known contemporary.

After the war many surplus J-1s were converted into three-seaters and used for barnstorming and joy-riding, Lincoln Aircraft being active in this field, their aeroplanes being known as the Lincoln-Standard. Others starred in several aviation films and today at least 34 survive in North America, most in private ownership and most in various degrees of completeness and originality.

The USAF Museum currently owns two Standards. '22692' was built in 1916 and originally restored by Roger Lorenzen and Fred Sonne during 1962; it had been previously displayed in the Hangar 9 Museum at Brooks Air Force Base in Texas. USAF Museum personnel completed a second restoration in 1979–81 and the result is one of the most authentic-looking examples of all the surviving Standards.

The second Standard J-1 displayed at Wright Patterson was donated to the Air Force Museum Foundation in 1962 by Mr Robert Grieger of Oak Harbour, Ohio. It is fitted with a Hall-Scott engine of 100 hp and has had most of its fabric removed to reveal internal structure and method of covering.

Another fine museum-owned Standard may be seen at the Henry Ford Museum at Dearborn, Michigan. Serialled 823H and finished in the post-war colours of the Hall Flying School, the machine is thought to have been built in 1916. It was last flown during the 1934 Cleveland Air Races by Ernest C. Hall, who later became director of the Ohio State Bureau of Aeronautics. When Hall donated the Standard to the Henry Ford Museum in 1938 he commented that he knew of no other J-1s in such good condition and recalled that he had personally flown over 1000 instructional hours on the type during the war and soloed over 100 student pilots. The museum example was originally fitted with a four-cylinder Hall Scott engine which was later replaced by a Wright Hispano A.

Thomas Morse S-4B

4328. Old Rhinebeck Aerodrome, New York, USA

The Thomas-Morse Aircraft Corporation was formed during January 1917 by the English Thomas brothers with support from the Morse Chain Co. Its chief designer, B. D. Thomas (no relation), had previously played a part in designing the Curtiss 'Jenny' and early in 1917 designed a single-seat trainer, the S-4, which flew for the first time in June. The aeroplane was accepted by the US Army as the S-4B, subject to various changes, including a shorter fusel-

This Thomas Morse S–4B resides with Cole Palen. It is seen here at Richland, Wisconsin, after restoration by its first owner, the late Dwight 'Doc' Woodard. (John Garwood)

age and redesigned smaller control surfaces.

In October 1917 the US Signal Corps ordered 100 S-4Bs for advanced flying training use. Aside from a tail-heavy tendency the flying qualities were reasonable, but trouble was experienced with oil leakages and other shortcomings of the 100 hp Gnome Monosoupape engine, and when 400 improved S-4Cs were ordered during January 1918 the more reliable 80 hp Le Rhône 9C was used, although the first 50 S-4Cs were completed with Monosoupapes.

Provision was made for a 0.30 Marlin machine gun on the starboard side or, alternatively, a camera gun could be fitted. In August and October 1918 further orders for 150 and 500 S-4Cs were placed, but after the Armistice the latter were cancelled and only 97 from the August order were completed. The S-4 was employed solely in the USA, mostly by the Signal Corps, but the US Navy received ten ex-Army S-4Bs and S-4Cs, and six twin-float S-5s. The final wartime variant, and the last single-seat 'Tommy', was the S-4E of 1918, which had a shorter span and tapered wings.

After the Armistice a large number of Thomas Morse S-4s appeared on the market and were subsequently used for racing and film purposes for many years. At least 15 examples of the Thomas Morse have survived in the USA, virtually all of them the S-4C variant.

Cole Palen's S-4B 'Tommy' has an interesting history. It was originally owned by Frank Sharpless of Neenah, Wisconsin, who purchased it in 1928 and later sold the aeroplane to Roland Jack of Hortonville two years later. In 1952 Mr Jack sold the S-4B to the late Dwight B. ('Doc') Woodard of Richland Center, who related the whole fascinating story of his acquisition to WWI aeroplane enthusiast John Garwood during lengthy correspondence in the mid-1950s.

After World War II, 'Doc' Woodard settled down to run a small airfield in Wisconsin, his life-long dream of owning a genuine WWI aeroplane as yet unrealized. In October 1952, a friend told Woodard

Champion Spark Plugs were not slow to capitalize on their involvement with Woodard's 'Tommy' restoration, as this 1957 magazine advertisement testifies. (Via John Garwood)

of an old biplane he recalled having seen in a barn near Hortonville during his youth. What stuck in his mind most was the fact that when the aeroplane's airscrew was turned, the engine went round with it. Not surprisingly this fired Woodard's interest and he decided to track down the machine if it still existed. What followed is best described in 'Doc' Woodard's own words:

'My friend and I were on our way to Hortonville on a thousand-to-one chance of the old airplane still being there. Upon arrival, we were advised by neighbours that the ship was still in the hayloft, but our chances of buying the old plane were very poor. Never having seen one of the old Thomas Morse military scouts, I still wanted desperately to see it, even though I resigned myself to the fact that I would, most likely, be unable to buy it.

'We went out to the farm of Mr Roland Jack, who owned the ship. Mr Jack was very agreeable when we asked to see the old ship and seemed proud to be able to show it to us. After crawling the full length of the dusty hayloft, and looking down into a dark corner, only the outline of the top of the fuselage and engine cowling was visible under 32 years' accumulation of

dust and chaff.

'The tail group was completely buried under the hay, and the wings were piled up and partly buried in another part of the loft. Everything looked rusty and in the worst possible state of repair. After talking and discussing the history of the old airplane with Mr Jack, I was very surprised when he asked me if I thought I had enough aviation background to be able to fly the old ship. I assured him that I would not get into trouble with it, as I had 23 years of flying experience.

'I was highly elated, therefore, when he asked me if I would consider paying 500 dollars for the old plane. I gave him 100 dollars on the spot, the balance to be paid two days later when I was to come back and take it away. It was told later that before I was out of the yard Mr Jack realized that he had sold his old pet, and had some misgivings.

'Two days later we went back to Mr Jack's with a truck, and not until after an all-day struggle of pitching hay to get the ship out of the loft were we able to get an idea of the real condition of my purchase.

'From a casual glance I could see that the landing gear was broken, and the obsolete 26 × 4 tyres were beyond repair. The complete tail group was broken off by a load of baled hay that had fallen on it years ago, and with most of the weight on one side, the fuselage had taken on a permanent twist. The propeller, while still in one piece, was split, and I could see broken wing spars and ribs sticking out through the old wing fabric, which looked and felt like a poor grade of leather. The reconstruction of the old ship was rapidly taking on the appearance of a project that would involve years of time and more money than a man of my means had to spend. But I was elated because the old ship was all mine.

'I brought the ship back to my little airfield and stored it for a month in the back of the hangar, while preparations were made for reconstruction, and we studied its construction and condition. Knowing that everything which would be needed would have to be hand-made, and as all woodwork was hand-fitted, it became increasingly obvious that months of painstaking labour had been spent on each airplane in 1916 and 1917.

'Work was actually started on 1 December, 1952, by ripping the old fabric off the fuselage and emptying out at least ten bushels of chaff and corn cobs that the rats and mice had carried in. From the condition that it was in, I would estimate that at least 5000 rats and mice were born, grew up and played in that old ship. During the 30-day period when we were looking it over, we were pouring penetrating oil in the old engine to free the valves and other moving parts. At the same time, we were studying the mechanics of it, knowing that we had no one to turn to for information, and having no knowledge whatever ourselves of rotary engines. As the whole engine rotated with

Cole Palen's S–4B at Old Rhinebeck in 1983. (H. Van Dyk Soerewyn)

the propeller on a stationary crankshaft, the functions of its working parts were vastly different from anything we had ever had any experience with.

'We started out by overhauling the magneto and cleaning up the ignition system, followed by the oil system. The tank held six gallons and metered the oil into the engine at a rate of one and a half gallons an hour, the surplus oil being thrown out as the engine rotated. If the engine is throwing oil the full length of the ship while in flight, everything is normal. If not, it is then time to become alarmed.

'We discovered, much to my concern, that no carburettor was used, but merely a slide valve for air, and a metering valve for fuel with a control for each in the cockpit. I then realized that just keeping the old ship in the air was not enough – the pilot had to mix his own fuel gas and air while in flight.

'Realizing that securing tyres of the correct size would present quite a problem, I wrote to every rubber company in the United States that manufactured tyres in the old days, only to learn from each that the moulds had been abandoned years ago. The Union Switch and Signal Company, of Swissdale, Pennsylvania, who manufactured the engine, advised me that in 1919 all parts were turned over to the Army. I was also advised by the Morse Chain Company of Ithaca, New York, an evolution of the original Thomas Morse Company, that all records were destroyed years ago. News of this nature, however, travels fast, and before long, letters offering assistance of one sort of another began coming from all directions.

'A Mr Moore from Pennsylvania furnished me with the rigging manual, and the original engine technical data manual was secured from the Air Force Technical Museum at Wright Patterson Air Force Base. The propeller was sent to the Morey Airplane Company of Middleton, Wisconsin, where many hours of work were spent on it; it came back two months later looking like new.

'One day, after we were all tired of working and fitting and scraping the fuselage, we decided that we needed some diversion, and wanted to see if the engine would run. We drained the oil tank and found that it had been running previously on steam cylinder oil instead of the castor oil originally used. We poured three gallons of No. 50 aircraft oil in the tank, installed new spark plugs, the overhauled magneto, and were ready to go. By this time the engine had become thoroughly soaked with the penetrating oil that we had been pouring over and in it to loosen it up. My friend Al used a hand squirt gun to prime the cylinders with fuel, and I was sitting in the cockpit minus all fabric and wondering what I would do if the darn thing *did* start!

'Of course, by this time we had quite a few spectators standing about, and I assigned one of them, Leon Smith, to stand in such a position that he could pull the hot wire off the magneto in case it did start, and the mixer valve or the old "blip" switch be faulty. Al turned the engine over a few times and called for "Contact". On the first pull the old engine let out a roar and nearly scared us all to death. I could see that the engine was turning too fast, and that a cloud of oil was flying all over everything. The air and fuel valves didn't seem to slow it down enough, so I reached over and cut the switch just as Leon pulled the magneto wire off. Al and I were very happy to realize that the engine would actually run, but poor Leon looked like an oil-soaked black man. We therefore decided to call it a day and head for the snack bar.

'As time went on and we worked on the fuselage, we realized that we had a very serious problem ahead of us. The original stabilizer had been mangled beyond repair by the falling hay bale, so a new one had to be constructed. Since the Thomas Morse stabilizer was sort of a moulded structure, made of wood and designed to act as an airfoil to carry the weight of the tail, we saw that building one would take weeks of work. I decided, therefore, to take a chance and run an ad. in *Trade-A-Plane*. Two weeks went by with no response, so I bought some aircraft spruce, and we started to work, gluing broken parts together, and trying to get something that would resemble a pattern to work from.

'After a further week's work, I received word from a Mr Watkins of Bellefontaine, Ohio, stating that he had a stabilizer he would sell. A telephone call confirmed the fact that it was what we wanted, and the next morning found us on our way to Ohio. After 1100 miles of driving over icy roads for three days, pulling a trailer, we returned with an old 1916 airplane stabilizer – a real prize.

'By this time the old ship had taken up so much time that my other maintenance responsibilities on the airfield were running behind. I built a small shop in the back of our big hangar, however, so that work could be carried on when possible. The shop was just large enough to accommodate the fuselage or one wing at a time, and all of the re-covering and most of the woodwork was done in there.

'In the meantime, the Air Force had heard of my reconstruction attempts on the old "Tommy", and in April some officers from Truax Air Force Base came out to look at it and ask if it could be displayed at Truax on 15 May, for Armed Forces Day. This meant working night and day to get it finished, and one week before the show we could see we had a 50/50 chance of completing the job in time.

'To add to our difficulties, the publicity which had been given the old ship resulted in people coming out by the hundreds to look at it. Both the Air Force and United Press were taking pictures while we were trying to get the ship rigged, and every time they appeared on the scene it meant putting the engine cowling and propeller back on and pushing the ship outside where it could be seen. Also, during this hectic period, I was sending numerous wires to the CAA in Washington, trying to get a number issued to the ship which was small enough so that both it and the insignia would fit on the same panel. At last they issued me N74W, which was just right.

'We set 12 May as the date on which to test-hop the ship, as the CAA inspectors would then be available. A crowd of at least 500 people were on hand at the field, including United Press and Movietone News from Chicago. Everything seemed to be working out fine, and the CAA instructed me to first make a fast taxi run, and then come back and take off. When what I thought a good taxi speed had been reached, much to my surprise the old plane left the ground. In setting it back down again on a short runway with a strong cross wind a vicious ground loop occurred. I then realized that a different tail skid had to be built to hold the ship straight on the ground. The landing gear was set so far forward that it threw a great deal of weight on the tail, and once it started to swing it was almost impossible to get it stopped.

'14 May dawned bright and clear, and the new tail skid had been installed. The great day had arrived to fly the old ship to Madison, Wisconsin, for the display at Truax. It seemed as if everyone in Richland County was on hand to see it leave, and hundreds were waiting at Madison to see it arrive. At 5 pm everything was ready to go and some Air Force jets were circling the field to escort me!

'As the old "Tommy" left the ground, turning up a good 1050 rpm, I had the elated feeling that all the time, worry and money had been well spent. The old engine ran fine, and when oil started to plaster the windshield and spatter up my goggles, I knew that the oiling system was OK. The ship flew better than I thought it would, even though it isn't very stable as modern ships go, and one wonders just what it is going to try and do next. The only anxious moments that I had was when two F-86s cut across my nose as I was crossing Truax field, and the old bus cut a few fancy capers going through their slipstream!

'The show at Truax was a huge success and thousands of people were present. With the old scout parked next to the modern jets, it presented a marvellous picture of aviation progress. I am very proud of my old airplane, and have enjoyed every minute that has been spent on it. There are several ways in which I could improve its flying characteristics, but in order to do so, changes from the original design would have to be made. The "Tommy" is now as nearly as possible as it came from the factory, and since I know what its shortcomings are, I intend to leave it as it is.

'To the best of my knowledge this airplane was manufactured in 1917, and was used by the Signal Corps for scout pilot training. At the end of the war it was purchased by Mr Jack and was kept and flown by him until 1921, when he removed the wings and stored it in his hayloft, where it remained for over 30 years before being flown again . . .'

Sadly, 'Doc' Woodard died in 1957, but in 1963 his widow loaned the Thomas Morse to the USAF Museum, where it remained for ten years. Cole Palen obtained the machine from the Woodard estate in 1973 and restored it once more to flying condition. Following damage sustained during a recent airshow, the 'Tommy' is currently a static exhibit in Old Rhinebeck's museum hangar.

Thomas Morse S-4C

SC.38934. Cradle of Aviation Museum, New York, USA

This 'Tommy' was built in Ithaca, New York, in 1918 by the Morse Chain Company and numbered 552. Powered by an 80 hp Le Rhône and armed with a 0.30 Marlin machine gun, it was apparently a war-surplus machine when purchased by two men in Hasbrouck Heights, New Jersey (and assembled by Clarence Chamberline and Basil Rowe), who subsequently sold it to Louis Meier of sky-writing fame for $250. Meier flew the 'Tommy' for a few years, during which time he took part in the filming of *The Sky Raiders* starring, amongst others, Captain Charles Nungesser, the 'Tommy' painted in German markings!

The S-4C's fourth owner was Paul Kotze of North Merrick, Long Island, who purchased it from August Hauck in 1928 for 500 dollars. The aeroplane was in perfect condition, with only 20 hours' flying time, and Mr Kotze was checked out on his new prize by Roger Q. Williams, who had flown it previously on occasion. Kotze subsequently joined a small air circus for a time and participated in several air shows alongside Bert Acresta, who owned a Fokker D.VII, and 'Sunny' Harris, who had a genuine 1912 Curtiss pusher bi-plane. The 'Tommy' later appeared at the Chicago World's Fair in 1936 and from there it was loaned to the Roosevelt Field Museum at Minesola, Long Island. In 1939 the aeroplane's sojourn at Roosevelt Field was over as the museum had to be disbanded and the Grumman Aircraft Corporation undertook to fully restore the 'Tommy' to airworthy condition. Mr Kotze generously donated the aeroplane to the National Air Museum, where it remained in storage for some years. Since 1979 it has been on loan to the Cradle of Aviation Museum at Mitchell Field, Garden City in New York.

Paul Mantz's workshops in 1957. From front to rear: two Thomas Morse S–4C trainers; a pair of Nieuport 28s; a Spad 7, and another S–4C. (John Garwood)

Tom Oviatt (left) and Jim Barton in suitably Gallic attire pose with a Thomas Morse S–4C used in MGM's 1936 film Suzy, which starred Jean Harlow. It is quite likely that the Tommy is one of the 17 examples of the type still extant in the USA. (Jim Barton via Harry Woodman)

The Tommy belonging to Jim Nissen of Livermore, California, seen here in 1956 wearing spurious colours and markings. (Via John Garwood)

Voisin LA.S B2

'V955'. Musée de l'Air et de l'Espace, Le Bourget Airport, Paris, France

In spite of their somewhat frail appearance the Voisin pusher biplanes, first designed in 1914, were in fact particularly serviceable machines as ably demonstrated by their continuous employment throughout the entire war. The basis of the type's success was its strongly built steel tube airframe and an ability to take advantage of successively more powerful motors which appeared as the war progressed.

A batch of Voisin LAs (Type 3s) with 120 hp Canton-Unne (Salmson) engines were awaiting delivery to Russia when war was declared, and immedi-

The USAF Museum's Thomas Morse S–4C SC38944. It was donated in 1965 by Captain R. W. Duff of Miami and restored by Aero Mechanics High School, Detroit, Michigan (H. Van Dyk Soerewyn)

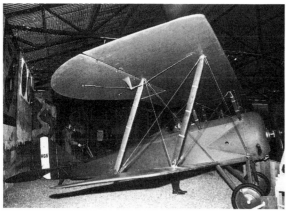

Thomas Morse S–4B seen in 1987 displayed at the US Marine Corps Museum at Quantico, Virginia, USA. (Stuart Howe)

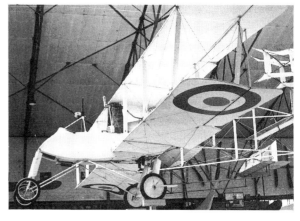

The Voisin LA.S B2 at the Musée de l'Air in 1974. These remarkable aeroplanes served throughout WWI and were more rugged than their appearance suggests. (Stuart Howe)

The LA.S B2 now exhibited at La Grande Gallerie, Le Bourget. *(J. L. Rosman)*

Currently stored away in the vaults of NASM is their Voisin LA3 seen here displayed in the Smithsonian after WWI. (John Garwood)

ately offered to the Government by Gabriel Voisin, who armed six of them with Hotchkiss guns obtained at his own expense. One of the machines, V89, flown by Frantz and Quenault, scored the first confirmed air victory for France on 5 October, 1914. Continuing their pre-war experiments with aeroplane cannons, the Voisin brothers produced the LB (Type 4), armed with a 37 mm Hotchkiss; virtually a Type 3 with staggered wings, a modified nacelle and additional bracing. A few examples had the 47 mm Hotchkiss, and while the *avion canon* was effective against stationary targets, it proved useless in air combat.

As they were developed, Canton Unne motors of increased power were fitted; the 150 hp engine powered the Type 5 or LA.S (S for *sureleve* or 'raised' – the power-unit canted forward to deliver its thrust in a downward direction), while the Type 6 (also LA.S) had the 155 hp motor with modified valves.

Escadrilles VB.1, 2 and 3 (later, 101–3) with 18 Voisins, formed the first *Groupe de Bombardement*, and the type also flew with the subsequently formed G.B.2, 3 and 4 on day-bombing raids. G.B.1's most successful attack was the poison-gas factory at Ludwigshafen on 26 May, 1915. In September 1915 the campaign was abruptly terminated, the French command having apparently lost faith in strategic bombing and thereafter Voisins bombed only at night.

At Le Bourget Airport, a superbly restored example of a Voisin LA.S B2 is displayed in *La Grande Gallerie* finished in the overall white scheme typical of many wartime machines. Built in 1915 it is fitted with a 140 hp Canton Unne. The museum also owned the nacelle and engine of a Voisin LA3 for many years, but this was transferred to the Royal Army Museum in Brussels during 1975. It is currently in storage. Another stored Voisin LA3, complete this time, belongs to the National Air and Space Museum, while at the Air Force's Red Banner Academy in Monino, near Moscow, an LA5 is displayed.

Zeppelin C.IV

55864. Musée de l'Air et de l'Espace, Villacoublay, France

The Zeppelin C.I and C.II (Ja) two-seaters were the brainchild of Paul Jaray and were constructed at the Zeppelin airship factory at Friedrichshafen during the autumn of 1917. The first series of six all-metal C.II machines were completed during early 1918 and were fabricated completely from duralumin profiles. The metal consisted of thin-walled, V-shaped and specially edge-beaded rolled shapes and the completed major components were fabric-covered. By June 1918 14 examples of the C.II had been delivered with the purpose of evaluating all-metal-built aeroplanes in combat conditions. By November the series of 20 C.IIs was complete but undelivered. After the Armistice the Allies sold 19 of the captured C.IIs to Switzerland, in whose service some of them remained until 1928.

The projected C.III was not built during the war, but one prototype C.IV was almost completed by November 1918. It was designed as an enlarged C.II, but no drawings of the machine have survived. The Musée de l'Air storage facility included the remains of this rare machine (Constructor's Number 01) until the disastrous fire at Le Bourget in June 1990 where it was destroyed along with many unique warplanes of later years – one of the most devastating blows to the aeroplane preservation scene.

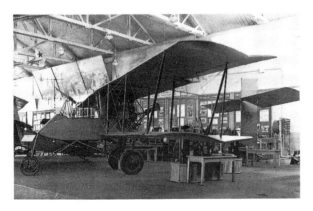

The Voisin LA5 displayed in Monino's 'Red Banner Academy' near Moscow. (Harry Woodman)

A wartime example of the Zeppelin (Jaray) C.II. The fuselage of a late-war prototype C.IV – similar to that illustrated – stored by the Musée de l'Air until 1990 when it was destroyed by fire. (Albatros/P. L. Gray Archive)

Bibliography

Publications and articles found to be the most useful to the author during research for this book are appended below. In no way is the list intended to be a definitive bibliography of WW1 aeronautical history.

BOOKS (Concerning museum aeroplanes)

Albatros D.Va, German Fighter of World War 1 by Robert C. Mikesh; published by Smithsonian Institution Press, 1980.
British Aviation Museums by Bob Ogden; published by Key Publishing Ltd, 1983.
de Havilland DH-4, From Flaming Coffin to Living Legend by Walter J. Boyne; published by Smithsonian Institution Press, 1984.
European Aviation Museums and Collections by Bob Ogden; published by Key Publishing Ltd, 1985.
Museum and Display Aircraft of the World by Stephen Muth; published by The American Aviation Historical Society, undated.
Museum and Display Aircraft of the United States by Bruce Wm Orriss; published by the American Aviation Historical Society, 1976.
Phoenix aus der Asche – Die Deutsche Luftfahrt Sammlung Berlin by Michael Hundertmark and Holger Steinle; published by Silberstreif Verlag GmbH, 1985.
Samoloty W Muzeach Polskich by Marian Krzyzan; published by Wydawnictwa Komunikaczii Lacznosri, 1983.
United States Guide to Aircraft Museums and Memorials, WWII Landmarks and Converted Aircraft by Michael A. Blaugher; published by the author, 1987.
Vintage and Veteran Aircraft by Leslie Hunt; published by Garstone Press, 1970.
Vintage Aircraft Directory by Gordon Riley; published by Aston Publications, 1985
Vintage Aircraft of the World by Gordon Riley; published by Ian Allan Ltd, 1983.

BOOKS (General WWI Aviation)

The Aeroplanes of the Royal Flying Corps (Military Wing) by J. M. Bruce; published by Putnam, 1983.
Albatros Fighters of World War I by Peter L. Gray and Ian R. Stair; published by Wingspan Publications, 1979.
Fokker Fighters of World War I by Peter L. Gray and Ian R. Stair; published by Wingspan Publications, 1976.
German Aircraft of the First World War by Peter Gray and Owen Thetford; published by Putnam, 1962.
Windsock Datafiles: Albatros DV; Bristol F2B; Fokker D.VII; Fokker E.III; Hanriot HD.1; LVG C.VI; Nieuport 17; RAF BE2e; RAF RE8; RAF SE5a; Sopwith 2F1 Camel; Sopwith Pup; Sopwith Triplane; and Spad 7.C1; published by Albatros Productions Ltd., 1986–90.

JOURNALS

To list each and every feature on WWI preserved aeroplanes that have appeared in the world's general and enthusiast press is obviously impractical, but the author has found the most well-researched and authoritative accounts to have appeared in past and present issues of the following: *Aeroplane Monthly* (UK); *Cross and Cockade* (USA); *Cross and Cockade International* (UK); *FlyPast* (UK); *NFF-Kontakt* (Norway); *Prop-Swing* (UK) and *WWI Aero* (USA). To keep up to date with current movements of WWI survivors the world over both the British monthly *FlyPast* and the American journal *WWI Aero* are particularly recommended, while detailed studies of WWI museum aeroplanes are frequently featured in *Windsock International*.

WW1 Survivors – by Museum

Aeroplane Type	Country of Origin	Reg./Serial No.	Constructor's No.	Remarks	Status

Argentina
Museo Nacional de Aeronautica, Aeroparque Jorge Newberg, Buenos Aires

Aeroplane Type	Country of Origin	Reg./Serial No.	Constructor's No.	Remarks	Status
Ansaldo SVA10	I	13164	?	Non-standard components. See page 30	Displayed
Nieuport 28.C1	F	N6993	?	Details lacking	Unknown

Australia
Australian War Memorial, GPO Box 345, Canberra ACT 2601

Aeroplane Type	Country of Origin	Reg./Serial No.	Constructor's No.	Remarks	Status
Airco DH9	GB	F1287	?	See page 15	Storage
Albatros D.Va	G	D5390/17	?	See page 21	Displayed
Avro 504K	GB	H2173	?	Now A3–4. See page 36	Displayed
Pfalz D.XII	G	2600/18	?	See page 96	Displayed
RAF SE5a	GB	'C9539'	?	A2–4. See page 106	Displayed

Harry Butler Memorial, PO Box 88, Minlaton, South Australia, 5575

Aeroplane Type	Country of Origin	Reg./Serial No.	Constructor's No.	Remarks	Status
Bristol M1C Monoplane	GB	C5001	2819?	Ex G-AUIH. Now VH-UQ1. See page 42	Displayed

Kingsford Smith Airport

Aeroplane Type	Country of Origin	Reg./Serial No.	Constructor's No.	Remarks	Status
RAF BE2c	GB	?	?	Ex G-AUOV. In Qantas colours	Displayed?

Royal Australian Air Force Museum, RAAF Base, Point Cook, Victoria 3029

Aeroplane Type	Country of Origin	Reg./Serial No.	Constructor's No.	Remarks	Status
Maurice Farman Seriè 11		CFS–15	?	Under restoration	Displayed

Austria
Heeresgeschichtliches Museum, Arsenal, Object 1, 1030, Wien

Aeroplane Type	Country of Origin	Reg./Serial No.	Constructor's No.	Remarks	Status
Albatros B.I	AH?	20.0I	1	See page 20	Displayed

Technisches Museum Fur Industrie und Gewerbe, Mariahilfer Strasse 212,1140, Wien

Aeroplane Type	Country of Origin	Reg./Serial No.	Constructor's No.	Remarks	Status
Aviatik (Berg) D.I	AH	101.37	?	See page 31	Displayed
Fokker D.III	AH?	?	?	See page 56	Displayed?

Belgium
Musée Royal de l'Armée, Parc du Cinquantenaire/Jubelpark 3, B1040, Brussels

Aeroplane Type	Country of Origin	Reg./Serial No.	Constructor's No.	Remarks	Status
Aviatik C.I	G	C227/16	832	Being restored 1987 – see page 31	Storage
Bristol F2B Fighter	GB	?	?	BAPC 19. Restored by Skysport Engineering – see page 40	Displayed
Caudron G.3	F	2531	?	From Musée de l'Air – see page 46	Displayed
FBA Type H(Schreck)	F/GB	5	55	Unrestored – see page 55	Displayed
Hanriot HD.1	F	HD.78	5153	Restored 1973 – see page 68	Displayed
Halberstadt C.V	G	3471/18*	?	*Has also carried 9471/18. See page 66	Displayed
LVG C.VI	G	5141/18	4981	Unrestored – see page 79	Displayed
Maurice Farman Serié 11A-2	F	?	?	Restored 1980 – see page 83	Displayed
Nieuport 23.C1	F	N5024	?	Being restored 1987 – see page 88	Storage
RAF RE8	GB	8	326	Restored – see page 102	Displayed
Sopwith LCT (1½ Strutter)	GB	S85	66?	Restored – see page 111	Displayed
Sopwith F1 Camel	GB	B5747	?	Restored – see page 117	Displayed
Spad 13.C1	F	SP.49	?	Restored 1975 – see page 139	Displayed
Voisin LA5B	F	?	?	Nacelle only	Displayed

Canada
National Aviation Museum, Rockcliffe Airport, Ottawa, Ontario, C1A 0M8

Aeroplane Type	Country of Origin	Reg./Serial No.	Constructor's No.	Remarks	Status
AEG G.IV	G	G574/18	?	Sole survivor – see page 13	Displayed
Avro 504K	GB	D8971	?	Marked 'G-GYCK – see page 35	Storage
Avro 504K	GB	H2453	2552	Ex – 5918, N8763R with parts from D8971 – marked as G-CYFG – see page 35	Displayed
Curtiss JN-4 (Can.)	USA	39158	?	Marked as C227 – see page 52	Displayed
Curtiss HS-2L	USA	A1876	2901-H.2	Wings from NC652; marked G-CAAC	Displayed
Fokker D.VII	G	10347/18	3659	Under restoration 1988 – see page 56	Storage
Junkers J.4 (J.I)	G	586/18	252	See page 72	Storage
Maurice Farman Serié 11	F	?	?	Finished as VH-UBC. See page 82	Displayed
Nieuport 12	F	'A4737'	?	See page 87	Storage
RAF BE2c	GB	4112	663	Under restoration – see page 96	Storage
Sopwith 2F1 Camel	GB	N8156	?	See page 123	Displayed

| Sopwith 7F1 Snipe | GB | E6938 | ? | See page 124 | Displayed |
| Sopwith 7F1 Snipe | GB | E8102 | ? | Fuselage only. Major Barker's – see page 126 | Displayed |

Brome County Historical Society Museum, 130 Lakeside, PO Box 690, Knowlton, Quebec, J0E 1U0

| Fokker D.VII | G | 6810/18 | ? | See page 56 | Displayed |

Reynolds Aviation Museum, 4110 571th Street, Wetaskiwin, Alberta, T9A 2B6

| Curtiss JN-4C | | 'C1347' | 1347? | Canuck, Ex. G-CABX, G-CATE | ? |

Private Ownership

| Curtiss JN-4D | USA | ? | 3793? | JF Johnson, Edmonton | ? |

Czechoslovakia
Národní Technické Museum, Kosteni 42, 170 78, Prague 7

Anatra DS	R	'11120'	3979	See page 25	Displayed
Hansa Brandenburg D.I	AH	28.68	?	Fuselage only – see page 71	Displayed
Knoller C.II	AH	119.15	?	Restored 1987–88 – see page 74	Displayed
LWF Model A	USA	?	4	See page 79	Displayed

Vojenske Museum, Expozicé Letectvá a Kosmonautiky, Kbely, Prague 9, 19706

| Spad 7.C1 | F | S11583 | ? | Restored 1980. Ex-L-B126 – see page 129 | Displayed |

Finland
Hallinportti Ilmailumuseo, 35600 Halli

Caudron G.3	F	IE18	?	Parts only	Displayed
Caudron G.3	F	?	?	Nacelle only, and some parts	Displayed
Rumpler 6B.1	G	5A1	?	Restored 1986–'87 – see page 108	Displayed

Keski-Suomen, Ilmailumuseo, PL1, 41661 Tikkakoski

| Avro 504K | GB | E448 | ? | Ex G-EBNU; IH–49; marked as AV–57 – see page 36 | Displayed |
| Martinsyde F.4 | GB | D4326 | ? | Marked as MA-24 – see page 80 | Displayed |

Vesivehmaan Varastohalli, c/o Matti Vahvaselka, Kariniemenkatu 28 B 65, Lahti: 14

| Breguet 14.A2 | F | 3C30 | ? | Status unknown | Storage |

Musée de l'Air et de l'Espace, 93350 Le Bourget

Airco DH9	GB	F1258	?	See page 19	Displayed
Breguet 14.A2	F	?	2016	Formerly F-WAHR – see page 38	Displayed
Caudron G.3	F	324	324		Displayed
Caudron G.4	F	C1720	?	See page 47	Displayed
Henry Farman HF.20	F	?	?		Displayed
Maurice Farman Seriè 7	F	?	446	Dismantled	Storage
Fokker D.VII	G	6796/18	?	See page 58	Displayed
Junkers D.I (J.9)	G	5929/18	?	See page 73	Displayed
LVG C.VI	G	9041/18	?	From Royal Army Museum, Belgium	Storage
Nieuport 11	F	'N976'	?	Restored – see page 86	Displayed
Paul Schmitt	F	?	?	Status unconfirmed	Storage
Pfalz D.XII	G	2690/18	3240	See page 96	Displayed
RAF BE2c	GB	9969	?	See page 98	Displayed
Sopwith 1A.2 (1½ Strutter)	GB	1263	?	Formerly 556. See page 112	Displayed
Spad 7.C1	F	S254	254?	Guynemer's machine. Restored – see page 127	Displayed
Spad 13.C1	F	?	15295	Restored as 'S5925' – see page 138	Displayed
Spad 13.C1	F	4377	?	On loan from Salis-airworthy	With the Memorial Flight Association, Meudon
Spad 13.C1	F	8340	?	Fuselage only	Storage
Voisin LA.S B2	F	955	?	Marked as 'V955' – see page 147	Displayed
Voisin LA10	F	?	?	Nacelle only	Storage
Zeppelin C.IV	G	55864	01	Destroyed, June 1990 – see page 149	Storage

West Germany
Deutsches Automuseum, Schloss Langenburg, 7183 Langenburg

| Halberstadt CL.IV | G | D-71 | ? | Air charter use 1920–1939 – see page 66 | Displayed |

Deutsches Museum von Meisterwerken der Naturwissenschaft und Technik, Museumsinsel 1, 8000 Munchen 22

Fokker D.VII	G	'4408/18'	?	Old civilian registration D-20 – see page 57	Displayed
Rumpler C.IV	G	?	310?/17	Restored 1986/7 – see page 106	Displayed

Hungary
Kozlekedesi Muzeum, Varosligeti Korut 11, Budapest 1146

Lloyd	AH	40.01	?	See page 76	Displayed

Italy
Aeritalia Collection, Corso Marche 41, 10146 Turin

Ansaldo SVA9	I	'13148'	89	Bought from the Fyfield Collection, January 1989 – see page 30	Used for travelling exhibitions

Museo Aeronautico Caproni, Aeroporto di Trento-Mettarello, Trento. (Probably opening 1991). Restoration facility: Masterfly, Via Zeni 8, 38068 Rovereto. (Venegono) Villa Caproni, Venegono Superiore, Varese. (Storage only – not open to the public). N.B. There are no aeroplanes left at the old Vizzola site.

Ansaldo A.1 Balilla	I	16552	63	Now at Rovereto – see page 26	?
Ansaldo SVA5	I	11777	?	At Gonalba for restoration – see page 28	?
Caproni Ca.22	I	?	?		Storage?
Caproni Ca.53	I	?	?		Storage
Fokker D.VIII	G	'MM194'?	2916?	Fuselage only. Destined for USAF Museum for restoration – see page 62	?

Museo Baracca, Castello di Lugo di Romagna

Spad 7.C1	F	S2489	?	See page 133	Displayed

Museo Nazionale della Scienza e della Tecnica, Via San Vittore 21, 20123 Milano

Junkers J.4 (J.I)	G	?	?	Fuselage only – see page 72	Displayed
(Macchi) Nieuport 10	I	15179	?	Previously I-BORA – see page 84	Displayed

Museo del Risorgimento di Bergamo, Città, Bergamo

Ansaldo A.1 Ballila	I	16553	?	See page 27	Displayed

Museo Storico dell'Aeronautica Militare Italiana, Aeroporto di Vigna di Valle, 00062 Vigna di Valle

Ansaldo SVA5	I	11721	?	See page 28	Displayed
Caproni Ca.3	I	23174	?	Marked as '4166' – see page 43	Displayed
Hanriot HD.1	F	19309	?	Marked as '515' – see page 67	Displayed
Lohner L.I	AH	L-127	?	Restored 1986–88 – see page 76	Displayed
Spad 7.C1	F	S.1420	?	See page 131	Displayed
Spad 7.C1	F	?	?	See page 133	Used for travelling exhibitions
Spad 13.C1	F	?	?	Marked as 'S.1420' – see page 138	Displayed

Museo Storico Italiano della Guerra di Rovereto, Castello di Rovereto, Via Castelbacco 7, 38068 Rovereto

(Macchi) Nieuport 10 (18mq)	I	13469	?	See page 85	Displayed

Museo Vittoriale di Gardone, Vittoriale degli Italiani, 25083 Gardone Riviera, Brescia

Ansaldo SVA10	I	12736	?	Restored 1988 – see page 29	Displayed

Japan
Army Air Base Museum, Jokorozawa

Nieuport 18.E2	F	?	?		Storage?
Salmson 2.A2	F	?	?	Parts only? Fuselage?	Storage?

Kotsu Transportation Museum, 1-25 Suda-cho, Chiyoda-Ku, Tokyo

Maurice Farman Serie 11	F	266	?	See page 83	Displayed?

J A S D F, Hamamatsu-South, Nishiyama-cho, Hamamatsu City, Shizuoku-Pref

Maurice Farman Serie 11	F	?	?	?	Storage?

Mexico
El Ebane Military HQ Museum, San Luis, Potosi

'Latino America'	M	?	?	Blt 1916 – Data invited	Displayed?

Santa Lucia Mexican Air Force Base, Santa Lucia

GAF 'Type A'	M	?	?	Blt 1916 – Data invited	Displayed?

Netherlands
Militaire Luchtvaart Museum, Kamp van Zeist, 3769 ZK Soesterberg

Fokker D.VII	G	7748/18?	?	Formerly N6268; N4729V – see page 58	Displayed

New Guinea
Port Moresby

Curtiss MF Flying Boat	USA	?	?	Owned by Major L G Halls? Details invited	?

New Zealand
Taranaki Museum, War Memorial Building, Akiri Street, New Plymouth

Avro 504K	GB	ex-NZRAF ? 202		ZK-ACH. Incomplete	Storage

Norway
Kongelige Norsk Luftforssvaret Collection, 'Flymuseet' 2062, Gardermoen Lufthavn

Avro 504K	GB	B4505?	?	Ex 504A. Marked 103	Storage
RAF BE2e	GB	A1380	?	Marked 131 – see page 100	Displayed

Norsk Teknisk Museum, Fyrstikkaleen 1, Etterstad, Oslo

Maurice Farman Serie 11 (MF1)	F	F.16	?		Storage
Haereas Flyvemaskinfabrik FF.7 'Hauk'	N	?	?	Fuselage only – Hannover CL.V licence blt.	Storage

Peru
Museum not known

Ansaldo SVA	I	?	?	Marked 'Cuzco' – details invited	Displayed?

Poland
Muzeum Lotnictwa i Astronautyki, Skr Pocztowa 17, Alega Planu 6-Letniego 17, 30–969 Krakow 28

Most of these aeroplanes, together with the four ex-Strähle Halberstadts, are destined for West Germany to the Museum für Verkehr und Technik, Trebbiner Strasse 9, D–1000 Berlin 61 in an ambitious restoration programme.

Albatros C.I	G	197/15	?	See page 25	Storage
Aviatik C.III	G	C1225/17	1996	See page 31	Storage
DFW C.V	G	C17077/17	473	See page 54	Storage
Grigorovich M-15	C	1?	R11 C262	See page ?	Storage
Halberstadt CL.II	G	C15495/17	'1046'	See page 65	Storage
LFG Roland D.VIb	G	D2225/18	?	See page 75	Storage
Sopwith F1 Camel	GB	B7280	?	See page 118	Storage
Zeppelin Staaken R.VI	G	R35/16	?	Nacelle/engines only	Storage

Ex-Deutsche Luftfahrt Sammlung, Berlin. 'Missing in Action' 1944–19??

AEG J.I	G	?	?	
Albatros C.IX	G	C4508/16	?	
Albatros D.III	G	?	?	
Albatros D.V.	G	'1916/17'	?	
Fokker Dr.I	G	528/17?	?	
Fokker D.VII	G	?	?	
Fokker D.VII	G	?	?	According to recent research, *all* removed from Berlin 1941–44.
Junkers J.9 (D.I)	G	?	?	Current status unknown
Junkers J.4 (J.I)	G	?	?	
Pfalz D.XII	G	?	?	
Rumpler C.IV	G	?	?	

Siemens Schuckert D.IV	G	?	?	According to recent research, *all* removed from Berlin 1941–44.	
Spad A-2	F	?	?	Current status unknown	

Portugal
Museo de Marinha, Praco de Imperio 9, 1480 Lisboa

Shreck (FBA)	F	2	203		Displayed

Republic of South Africa
South African Museum of Military History, PO Box 52090, Saxonwold, Transvaal 2132

Airco DH9	GB	2005	?	Ex ZZ-A01. Marked I.S8. See page 15	Storage?
RAF SE5a	GB	F7781/3?	?	Marked A.24. See page 106	Storage?

Sweden
Flygvapenmuseum Malmen, Box 13300, S580 13 Linkoping

Albatros SK-1	G	04	?	See page 24	Displayed
Thulin Type G	SW	15	?	On loan from Tekniska Museet, Stockholm	Storage?

Industrimuseet, Box 5037, S 402 21 Goteborg

Albatros B.II	G	SE-ACR	?	Formerly, SE-94	Storage

Landskrona Museum, Slottsgatan, Landskrona S 261 31

Thulin Type NA	SW	?	?	1918-built.	Displayed

Luftfartmuseet, Stiftelsen Luft-och Rymdfartmuseet c/o Tekniska Museet, Museivagen 7, S 115 27 Stockholm

Thulin Type A	SW	?	?	On loan from Tekniska Museet, Stockholm	Displayed
Thulin Type N	SW	1–59	?	On loan from Tekniska Museet, Stockholm.	Displayed

Tekniska Museet, Box 406, Malmohusvagen, S 211 24 Malmo.

Thulin Type A	SW	?	?	Forward fuselage only.	Displayed
Thulin Type B	SW	?	?	On loan from Tekniska Museet, Stockholm.	Storage

Switzerland
Museum der Schweizerischen Fliegertruppe, Abteilung der Militarflugplatz, 8600 Dubendorf

Hanriot HD.1	F	653	?	Macchi built – see page 69	Displayed
Nieuport 28.C1	F	607	?	See page 90	Displayed

Verkehrshaus der Schweiz, Lindostrasse 56006, Luzern

Nieuport 28.C1	F	688	?	See page 91	Displayed

Turkey
Turk Hava Kuvvetleri Hava Muzesi, Hava Harp Okulin Komutanligi Hava Muzesi, Yesilyurt, Istanbul

Grigorovich M5	R	?	?	Built 1914	?

Union of Soviet Socialist Republics
Air Force Museum, 141170 Monino, Moskovskii Oblast

Voisin LA5	F	?	?	See page 149	Displayed
Sopwith Triplane	GB	N5486	?	See page 115	Displayed

United Kingdom
Fleet Air Arm Museum, RNAS Yeovilton, Ilchester, Somerset BA22 8HT

Short 184	GB	8359	?	From IWM. Forward fuselage only – see page 109	Displayed
Sopwith Baby	GB	'N2078'	?	Parts from 8214 and 8215. See page 110	Displayed

Imperial War Museum, Duxford, Duxford Airfield, Duxford, Cambridgeshire CB2 4QR

Bristol F2B Fighter	GB	E2581	?	See page 39	Displayed
RAF RE8	GB	F3556	?	See page 101	Displayed
Spad 7.C1	F	'S.4523'	248	'N9727V'. Ex Wings and Wheels – see page 130	Displayed

Imperial War Museum, Lambeth, Lambeth Road, London SE1 6H2

RAF BE2c	GB	2699	?	See page 97	Displayed
Sopwith 2F1 Camel	GB	N6812	?	See page 120	Displayed

Mosquito Aircraft Museum, Box 107, Salisbury Hall, London Colney, Hertfordshire AL2 1BU

RAF BE2e	GB	A1325	?	Awaiting restoration – see page 99	Displayed

Museum of Army Flying, Army Air Corps Centre, Middle Wallop, Stockbridge, Hampshire SO20 8DY

Sopwith Pup	GB	N5195	?	Rebuilt. Airworthy – see page 112	Displayed
Sopwith Pup F.1 Camel	GB	B6291	?	Rebuilt. Airworthy – see page 115	Displayed

Royal Air Force Museum, Hendon, London NW9 5LL

Airco DH9A	GB	F1010	'WA/8459/AMA'	Rebuilt. Ex-Krakow. See page 19. In Bomber Command Hall.	Displayed
Avro 504K	GB	E449	927	Ex. RAeS, Nash. See page 34. In Bomber Command Hall.	Displayed
Bristol F2B Fighter	GB	'E2466'	?	Part restoration – see page 41	Displayed
Caudron G.3	F	'3066'	5019	See page 45	Displayed
Hanriot HD.1	F	HD.75	75	Formerly 00–APJ, G-AFOX – see page 69	Displayed
Morane Saulnier Type BB	F	A301	?	Fuselage only – see page 82	Displayed
RAF SE5a	GB	'F938'	687/2404	Formerly B4563, G-EBIC – see page 104	Displayed
Sopwith Triplane	GB	N5912	?	See page 113	Displayed
Sopwith F1 Camel	GB	F6314	?	See page 115	Displayed
Avro 504K	GB	H2311	?	Ex-Henlow, now Manchester. See page 34.	Storage
Curtiss JN-4	USA	?	?	At Henlow?	Storage
Fokker D.VII	G	8417/18	?	At Cardington – see page 57	Storage
RAF FE2b	GB	?	?	At Cardington. Nacelle only.	Storage

Reserve Collection (applies to Curtiss JN-4, Fokker D.VII, RAF FE2b)

Museum of Scotland, Chambers Street, Edinburgh, EH1 1JF, Scotland.

Avro 504K	GB	?	?	Forward fuselage/nose	Displayed

The Science Museum, Exhibition Road, South Kensington, London SW7 2DD

Avro 504K	GB	D7520	?	See page 34	Displayed
Fokker E.III	G	210/16	509	See page 64	Displayed
RAF SE5a	GB	?	688/2404	Ex G-EBIB – see page 105	Storage

The Shuttleworth Collection, Old Warden Aerodrome, Biggleswade, SG18 9ER

Avro 504K	GB	H5199	?	Ex 3404 – see page 33	Displayed
BAT Bantam	GB	?	PK 23/15	Ex K123. Remains. Being rebuilt?	Storage
Bristol F2B Fighter	GB	D8096	3476/7575	See page 40	Displayed
LVG C.VI	G	7198/18	4503	See page 76	Displayed
RAF SE5a	GB	F904	654/2404	Ex G-EBIA – see page 102	Displayed

Private ownership – various

Bristol F2B Fighter	GB	G-AANM	67627?	Being restored to fly. Vintage Aero Ltd. See page 39	Storage
Curtiss JN-4D	USA	?	?	Vintage Aero Ltd. Being restored	Storage
Nieuport 28.C1	F	N5246	?	Ex Wings and Wheels. Vintage Aero Ltd. – see page 91	Storage
Sopwith Pup	GB	B1807	?	Mr K M Baker? Parts located 1977.	Storage

United States of America
University of Alaska Museum, 907 Yuban Drive, Fairbanks, Alaska 99701

Curtiss JN-4D	USA	?	?	Fuselage only	Displayed

Champlin Fighter Museum, 4636 Fighter Aces Drive, Mesa, Arizona 85205

Aviatik (Berg) D.I	AH	101.40	?	See page 31	Displayed
Pfalz D.XII	G	2848/18	3498	Formerly N43C – See page 93	Displayed

Planes of Fame Air Museum, WWII Cal-Aero Field, 7000 Merrill Ave., Chino, California 91710

Hanriot HD.1	F	'5624'	1398	Nungesser's aeroplane – see page 70	Displayed

San Diego Aerospace Museum, 2001 Pan American Plaza, Balboa Park, California 92101

Curtiss JN-4C	USA	?	?		Displayed
Curtiss JN-4D	USA	N5391	396		Displayed

Spad 7.C1	F	?	?		Displayed
Standard J-1	USA	N2826D	1598		Displayed
Thomas Morse S-4C	USA	34544	A51		

The Fyfield Collection, Washington, Connecticut, 06793 (As of September 1989)

| Curtiss JN-4D | USA | 34091 | ? | Plus fuselage, wings of a second a/c | Storage |
| Thomas Morse S-4C | USA | SC 38910 | ? | Ex. C1358 | Storage |

New England Air Museum, Bradley International Airport, Windsor Locks, Connecticut 06096

| Standard J-1 | USA | 129 | ? | | Displayed |
| Thomas Morse S-4C | USA | 38910 | ? | | Displayed |

National Air and Space Museum, Smithsonian Institution, Independence Avenue SW, Washington DC 20560

Albatros D.Va	G	7161/17	2004	See page 23	Displayed
Caudron G.4	F	2170	C-4263	See page 48	Displayed
Curtiss F5L	USA	A 3882	?	Hull only	Displayed
Curtiss JN-4D	USA	'4983'	?	At Silver Hill	Displayed
De Havilland DH4	USA	'No. 1'	A15101?	See page 54	Displayed
Fokker D.VII	G	4635/18 (OAW)	3533	See page 59	Displayed
Halberstadt CL.IV	G	8103/18	?	To Berlin for restoration 1989. See page 65	Storage?
Nieuport 28.C1	F	'N4123A'	?	Ex Palen, see page 90	Displayed
Sopwith 7F1 Snipe	GB	E8105?	?	From Old Rhinebeck, being restored – see page 126	Storage
Spad 7.C1	F	?	?		
Spad 13.C1	F	S7689	?		Displayed
Standard J-1	USA	N1375	?		Displayed
Voisin LA3	F	?	?		Storage

Weeks Air Museum, 14710 SW, 128th Street, Miami, Florida 33186

Avro 504J/K	GB	B3182	?	N3182C. See page 36	Displayed
Orenco F	USA	N2145	45		Displayed
Sopwith LCT (1½ Strutter)	GB	?	?	Ex-J. Jurist	Storage?
Spad 7.C1	F	193	?		Displayed
Standard J-1	USA	N2825D	1582		Displayed
Thomas Morse S-4C	USA	?	?		Displayed

U.S. Naval Aviation Museum, Pensacola, Florida 32508

Curtiss JN-4D	USA	'A995'	?		Displayed
Curtiss MF IP	USA	A-5483	?		Displayed
Curtiss NC-4	USA	?	?		Displayed
Curtiss N-9H	USA	?	?	Loaned from NASM	Displayed
Thomas Morse S-4C	USA	A5858	235	Ex N5858	Displayed

Museum of Science and Industry, 57th Street and S. Lake Shore Dr., Chicago, Illinois 60637

| Curtiss JN-4D | USA | 2421 | 533 | | Displayed |

Airpower Museum Inc., PO Box H, Ottumwa, Iowa 52501.

| Standard J-1 | USA | ? | ? | | |

Combat Air Museum, Forbes Field, PO Box 19142, Topeka, Kansas 66619

| Curtiss JN-4D | USA | ? | ? | | Displayed |

Owls Head Transportation Museum, Box 277, Owls Head, Maine 04854

Curtiss JN-4S	USA	N94JN	?	Ex 34094, N34094	Displayed
Standard J-1	USA	N22581	581	Ex – N.S. Sorensen	Displayed
Thomas Morse S-4	USA	Ex NR667	?	Prototype; Ex-Wings and Wheels Museum	Displayed

Henry Ford Museum and Greenfield Village, 20900 Oakwood Boulevard, PO Box 1970, Dearborn, Michigan 4812

Curtiss MF	USA	257	?	Modified Seagull. Built 1916	
Curtiss JN-4D	C	8428	?	Canadian built	
Laird Biplane	USA	?	?	1915 built. 'Aerobatic' display aeroplane	

| Standard J-1 | USA | '823H' | ? | See page 142 | |

Harold Warp Pioneer Village, Minden, Nebraska 68959

Curtiss JN-4D	USA	1350	3044		Displayed
Curtiss JN-9	USA	?	?		Displayed?
Standard J-1	USA	?	?		Storage

Harrah's Automobile Museum, PO Box 10, Reno, Nevada 89504

| Curtiss JN-4D | USA | N5162 | 278–506 | | At Int. Airport |

Buffalo and Erie County Historical Society Museum, 25 Nottingham Court, Buffalo, New York 14216

Standard H-2	USA	?	?		Displayed?
Standard H-3	USA	?	?		Displayed?
Standard J-1	USA	5957	?	Cut up, modified to resemble JN-4D!	

Cradle of Aviation Museum, Museum Lane, Mitchell Field, Garden City, New York 11530

Curtiss JN-4C (Can)	USA	1187	?	Flown by Lindbergh	Displayed
Curtiss JN-4D	USA	10726?	3334	Fuselage only	Storage?
Thomas Morse S-4C	USA	SC38934	552	Ex-Paul Kotze	Displayed

Glenn H. Curtiss Museum of Local History, Labe and Main Streets, Hammondsport, New York 14840

| Curtiss JN-4D | USA | ? | ? | Complete | Displayed |
| Curtiss JN-4D | USA | ? | ? | Fuselage only | Displayed |

Old Rhinebeck Aerodrome, PO Box 89, Rhinebeck, New York 12572

Curtiss JN-4H	USA	'38278'	3919	Ex-N3918. See page 53	Displayed
Morane Saulnier Type AI	F	MS1591	?	Ex-Wings and Wheels. N1379M – See page 81	Displayed
Nieuport 10/83	F	'503'	?	N680CP – See page 85	Displayed
Spad 13.C1	F	'S16541'	?	Recently restored to static condition	Displayed
Thomas Morse S-4B	USA	4328	153	N74W	Displayed

Bonanzaville Museum, West Fargo, North Dakota 58078

| Standard J-1 | USA | N9477 | 2434 | Ex 2434 | Displayed |

The Western Reserve Crawford Auto Aviation Museum, 10825 East Boulevard, Cleveland, Ohio 44106

| Curtiss MF | USA | NC903 | ? | Ex-A5543 | Displayed |
| Thomas Morse S-4C | USA | SC44610 | 633 | Ex-N5452 | Displayed |

US Air Force Museum, Wright Patterson AFB, Dayton, Ohio 45433

Caproni Ca 36	I	2378?	?	On loan from Museo Caproni – see page 44	Storage
Curtiss JN-4D	USA	2805	?	See page 51	Displayed
Halberstadt CL.IV	G	4205/18	?	See page 65	Storage
Halberstadt CL.IV	G	?	?	See page 65 — To Berlin for restoration, 1989	Storage
Halberstadt CLS.I	G	?	?	See page 65	Storage
Nieuport 28.C1	F	N8539	?	See page 89	Displayed
Packard Le Pere Lusac II	F	SC42133	?	From Musée de l'Air – see page 92	Storage
Spad 7.C1	F	'AS 94099'	?	See page 134	
Spad 16.A2	F	A59392	939	Loaned by NASM for restoration – see page 139	Storage
Standard E-1	USA	AS49128	?	See page 141	Displayed
Standard J-1	USA	11	?	Marked as 'AS22692' – see page 142	Displayed
Standard J-1	USA	1141	?	See page 142	Displayed
Thomas Morse S-4C	USA	SC38944	160		Displayed

Edward White II Museum, Hangar 9, Brooks AFB, San Antonio, Texas 78235

| Standard J-1 | USA | 22690 | ? | | Displayed |

USAF History and Traditions Museum, Lackland AFB, San Antonio, Texas 78236

| Curtiss JN-4D | USA | ? | ? | Fuselage and wings only | Storage? |

Virginia Air Museum, PO Box 787, Ashland, Virginia 23005

Standard E-1	USA	?	?	Carries no identity/serial numbers	Displayed

Marine Corps Air-Ground Museum, Brown Field, Elrad Avenue, Quantico, Virginia 22134–5001

Sopwith F1 Camel	GB	N6254	?	Ex-Jarrett, see page 119	Displayed
Thomas Morse S-4B	USA	NR66Y	?		Displayed

EAA Aviation Center and Air Museum, Wittman Field, Oshkosh, Wisconsin 54903–3065

Curtiss JN-4D	USA	5357	4904		Displayed
Curtiss JN-4D	USA	5360	2402		Displayed
Pfalz D.XII	G	2486/18	2936	On loan from NASM – see page 96	Displayed
Standard J-1	USA	N6948	1956	In flying condition. Ex – Klessig.	Displayed

Private Ownership

Caudron G.3	F	?	?	
Curtiss JN-4	USA	4769/47529	?	E S Yandik, NY. Possibly three others also.
Curtiss JN-4	USA	4769/38156	?	E S Yandik, MY.
Curtiss JN-4C	C	1122	?	E Carlson, Wa.
Curtiss JN-4C	C	1639	?	C Mael, Wi.
Curtiss JN-4C	C	496	?	R McDaniels, Ill.
Curtiss JN-4C	C	?	?	H Wells, Ca.
Curtiss JN-4D	USA	N 7628B	?	Stapleton International Airport, Denver, Co.
Curtiss JN-4D	USA	?	?	3.M Airport, NJ.
Curtiss JN-4D	USA	N 6898L	?	Ex 34135, Arkansas ANS, Adams Field, Ark. See page 51
Curtiss JN-4D	USA	?	123	D Fischer, Lancaster, Ca.
Curtiss JN-4D	USA	3712	?	R and J Folsom, Ca.
Curtiss JN-4D	USA	7710	?	R and J Folsom, Ca.
Curtiss JN-4D	USA	?	?	R and J Folsom, Ca.
Curtiss JN-4D	USA	?	?	G Frank, Id. Aeroplane is 'Basket Case'.
Curtiss JN-4D	USA	?	?	G Frank, Id. Aeroplane is 'Basket Case'.
Curtiss JN-4D	USA	?	?	E M Freeman, Ca.
Curtiss JN-4D	USA	12205	?	D C Gilmore, Ia.
Curtiss JN-4D	USA	?	?	V Grahn, Mi.
Curtiss JN-4D	USA	4236	?	J H Green, Pensacola, Fl.
Curtiss JN-4D	USA	?	?	F P Higgins?
Curtiss JN-4D	USA	?	?	K Hyde, Va.
Curtiss JN-4D	USA	?	5360	K Hyde, Va. Plus one other, possibly c/n 450?
Curtiss JN-4D	USA	?	?	F Johnson, Portland, Or.
Curtiss JN-4D	USA	3862	400/700)	P H Knepper, Pa.
Curtiss JN-4D	USA	?	?	M L McClure, Ill.
Curtiss JN-4D	USA	?	?	D F Neumann, Mn.
Curtiss JN-4D	USA	?	5002	J M Nissen, Ca.
Curtiss JN-4D	USA	?	?	W Olsen, Wa.
Curtiss JN-4D	USA	?	?	H Snow.
Curtiss JN-4D	USA	?	?	D Trone, Ca?
Curtiss JN-4D	USA	?	?	R Watkins, Oh.
Curtiss JN-4D	USA	?	?	B Wiesener, Tx.
Curtiss JN-4D	USA	?	?	Dr A L Wood
Curtiss JN-4H	USA	?	?	R Hazuka, Ca.
Curtiss JN-4H	USA	?	?	F Schelling.
Nieuport 11	F	?	?	Ex-Aeroflex.
Nieuport 12	F	?	?	D Groves; fuselage only?
Nieuport 28.C1	F	?	?	E Carlsen?
Nieuport 28.C1	F	N28GH	?	R Folsom
Nieuport 28.C1	F	?	?	R Folsom
Nieuport 28.C1	F	6367?	?	R Rust. In *The Dawn Patrol*.
Nieuport 28.C1	F	6493?	?	R Rust. In *The Dawn Patrol*.
Standard J-1	USA	N28250	?	Ex-Movieland of the Air Museum?
Standard J-1	USA	?	?	Ex-Movieland of the Air Museum?
Standard J-1	USA	?	?	G Babwell, Wa.
Standard J-1	USA	?	?	P J Baker. Fuselage only.
Standard J-1	USA	?	?	E Carlsen, Wa. This or the next machine is a 'Basket Case'.
Standard J-1	USA	?	?	E Carlsen, Wa.
Standard J-1	USA	N6250S	?	R Fulsom. Flown in *The Great Waldo Pepper*.
Standard J-1	USA	T4732	?	R Fulsom.
Standard J-1	USA	7710	?	R Fulsom.
Standard J-1	USA	T4595	?	R Fulsom?
Standard J-1	USA	N62505	?	Ex-Movieland of the Air.
Standard J-1	USA	?	?	E M Leadon, Wa.
Standard J-1	USA	N6093V	?	M McClure, Ill.
Standard J-1	USA	?	?	M McClure, Ill.
Standard J-1	USA	2904	?	C L Peck.

Standard J-1	USA	?	?	C L Peck.
Standard J-1	USA	?	?	P Taylor.
Standard J-1	USA	1000	?	J M Miller.
Standard J-1	USA	?	?	P Jordin, Ct.
Standard J-1	USA	?	?	R Watkin, Vi.
Standard J-1	USA	?	?	W Garrett.
Thomas Morse S-4B	USA	?	305	Ex-Wings and Wheels.
Thomas Morse S-4C	USA	SC 38898	?	E W Carlsen, Wa.
Thomas Morse S-4C	USA	SC 41382	?	E M Freeman, Ca.
Thomas Morse S-4C	USA	?	?	E M Freeman, Ca. Fuselage only; ex-Mantz.
Thomas Morse S-4C	USA	SC 38802	?	R Hazuka, Ca.
Thomas Morse S-4C	USA	3932	?	R Hazuka, Ca.
Thomas Morse S-4C	USA	?	?	R Hazuka, Ca.
Thomas Morse S-4C	USA	SC 38669	235	J M Nissen, Ca.
Thomas Morse S-4C	USA	Ex NR502	?	Ex-Movieland of the Air.

Venezuela
VAF Technical School, Escuela Technica FAV, Secciòn Metalmecanica, Base Aerea Mariscale Suere, Buca del Rio, Maracay, Edo, Aragua, 2104.

Hanriot HD.1	F	?	?	Last reported displayed in 1983	?